ETHICAL CONCERNS IN PSYCHOTHERAPY AND THEIR LEGAL RAMIFICATIONS

Andrew Thompson

UNIVERSITY PRESS OF AMERICA

LANHAM • NEW YORK • LONDON

University Press of America,™ Inc.

4720 Boston Way
Lanham, MD 20706

3 Henrietta Street
London WC2E 8LU England

Printed in the United States of America

Library of Congress Cataloging in Publication Data

Thompson, Andrew, 1932-
Ethical concerns in psychotherapy and their legal ramifications.

Includes index.
1. Psychotherapy ethics. 2. Psychotherapists—Legal status, laws, etc.—United States. I. Title.
RC455.2.E8T48 1983 174'.2 83-6823
ISBN 0-8191-3241-1
ISBN 0-8191-3242-X (pbk.)

All University Press of America books are produced on acid-free paper which exceeds the minimum standards set by the National Historical Publications and Records Commission.

To Marie-Anne

the best Swiss of all

ACKNOWLEDGMENTS

It is both my ethical duty and my pleasure to acknowledge those who provided primary assistance in the formation of this book.

Peter Ozanne, a faculty member at the University of Oregon Law School, wrote the initial drafts of the chapter on malpractice, as well as providing counsel on several portions of the book. Donna Bruyere, of the Illinois State University Counseling Psychology faculty, wrote an initial draft of the chapter on groups, and thus was instrumental in its creation. The graduate students in my course on ethical and legal issues in counseling and psychotherapy provided numerous suggestions and much encouragement as they struggled with earlier versions of the chapters; some even demonstrated considerable editing skills. Richard Francisco, a co-worker in the University of Oregon Counseling Center, and Carol Dawes, a psychologist in full-time private practice, also faithfully read and commented on most of the book.

Finally, my two main typists deserve honorable mention. Sally Franzoni demonstrated admirable, good-natured patience as she typed and retyped most of the drafts of the chapters. My wife, Marie-Anne von Rechenberg, not only typed the final version, but edited it, during which process I learned a great deal about English from one who had to learn it as a foreign language, thus being more sensitive to idioms and grammatically suspect constructions.

I wish to thank these individuals and everyone else who has contributed time and effort towards this book.

CONTENTS

FOREWORD

Recent years have seen an upswelling of ethical and legal concern and sensitivity on the part of counselors and psychotherapists, with the result that the major ethical codes have recently undergone substantial revision. Since 1980 new codes have been adopted by the American Personnel and Guidance Association, the National Association of Social Workers, the American Psychiatric Association, and the American Psychological Association. This parallels adoption of new federal regulations, such as those on research with human subjects by the Department of Health and Human Services. As a result previous books in this field are seriously outdated in selected areas.

The field has not only been renewed, it has been expanded, with the result that it is no longer possible, if it ever was, to meaningfully cover all the ethical issues that may arise in one text. The variety of disciplines, of philosophical schools, of "brands" of therapy and of settings in which therapists work is too great. Accordingly, I have chosen to restrict the focus of this book to generic issues that cut across disciplines, schools, brands, and settings. Since I am most familiar with the ethical codes and literature of psychology, most of the references will be to these sources; however, parallel, if not identical expressions of these issues arise in psychiatry, clinical social work, marriage and family counseling and the other mental health fields.

But in spite of this expansion and this renewal, some issues have been raised inadequately, if at all, and many of them could profit from a skeptical, analytical approach. Consider, for example, the concept of confidentiality--the promise by the therapist that she will not divulge anything revealed to her by the client within the confines of the therapy hour without the client's express consent. Discussion of this issue almost always revolves around under what conditions it is permissible and prudent for the therapist to breach these "holy" secrets and to whom. Very little attention has been paid to the question of whether confidentiality is a good thing in itself, to its negative features, to whether we might be better off without invoking it, and to the fact that much of modern practice is conducted without any apparent need for such a contract. Throughout this book I have taken the liberty to gently question the revered tenets, the traditional ways of conceptualizing ethical issues. Although the primary task is to elucidate that which now exists, I have not hesitated to take a fresh look at old concepts or to challenge the accuracy of newly adopted "truths."

Consistent with this approach the book is organized in terms of generic issues rather than more conventional categories. Thus, one chapter identifies potentially false expectations clients may have regarding therapy and their therapists, and therapist regarding the effectiveness of therapy; it also describes ways of correcting such expectations. Another chapter depicts the effects of third-party payments on the practice, teaching, and development of theories of psychotherapy.

Some of the ethical issues have clear legal implications and, when this is the case, these implications are noted. Included is a chapter on tort law, the basic system of law used in malpractice suits, in order to provide the reader with the background necessary to understand the function of law relative to the practice of the profession. There is also a chapter on licensure, both its statutory and its ethical implications.

The emphasis remains, however, on the ethical issues and not the law. Although the profession of counseling and psychotherapy operates withing a legal context, I believe that any profession should first develop a set of ethical standards on its own and enforce them among its members instead of reacting defensively to regulatory legislation or what juries do in malpractice cases. The public, as consumer on the skills we hold out as special, has a right to expect no less from us.

This book is intended for the professional practitioner, those that train such practitioners, and the trainees. It has been and is being used, in its various preliminary forms, as the text for my graduate level course on ethical and legal issues in counseling and psychotherapy, which is required of all first year graduate students in Counseling Psychology at the University of Oregon.

Most chapters follow the same general format. After a brief introduction which states the issue and explains its relevance and importance, the reader is confronted with a number of "actual" situations, referred to as "Illustrative Cases." These situations pose ethical dilemmas which the reader is asked to resolve. Several options and questions are listed as means of prompting reader response. The following commentary sections analyze the overall issue into various components, present the formally applicable ethical and legal principles, if any, as well as extrapolations thereof. The illustrative cases are referred to, as appropriate, during the course of this analysis.

Terminology

"Counseling"/"Psychotherapy": To simplify matters, I have used the terms "psychotherapy" to stand for both "counseling" and "psychotherapy", and "psychotherapist" or "therapist" to stand for "counselor." Exceptions are made when the terms "counseling" and "counselor" are conventionally used terms, as in "marriage and vocational counseling." This is not intended to be interpreted as taking a position in the unresolved dispute over the proper use of these terms.

"He"/"She": Rather than adopt the "he or she" convention I have attempted to assign third party roles in an even-handed manner.

> The ideal patient must be <u>suggestible</u>. He should be able to easily absorb dogma and ideas of the most abstract, even outlandish dimension. He should be philosophically adaptable and able to ape the therapist's value system and biases. The more he agrees with the therapist, the better his chances of being helped. (Gross, 1978)

CHAPTER I

ONSET OF THERAPY: THE THERAPIST AS A MORAL AGENT

A central concern of therapy is the transmission of the therapist's values and life view to the client. There are many facets to this concern, only a few of which will be considered in this chapter. One basic issue is whether or not the therapist has the moral right to impose her values and perspective upon the client "for the client's own good." Some would argue, as Martin Gross does in the quote above, that imposing the therapist's values on her client is the essence of psychotherapy. I adopt a different view as a starting point. I believe that therapists should help their clients become self-governing individuals, who can pursue their own, freely-chosen values and goals. The question then becomes: How can therapists reduce the impact of their own values and goals upon their clients? This chapter first examines which types of therapist values are most apt to be imposed, wittingly or unwittingly. The section, Illustrative Cases, invites the reader to participate in identifying how therapist values may be imposed in particular situations and to find ways to reduce this impact. The following commentary section broadens the scope of the discussion and presents one method whereby client autonomy may be facilitated.

Traditionally it was thought that therapists, while acting as therapists, could be morally neutral or objective. The method to achieve this state of mind was a deliberate suspension of judgment and suppression of immediate emotional reactions until a deeper level of understanding and acceptance of the client was achieved through empathy and intuition. In using this method, the therapist spoke little, listened, and suppressed nonverbal responses. The therapist was particularly careful to avoid revealing her own personality characteristics, including her likes and dislikes. Freud stated: "The physician should be impenetrable to the patient, and, like a mirror, reflect nothing but what is shown to him." (1912/1959 p. 331). Carl Rogers states: "To me it appears that only as the therapist is completely willing that <u>any</u> outcome, <u>any</u> direction, may be chosen--only then does he realize the vital strength of the capacity and potentiality of the individual for constructive action." (1951, p. 48).[1] An introductory clinical psychology text recommends that, "the therapist should be accepting of the client, a sympathetic and non-moralistic listener who can react in a meaningful but objective manner." (Garfield, 1957, p. 254).

In recent years this image of the therapist as a neutral, unbiased observer has come under severe attack. Perry London (1964), the first modern writer to thoroughly examine this issue, claims that no therapist can be morally neutral:

> Moral considerations may dictate, in large part, how the therapist defines his client's needs, how he operates in the therapeutic situation, how he defines "treatment," and "cure," and even "reality." . . . Students of mental health find that it is difficult to <u>define</u> such terms as "health," "illness," and "normality" without some reference to morals; and worse still, they cannot discuss the proper treatment of what they have defined without recognizing and involving their own moral commitments.
>
> The issue is the same whether the problem is a social one like prostitution or an apparently individual one like obsessional neuroses. Neither can be called an illness on the grounds of invasion by a foreign body or of the malfunctioning of specific organs. Nor do people die directly from them. They may be abnormal in a statistical sense, but this is hardly a basis for worry. Living one hundred years or making a million

---

[1] Carl Rogers has altered his views considerably over the years and may be less willing to subscribe to this particular expression today.

> dollars is also deviant in that sense. The objectionable feature of these problems concerns the violation of the public moral code, in the one case, and the experience of apparently unnecessary personal anguish--in the other. In both, the assumption of a moral desideratum underlies the definition. (p.5)

Allen Bergin (1980) of Brigham Young University argues that no therapist, including Carl Rogers, practices value-free therapy. His published analysis of verbatim transcripts supports his claim that Rogers ". . . systematically rewarded and punished expressions that he liked and did not like in the verbal behavior of clients." (p. 37). He further contends that most therapists, wittingly or unwittingly, espouse secular moralities at the expense of the traditional religious values of many of their clients.

Richard Kitchener (1980), a philosopher, argues that behavior therapists believe that value judgments are relative to the individual and to the culture and fail to recognize that their basic assumption that "good" means "positive reinforcer" is inconsistent with this position. A number of psychologists have disputed some of Bergin's and Kitchener's specific assertions (for Bergin, see Ellis, 1980, and Walls, 1980; for Kitchener, see Ward, 1980). However, the critics do not dispute the basic contention that there is no value-free brand of psychotherapy, and thus no morally-neutral therapists.

Illustrative Cases

In order to appreciate the practical relevance of the above discussion and to identify some of the main issues that are apt to arise during the initial stages of therapy, place yourself in the role of the therapist or counselor in the following client interviews and consider the questions that follow each case.

The Aspiring Seducer: John complains to you of unsatisfactory heterosexual relations. He is unable to "make it" with enough women. He knows a sufficient number of women, but seldom is able to convince them to go to bed with him. He wants you to help him become more successful. He is set on this particular goal. John says he doesn't need help making friends and is not interested in developing a single, deep relationship. How will you respond?

1. Do you see John's request as psychologically normal or as evidence of a mental disorder? What criteria do you use to make this decision?

2. If you believe John's request reflects a distorted, destructive perspective, how will you communicate this to John and when? Will you simply state this belief at the outset, or somehow subtly persuade him to change it during the course of working "with" him?

3. If you are unwilling to help John achieve his goal and he is unwilling to change to a mutually acceptable one, do you think it is ethical to refer him to some other therapist who might help him achieve the goal?

The Homosexual Client: Ann tells you she is a homosexual with a dilemma. She has found her current life style and sexual relationships unsatisfactory. From her perspective there are two ways out--she can either "go straight" or she can somehow reduce the shame and secrecy of her present life and develop better homosexual relationships. Ann is not sure she can succeed at either and is seeking help in making a decision and implementing it. What is your response?

1. Do you believe homosexuality to be a psychologically normal, albeit a statistically infrequent, phenomenon, or do you believe it to be a psychological disorder? Do you consider it important to communicate this belief to Ann?[2]

2. Do you intellectually hold that homosexuality is, or can be, a psychologically normal sexual preference but find yourself personally repulsed by any overt demonstration of it and feel very uncomfortable with this client? If so, should you reveal this to Ann and if so, how?

The Religious Client: Carla has fallen in love with Harold, a married man with children, who is separated from his wife and claims to be working toward a

---

[2] For an extensive discussion on this and other issues that arise with regard to homosexuality see the series of articles on this topic in the April, 1976 Journal of Consulting and Clinical Psychology.

divorce. Carla is in her early twenties and has never been married or engaged to be married whereas Harold is in his early thirties and has been married for eight years. Carla was raised a Catholic and knows the church would never condone her relationship with this man. She is also having doubts about her religious faith, and gives that as another reason for not seeking counseling from a priest. What is your response?

1. Do you think this client is apt to be naive with regard to the intricacy of the bonds that exist in such a marital relationship? If so, is it appropriate to place a priority on the early investigation of her sophistication in such matters and then to educate her? Is it ethical to pursue this approach without first checking with her about doing so?

2. How would you handle Carla's religious conflict? Do you suspect Carla's decision not to see a priest is an attempt to escape her sense of guilt about interfering with a marital relationship and contemplating adultery? Or is it the result of a mature decision to get a different "unbiased" perspective? If you suspect Carla is motivated by guilt should you confront her with your suspicion?

3. What bearing do your religious beliefs, or lack of them, have on your attitudes towards her seeking secular counseling and her relationship with this man? Should you inform her of these beliefs?

4. Do you think it possible that one of the long-term secondary effects of secular counseling will be that Carla's ties with her church will be broken? If so, is it your responsibility to warn her of this possibility?

<u>The Dissatisified Wife</u>: Kay and Don request counseling to determine if and how their marriage can be saved. Don is relatively content with the marriage, but Kay is dissatisfied and will seek a divorce if there isn't a change soon. She complains of his insensitivity, his taking her for granted, and his unwillingness to share his feelings with her. Kay says Don spends most evenings watching TV and reading. He has promised to change, but all changes are short-lived, and the old rut is soon again established. Don tells you that he sees nothing wrong

with his behavior, except that Kay doesn't like it. He is willing to change, but is not sure what exactly would please Kay. He suspects nothing would help since the changes he has made in the past have been neither acknowledged nor appreciated.

1. What is your basic attitude towards the value of the institution of marriage? How will your attitude influence your behavior in this case? Do you believe marriage is usually a good thing and marriages ought to be saved if at all possible? Or do you think that most people get married, at least the first time, for the wrong reasons and it would probably be best if most of them divorced? Are you indifferent to the issue of divorce and only concerned with each client's individual stability and happiness? If so, is this a morally neutral stance?

2. Are you inclined to identify more with one party than with the other? Might it be best to see only one member of the pair and to refer the other to another counselor? Would bringing in a co-counselor reduce the probability that one party would be favored?

Commentary

There are no absolutely "correct" answers in these situations. At the end of the chapter I will suggest some ways of viewing them that might be helpful. But for now, the purpose of raising the questions is to expose the multitude of moral and ethical decisions which must be made during the beginning phase of counseling and therapy. No one claims that therapists are by nature morally neutral and objective. But at one time it was thought that they, by nature of their training and their methods, could somehow transcend their subjective reactions during the course of therapy. Therapists were expected to act as near-perfect mirrors of their clients' projections and as non-directive facilitators of client integration and development of their own values. As we have seen in the introduction to this chapter, the reality of accomplishing these objectives is doubtful.

Certain basic beliefs of the therapist are bound to affect her behavior, such as beliefs as to what is psychologically normal and desirable and what is abnormal and undesirable. On the other hand, there are other responses that are short-lived and have no significant or enduring effects on the course of counseling or therapy; responses such as instant liking or disliking, interest or disinterest. Typically, but not always, these reactions are transformed or greatly reduced in impact by getting to know the client. An experienced therapist presumably is able to discern her transitory reactions from those that will continue to be a significant factor throughout therapy. But no therapist can be aware of all of the ways in which she subtly structures the therapeutic situation and orients her clients to certain perspectives or of all the potential effects of such changed modes of thinking and feeling on the clients' subsequent lives. It is hoped that this and subsequent chapters will raise your level of awareness of such matters.

Assuming that the therapist is aware that she has some non-transitory reactions that may significantly affect the course of therapy, what courses of action are open to her? If she is secure in the belief that she knows what is best for the client she will not be especially concerned about attenuating the effects of her attitudes and values. If, on the other hand, the therapist wants to preserve the client's freedom and autonomy she has two choices: she can suppress, as best she can, the manifestation of her attitudes and values and remain essentially silent about them, or she can fully and openly reveal and discuss her attitudes and values with the client. The second choice has been promoted as an ethical option in recent years.

<u>The Principle of Informed Consent</u>: The principle of informed consent is based on the belief that the client, as a free and autonomous individual, should be a full participant in therapy. In order to accomplish this objective, the client needs to know what the therapist proposes to do and why, what the likely consequences are, and what the alternatives are. Only then will the client be able to make an informed choice.

One method for obtaining informed consent is a client-therapist contract.

> Most therapy contracts specify some or all of the following: the methods of therapy, its goals, the length and frequency of sessions, the duration of treatment, the cost and the method of payment, provisions for cancellation and renegotiation of the contract, the extent of each person's

responsibility, and the degree of confidentiality." (Hare-Mustin, Marecek, Kaplan, and Liss-Levinson, 1979, pp. 8-9)

The Specialty Guidelines for the Delivery of Services by Clinical Psychologists (Appendix B, hereafter referred to as the Specialty Guidelines) published by the American Psychological Association in 1981 support the establishment of specific, written client-therapist contracts:

> . . . A clinical psychologist develops a plan that describes the psychological services, the objectives and the manner in which they will be provided. This plan is in written form; it serves as a basis for obtaining understanding and concurrence from the user [includes recipients of clinical psychological services] and provides a mechanism for subsequent peer review.[3]

The official guidelines do not suggest informing clients of possible side effects of therapy or counseling. However, Hare-Mustin, et al., (1979) recommended that married people receiving individual therapy be warned that progress in individual therapy might disrupt their marital relationship. This would seem to be applicable to the case of The Dissatisfied Wife (p. 5). Coyne and Widiger (1978) also believe the therapist to be ethically responsible for warning clients about possible secondary effects on important beliefs and social relationships that are not targeted for change.

Hare-Mustin, et al. (1979) recommended a number of additional provisions as well:

> Techniques that might be at odds with the client's values should be specified. The client should know whether the therapy will consist of talking, role playing, or body work, if aversive techniques will be used,

---

[3] The corresponding guidelines for counseling psychology (American Psychological Association, 1981, pp. 652-663) are quite similar in this and in all other sections with which we will be concerned throughout this book. Therefore, only the guidelines for clinical psychology will be referred to.

> if he or she is expected to take medication, if others, such as family members, will be involved, and if he or she will be expected to join a group. Therapists who follow up on clients should secure their permission in the contract, even if this might bias future responses. Some practices, such as sexual relations with clients, are unethical and remain so whether or not the client agrees to them. (pp. 8-9)

It is not possible to anticipate every potential exigency of therapy in a contract. A therapist may want to try out a technique that is suggested by the immediate context or to follow a hunch and change the focus. In such cases informed consent would consist of immediately checking with the client to see if he is ready and willing to participate in this change of tactic or focus. But even this is often unwieldy and may destroy the on-going therapeutic process. At times it is necessary to proceed without specific, informed agreement, but this will vary according to the situation and therapist.

Many therapists find it unrealistic and countertherapeutic to establish contracts that specify the goals and means of treatment. For some, by the time the real goals are clear, a succession of in-the-moment, intuitive treatments will have already been invoked and much of the therapy completed. As one practitioner stated:

> To make a requirement that goals be discussed with the patient and the patient sign a form to that effect seems to me a blatant violation of the integrity of the work and the necessity of a "container" within which secure and protected space the work of transformation may take place and the healing occur. (Jaffe, 1981)

When to Refer: How does the ethical therapist handle an apparent mismatch of values, personality or goals between herself and the client? When should referral to another therapist be made? The answers to these questions are not always simple. They depend on at least three factors: (1) the importance of the mismatch; (2) the availability of suitable referral sources, and; (3) the degree of client-therapist involvement at the time of the recognition of the mismatch.

The official guidelines offer little direction in deciding when to make a referral, especially if the referral is based on a conflict of values. Principle 6e of the Ethical Principles of Psychologists (Appendix A; hereafter referred to simply as the Ethical Principles) states merely:

> . . . Psychologists terminate a clinical or consulting relationship when it is reasonably clear that the consumer is not benefitting from it. They offer to help the consumer locate alternative sources of assistance.

Several sections of the Specialty Guidelines (Appendix B) are relevant here. Section 2.2.5. states:

> Consultation is sought or referral made within the public or private network of services whenever required in the best interest of the users.

Psychologists are expected to have previously informed themselves about the network of services in their area. Section 3.1. advises psychologists to withhold services "in specific instances in which their own limitations or client characteristics might impair the effectiveness of the relationship."

A somewhat more specific statement is found in the article by Hare-Mustin et al. (1979) in the section entitled, What if the therapist has personal or moral problems with the client's goals? Therein they propose:

> Therapist and client together need to examine the likely consequences, both positive and negative, of achieving the goals the client seeks. If the therapist feels that he or she cannot agree with the client's goals, the therapist should not work with that person and should make a referral.

This may well be the case for some therapists when confronted with either with the "Aspiring Seducer" (p. 3) or the "Homosexual Client" (p. 4).

When not to Refer: None of these proposals seems to recognize that it might be unethical for the therapist to further what she considers to be an immoral goal of a client by referring that client to someone who might help the client achieve that goal. A similar situation arises if a client insists on a form of treatment that the therapist considers psychologically dangerous for the client, such as encounter group experience for someone who appears to be psychologically fragile. Is it really ethical to refer the client to someone who would provide such an experience, even though you wouldn't risk it yourself? One way to "resolve" this issue would be for the therapist to quite openly inform the client of the reasons for not treating or referring the client for treatment. This should not be done in an accusatory or condemning manner, but rather be presented simply as a result of a conflict of values and of judgment between the therapist and the prospective client.

Discussion of the Illustrative Cases

The Aspiring Seducer (p. 3): Our current culture advocates the equality of women and it would be the rare therapist who would dare to support a client whose intention is to seduce women at will, and, in effect, to treat them as objects. One could argue that some women already do that to men, but two wrongs do not make a right and the broader ethic frowns on any such unequal relationships.

One way in which the therapist could approach the problem would be to express some reservations about the specific goal of the client, but offer to help John to reach the general goal of more satisfactory relationships with women. The therapist may even express her belief that such relationships will involve more "give and take" on both parties' parts. Such a proposal is apt to spring from the therapist's ethical conviction that John's goal reflects an unhealthy or abnormal attitude and an impoverished background with respect to experiencing affectionate relationships. However, the philosophically sophisticated therapist will recognize that her conviction is based on her experience and her values, which are not necessarily valid for the client, and will be prepared to fail to reach a mutually satisfactory working agreement with the client.

The Homosexual Client (p. 4): Here, again, current cultural norms have an impact. There are many people in society and many sub-cultures and areas in our major population centers which tolerate, if not support, openness regarding homosexual orientation. Our profession has chosen to remove homosexuality from among the "mental illnesses" and to accept it as quite normal for some people. This does not stop researchers from attempting to find the contributing genetic, biological and environmental factors that determine sexual orientation, nor should it; but it does, and, in my mind, it should make it possible to conduct such research in an objective manner. To "excuse" homosexual orientation by attributing it to a "faulty" gene, or a biological "defect" would be to remove the prejudice from one level only to reflect it on another. Even the "survival of the species" argument does not hold up in view of modern developments in the reproduction of the human species and the fact that homosexuals are quite capable of having their own children, and often do.

With respect to Ann's dilemma, the answer, if any, would lie in the particularities of her situation and her psychological functioning. It may be she can find a more tolerant social environment by changing where she lives or where she works. It may be her choice of sexual partners is more a matter of fear than of positive attraction, in which case this might be a fruitful area on which to focus and work. This could be true of heterosexual relationships as well. The one thing on which I believe most modern therapists would agree is that it would be precipitious to help her to "go staight" without a great deal of evidence that this is what she really wants and that her present orientation is clearly the result of mistaken attitudes and crippling fears. I would add that heterosexually oriented individuals are equally apt to be miscast in their sexual roles.

<u>The Religious Client (p. 4)</u>: In this case the therapist's attitudes towards the sanctity of marriage and the role of religious conflict are crucial in how he responds to Carla. Society does not speak with a single voice on such matters, nor does our profession. My own preference is to openly express my views and my hypotheses to the client, inviting her to explore her attitudes and confirm or disconfirm my hypotheses. Thus, if I thought she was naive regarding the nature of the relationship that Harold has with his wife, and consequently the nature of the relationship he might have with her, I would express this, being careful to provide the basis for my hypothesis and agree to explore its validity in some mutually determined way. I would not want to assume that she was naive and operate

on that assumption without her knowledge.

Similarly with her religious conflict I would share my concern that she was avoiding confronting her sense of guilt by seeking me out instead of a priest. Again she would decide on the truth or falsity of my supposition and whether or not to test it out in some way. I would also warn her of the possible effect of secular counseling from me upon her religious convictions.

My preference for such openness is because I believe that ultimately the client knows what is true/not true, best/worst, appropriate/inappropriate for herself, and that while therapy may be a process by which these decisions are made clearer, the process, itself, must not be dominated by a conflicting orientation--namely, that the therapist knows what is best for the client.

This does not mean the therapist must make a point to proclaim all his potentially relevant beliefs at the first occasion, only that, as a particular belief, bias, or hypothesis obviously is going to dictate how he responds to a particular client, he consider how best to provide the client with the opportunity to correct such belief, bias, or hypothesis and choose an alternative course of action or perspective.

The Dissatisfied Wife (p. 5): This case belongs equally well in the next chapter on expectations and their influence. Obviously, an important factor in determining the satisfactoriness of a resolution to this typical marital conflict is the expectations of the three participants regarding what would be a satisfactory process and resolution. Suppose the wife expects the counselor to side with her and get her husband to see "reason." The husband, on his part, expects the same, only with respect to his spouse doing the changing. Both would consider divorce a bad resolution. If the counselor does not clarify her role and her attitudes about process and satisfactory resolution, the counselor risks being trapped by an unrealistic matrix of expectations.

Moreover, the counselor risks imposing her values as to what are "healthy" or "realistic" expectations for each spouse to have regarding the other spouse and the value of marriage. It can be argued that such imposition will take place regardless of any clarification by the counselor, and that, in any case, it is the proper role of the counselor to influence their clients in such matters.

I agree that counselor-client interactions inevitably involve such imposition of counselor values--the question is then not whether imposition should occur, but how. Again, if clients are encouraged to become informed rather than passive participants in the process of change, then it seems to me their capacities for self-direction are being respected, rather than being abrogated by the counselor.

As to the necessity or advisability of calling in a co-counselor, one who can represent the "other" spouse, whoever that may be, this is a judgment call that depends very much upon the degree to which the counselor finds herself identifying with one spouse and not with the other, and the likelihood of this identification being more than transitory. My experience is that such identification is frequent, but also quite transitory, often changing from one interview to the next, especially in the early stages of counseling. Calling in a co-counselor may only compound the problem as there is no guarantee that the co-counselor will identify with the other spouse. Avoiding, coping with, analyzing and resolving such identifications are themes of sufficient importance to be dealt with at length in the multitude of marriage counseling books on the market. What is important here to recognize is that it is basically an ethical question, and not just a matter of logistics.

This concludes our analysis of the general issue of the therapist as a moral agent. The following chapters are concerned with more specific dimensions of therapist values and their communication to the client.

Blessed is he who expects nothing, for
he shall never be disappointed.
(Alexander Pope)

CHAPTER II

ONSET OF THERAPY: COPING WITH EXPECTATIONS

One of the most interesting psychological phenomena is the effect of beliefs upon reality. Not only do people distort reality to conform to their beliefs, but, in some instances, they actually create the situation they fear or hope will occur by acting on their expectations. When this occurs we call it a self-fulfilling prophecy. We utilize this phenomenon when we ask clients to imagine how they would act in anticipated situations if they were confident and were to be successful, and then suggest that they will be able to transfer this attitude to the actual situation.

However, not all expectations are realistic, or can be, and not all self-fulfilling prophecies are positive. This chapter is concerned with potentially unrealistic expectations about therapy and about therapists and how they may be forestalled and corrected in an ethical manner. First some client situations will be described in the illustrative cases section in which it is clear that the clients' expectations of therapy and the therapist's role are in error. The question is whether the therapist can correct these expectations and still retain the possibility of working with the client. In The Therapist as Friend the client expects the therapist to become her personal friend, even, as she claims, her previous therapists have done. In The Therapist as Advice-Giver the therapist is cast into the role of an expert in human relationships and is expected to provide ready-made advice as to how to resolve a long-standing, difficult co-worker situation. In The Therapist as Headache-Remover the client expects the therapist to relieve her tension headache through hypnosis or biofeedback training, neither of which techniques is in the repertoire of the therapist.

The first commentary section which follows will examine the underlying expectation of all psychotherapy -- namely, that it is a beneficial form of treatment for many, if not all, kinds of psychological problems. The pro and con positions will be briefly depicted along with the implications for trying to correct the potentially false belief in the general efficacy of psychotherapy.

Next, some more specific, but still pervasive beliefs regarding the magical powers and expertise of psychotherapists will be listed, and the "traps" they constitute for the unwary therapist. Therapists' own tendencies to exaggerate their effectiveness, and the basis for these tendencies will also be examined. This is followed by a review of the official precautions and injunctions that the profession provides as a way of controlling such tendencies.

The final two sections describe three ways of assessing and correcting client expectations during therapy, as well as how to apply them to the illustrative cases.

Illustrative Cases

Here are some situations in which clients have potentially unrealistic expectations of the therapist or of the therapy.

> The Therapist as Friend: Joan comes in to "work on emotional problems." She has stated on the intake form that she has had previous therapy and in the course of the initial interview she admits to having had three previous therapists, all of whom she saw for a year or more, and all of whom she considered as friends. She claims that the therapy relationship developed into full-fledged social relationships after the termination of therapy, and that she still corresponds with one of the therapists. With regard to her problems, the particulars have changed, but she considers her overall problem to be the same as before--how to control her moodiness. She sees this as a long-term endeavor, perhaps a life-time one. Based on both her verbal statements and her general demeanor you suspect she is looking forward to forming yet another friendship, this time with you. What should you do?
>
> 1. Is it improper for you to be her confident, her "friend," to which she reports weekly as long as you restrict your contacts to the official sessions? If she is content with such a relationship, is there anything intrinsically wrong in maintaining it?[1]

[1] see footnote on next page

2. Suppose you tell her you will not be a friend of hers in the usual sense, and find it best to abstain from forming such friendships until after termination, but are willing to work with her on her problem. She accepts, but adds that she hopes this doesn't mean you wouldn't be concerned about her welfare--for example, she would like to be able to call upon you if an emergency arose or to chat with you if you met in the supermarket. How would you respond if your intent is to maintain a clear distinction between being her friend and being her therapist?

3. How would you handle her expectation of lifelong therapy? Do you believe it might actually be necessary or desirable? Or do you see this as a case of "therapy addiction" that needs to be countermanded in some way?

The Therapist as Advice-Giver: A mill worker is having problems in his work situation. He complains of being the "butt" of numerous jokes and of being laughed at and talked about behind his back. He does not like or respect his co-workers and claims he wants nothing to do with them and wishes they would leave him alone, as he does them. He says all this in a tense, aggrieved tone. He reluctantly provides additional details upon your request and then expectantly turns to you and says, "What do I do, Doc?" It is clear that he thinks he has done his part and the rest is up to you. You have the strong impression he is expecting some concise instructions. He seems to believe or hope that his problems are resolvable through a simple change in his behavior which you can prescribe. You also suspect if you don't "come through" he is apt to "write you off" as being inept and not come back. On the other hand you believe mere advice-giving to be superficial and essentially non helpful since his real problem, as best you can judge, consists of some well-entrenched faulty attitudes and tendencies to mis-perceive the nature of social interactions.
How would you handle the situation in an ethical manner? Your problem is that if you don't give him the

---

[1] (see p. 16) The pervasiveness of the perception of psychotherapists as special friends is manifested by the title of W. Schofield's book, Psychotherapy: The Purchase of Friendship (1964)

advice he expects he may walk out on you and not come back, and thus not work through his difficulties. But there isn't any advice you can give him that you think would really work since he would not be able at this point to implement the changes you believe necessary.

1. Would you temporarily deceive him--i.e., play along with his belief for now that he only needs advice and keep providing it at the rate necessary to keep him coming back (telling him to expect that it may take a while to find the right advice for the situation), but using whatever opportunities that present themselves to start exploration of the precipitating attitudes?

2. Would you be open with him and share your belief that such advice would be of little or no value since you suspect the problems he has arise from faulty attitudes and perceptions which will take a long time to identify and for him to acknowledge, and still more time to correct?

What criteria did you use to decide between the options above? Is this a case of the end justifying the means?

The Therapist as Headache-Remedier: A woman has been referred by her physician for aid in handling her headaches, which have been diagnosed as "tension headaches" by her physician. You have had no experience in treating such symptoms but in the process of interviewing the client you discover she is in a power struggle with her teenage daughter and has several unrealistically high expectations--potential sources of tension with which you have dealt as a therapist in the past. The client has heard of hypnotherapy and biofeedback and expects you to work with her in these ways, but you possess no expertise in either technique. Where would you go from here?

1. Would you simply admit your lack of expertise in the area of treating tension headaches and in the use of hypnosis and biofeedback and offer to refer her elsewhere?

2. Would you emphasize that the "real" sources of her tension would probably not be dealt with by the use of hypnosis and biofeedback and that such techniques could result in only short-term relief and

the development of other symptoms?

3. Might you simply offer to work with her on what you perceive to be the sources of her tension in the hope that this will eventually result in reduction of tension headaches and in the belief that this will be useful to her even if the headache persists?

4. Would you tell her you will help her and then start a "crash course" in learning how to use hypnosis and biofeedback? If so, how much of that would you admit to the client?

Commentary

Three kinds of faulty client expectations were illustrated above: confusion of the therapist's professional role with her social role; reduction of the therapist's professional role to information-giving; and attribution of competencies to the therapist which she does not possess. As shall soon be evident, this by no means exhausts the types of faulty expectations, but it should provide a flavor of how they may be manifested in particular situations and of the ethical issues that are involved.

Before we further examine the parts of the whole, let us step back for a moment and consider the expectation that underlies all psychotherapy--the expectation that it is, or can be, a beneficial treatment process for psychological ailments.

Warning: Psychotherapy may be Dangerous to your Health

In a recent best-selling book Martin Gross (1978) attacks the role of psychiatrists, psychoanalysts and other psychotherapists in our society. He sees them as agents of the psychological establishment that has transformed our society into one where everyone is sick, where normality is depicted as almost unobtainable and what is normal is seen as pathological. "Natural emotions such as outrage, despair, grief, jealousy, suspicion, disappointment and passing depression are made to appear not only undesirable but abnormal." (p. 17) He further claims that the "cures" that are achieved are fully accounted for by the factors of spontaneous remission and placebo effects. He documents this claim carefully by reference to numerous studies (for example: Eysenk, 1952, 1965; Frank, 1973; and Brill, Koegler, Epstein, and Forgy, 1964). Gross also challenges the view that psychotherapy, even if ineffective, is benign. He points to studies and quotes experts who have found that therapy can have a "psychonoxious" effect, such as the precipitation of psychotic breakdowns, the break-up of "balanced" marriages, and the creation of "therapy-addicts"--patients who lose their self-sufficiency in dependent relationships with their therapists (p. 41).

The philosopher, Michael Scriven, who was the first nonpsychologist to serve on an APA board had this to say in a letter to the editor of the APA Monitor (1975):

> On the more serious side, two issues that I fathered in BSERP [Board of Social and Ethical Responsibility] are going to starve to death without other support, and I don't know if APA's membership will find any redeeming charm in these ugly orphans. The first is the question of the moral justification for dispensing psychotherapy given the state of the outcome studies which would lead the FDA to ban its sale if it were a drug. As entertainment or placebo or research (not as education), it might be justified--but that's not how it's represented. "Honest conviction of meliorative effects" does not distinguish psychotherapy from snake-oil. I think a radical shift in what "informed consent" means for psychotherapy clients/patients is needed--perhaps they should be shown a standardized card expressing patients' rights and reasonable expectations, in the initial interview. The level of discussion of this issue by practitioners rarely exceeds crude rationalization, of income or tradition. (pp. 2-3)

Of course, there are many defenders of the efficacy of psychotherapy. Several recent reviews present a positive view of the value of psychotherapy, both in general and with regard to specific treatments for particular problems (Smith & Glass, 1977; Parloff, 1979; Frank, 1979; Beutler, 1979). Smith and Glass's statistical analysis of almost 400 studies led them to conclude: "On the average, the typical therapy client is better off than 75% of untreated individuals" (p. 752). A reader's review of the same data led him to the conclusion that the study sounded a "death knell for psychotherapy" in view of the null correlations between effectiveness of therapy and both length of therapy and professional status of therapists (Rimland, 1979). Thus the question of whether or not expectations regarding the positive value of psychotherapy are well founded is still being debated.

The ironic aspect of this issue is that even if all or most of the positive changes that occur during or following psychotherapy were to be due to placebo effects, it might still be advantageous for clients to believe otherwise, in that the belief in the efficacy of the therapy may be essential to its effect. In other words, therapists who follow Scriven's advice and inform their clients that if they improve at all it is more likely to be as a result of their belief in the therapist and the therapy than as a result of the actual treatment might well prevent both the positive placebo effects and any intrinsic treatment effects from materializing. Thus one can argue that it is unethical to inform clients that therapy, per se, may be of no value, or not to inform them of that possibility. It may be that the more ethical course of action will depend on the particular situation.

One consideration is that there is no single entity that is called "psychotherapy," so a lumping together of all the multitude of theoretical approaches and specific interventions, such as Smith and Glass have done, for the purpose of determining the efficacy of "psychotherapy" is somewhat misleading and says very little about any particular therapy. Some specific treatments for specific problems may indeed have a very high rate of success, according to replicated studies in real-life situations. Others may never have been researched, or researched only incidentally. As of this point no whole therapeutic approach, with all its variations, can be said to be effective with most, or even a particular subset of clients--that is, more effective than lack of formal therapeutic intervention.

Another factor that confounds any prediction of the efficacy of a therapy for a client is the client herself, or more precisely the client's willingness to assume an active role and make a concerted effort to bring about the desired changes. This is something difficult to judge within the first few interviews.

Finally, the therapist must take into account the potential receptiveness of the client in the first interview to the provision of information regarding probable outcomes. If the client is in a crisis situation, or actively psychotic, or otherwise preoccupied with her own thoughts and emotions, then communication of such information is apt to be either infeasible or counter-therapeutic.

Alleged Expertise of Therapists

Having examined the general issue of the effectiveness of psychotherapy we are now in the position to return to examination of more particular expectations that are common to our culture and which may well be faulty. Four types of expertise that are often attributed to, and sometimes assumed by, psychotherapists are listed below:

1. Mind-Reader--having the ability to decipher thoughts and feelings of others without it being necessary for them to express them. This can be a real liability in interview situations since it supports some clients' inclination to hide their feelings and only hint at their problems.

2. Psychoanalyst--dedicated to, and especially adept at, uncovering of the unconscious, repressed traumas that are the roots of current problems. Such expectations can interfere with non-analytic forms of treatment and lead to rejection of the therapist as incompetent and the therapy as superficial when the focus is maintained on current events and feelings.

3. Crisis-Intervener--able to efficiently and effectively intervene in interpersonal altercations, talk potential suicides off ledges, persuade people in psychotic states to quit harassing others, etc. Therapists are more apt to be equipped, both by temperament and by training, to assess and intervene at a more leisurely pace than such situations permit.

4. Social Expert--knowledgeable in the skills of "how to win friends and influence people." Although many therapists and counselors have studied various aspects of the communication process, others have not. Also there are many kinds of interpersonal relationships, each of which may require a different set of skills, and it may be that some capabilities are only incidentally affected by skill training. In any case I am unaware of research that demonstrates that therapists, as a group, are more proficient in all such

skills than other professionals. The case of The Therapist as Advice-Giver is relevant here. The therapist's expertise may not lie in telling the mill worker how to interact with his co-workers, but rather in helping him explore, define and change his interfering attitudes.

Clients are not the only ones to ascribe expertise to therapists. Therapists often attribute special knowledge and skills to themselves, whether or not they possess them. There are several reasons. A major reason is the lack of criteria for expertise and effectiveness.

Another reason is the "regression to the mean" phenomenon in psychotherapy. Many, perhaps most clients, come in at moments of peak stress in their lives. A number of environmental pressures, most of them temporary in nature, have combined to make it difficult for them to function effectively. They may be facing a momentous decision, an important challenge, financial or personal loss, or difficulties in interpersonal relationships. Regardless of how these matters turn out, the chances are that the client will be able to adjust to the outcome and feel better about herself within the near future, if for no other reason than that the uncertainty is reduced. However, if this improvement occurs during the course of therapy it may be attributed to the therapy (and hence to the therapist), rather than to the inevitable rduction of environmental stress.[4]

Another factor that, if true, could well contribute to both general and specific expectations of therapeutic effectiveness is the alleged tendency for editors of professional journals to publish studies that report positive findings and reject those that report negative ones. A recent study found that when referees read manuscripts which were identical except for their results and discussions, positive (confirmatory to the

---

[4] Jerome Frank made a similar observation about the statistical probability of spontaneous recovery. ". . . from a statistical standpoint, most people come to psychotherapy when they are in the throes of a crisis or recovering from one . . . they will be more distressed and incapacitated than they were a few months before or will be a few months after regardless of any intervention." (1968, p. 386)

hypotheses) data were much better received than negative results. (Mahoney, 1977)

Still another possibility is that researchers tend to send in only these studies that confirm their hypotheses of successful treatments. This would certainly be true of case studies.

Finally, in view of the financial and prestigious rewards involved it may well be that many therapists find it easier to accept flattering portrayals than to contest their accuracy.

Control of Promotion and Development of False Expectations: Official Recommendations from the Guidelines

Given that there are pressures and tendencies to overestimate our efficacy and competencies as practitioners, what regulatory advice does the profession provide to help us control such tendencies? There are at least four areas addressed by the various ethical codes and guidelines: public statements, evaluation research, continuing education, and limiting of services to areas of competency.

Public Statements: Perhaps the first opportunity to err ethically occurs when the practitioner advertises or is asked to describe his services to the public. Principle 4, Public Statements, of the Ethical Principles should be read in entirety by practitioners prior to making any such description. Here I will note just two of the most commonly relevant portions from sections b and d.

> They [public statements] do not contain (iv) a statement intended or likely to create false or unjustified expectations of favorable results; (v) a statement implying unusual, unique, or one-of-a-kind abilities. (Section b)
>
> Announcements or advertisements of "personal growth groups," clinics, and agencies give a clear statement of the purpose and a clear description of the experiences to be provided. The education, training, and experience of the staff members are appropriately specified. (Section d)

Here is a statement found in a recent brochure. How well does it fit the guidelines?

> SUPPORT-THERAPY GROUP FOR WOMEN
> Feeling lonely, depressed, or just plain stuck? This group provides a supportive place where you can learn about yourself, meet others, and get going on those desired changes you want to make in your life. Using techniques such as Gestalt therapy, Art therapy, Guided Fantasy, and Psychodrama, women progress individually and as a group. Specific skills in assertiveness training, interpersonal communication and problem solving are taught. The group is creative, fun and growth producing.

Evaluation Research: Perhaps the single most effective way of keeping oneself humble is by conducting follow-up research on one's clients. Unfortunately, it can also be a very time-consuming project, at least until a workable set of procedures has been established. Such research is not required of individual practitioners, but it is advocated for psychological service units which are components of larger organizations. The *Specialty Guidelines* state:

> There are periodic, systematic, and effective evaluations of clinical psychological services . . . . Thus evaluation includes an assessment of effectiveness . . . , efficiency . . . , continuity . . . , availability . . . , accessibility . . . , and adequacy. . . . (Section 3.3)

Continuing Education: It has long been recognized that a professional's education is never completed, but it is only recently that continuing education has become a formal requirement in order to maintain licensure as a psychologist in certain states. Thus "teeth" have been added to the statements in Principle 2 of the *Ethical Principles* and Section 15 of the *Specialty Guidelines* that require that psychologists maintain current knowledge of scientific and professional developments. Section 5 of *The Principles of Medical Ethics: With annotations especially applicable to Psychiatry* and Section 5: 01 of the *Code of Ethics of the National Association of Social Workers* contain similar injunctions.

Competency Requirements: Another aspect of assuring competency is the requirement that practitioners limit their services to areas in which they have acquired adequate knowledge and skills. Again this is a concern of all mental health professionals. Psychologists recognize the importance of this issue in Principle 2 of the Ethical Principles which states in part:

> Psychologists recognize the boundaries of their competence and the limitations of their techniques. They only provide services and only use techniques for which they are qualified by training and experience. In those areas in which recognized standards do not exist, psychologists take whatever precautions are necessary to protect the welfare of their clients. They maintain knowledge of current scientific and professional information related to the services they render.
>
> a. Psychologists accurately represent their competence, education, training, and experience . . . .

The Specialty Guidelines (Section 1.6) provide specific instruction regarding offering services outside of demonstrated competencies.

> Clinical psychological services are offered in accordance with the providers' areas of competence as defined by verifiable training and experience. When extending services beyond the range of their usual practice, psychologists obtain pertinent training or appropriate professional supervision. Such training or supervision is consistent with the extension of functions performed and services provided. An extension of services may involve a change in the theoretical orientation of the clinical psychologist, a change in modality of techniques, or a change in the type of client and/or the kinds of problems or disorders for which services are to be provided (e.g., children, elderly persons, mental retardation, neurological impairment).

Three Ways to Assess and Correct Client Expectations

We have seen how therapists can, to a degree, protect both themselves and their clients from false expectations. However, despite all these precautions clients will continue to have false expectations of therapy, some of which will be immediately apparent, and others which will arise throughout therapy. How can the ethical therapist respond to such false expectations? This last section provides three different ways in which therapists can assess and respond to client expectations, plus some comments as to the possible ethical implications of choosing one as opposed to the others.

The three different methods described below differ primarily in the degree of explicitness with which client and therapist expectations are communicated.

1. Subtle Shaping: This process is an inevitable and intricate part of any client-therapist interaction. It is mutual in that both parties shape each other's expectations. It may or may not be a consciously controlled process. It consists of providing subtle indications to the other party, both non-verbal and verbal, that certain expectations are accurate and will be met and that others are inaccurate.

Example: Kay and Don, the married couple referred to in the case of The Dissatisfied Wife in the last chapter (p. 5) are prone to talk to and look at their counselor, you, while talking about each other, as if the partner weren't present. From this and other indications you hypothesize that they expect you to act as a go-between, perhaps as a referee. You believe this to be an inappropriate role and wish to bring about more direct exchanges between the couple. You avoid responding to comments unless they are explicitly directed to you, avert your eyes when looked at, and look to the spoken-about party to respond.

Example: The mill worker referred to in The Therapist as Advice-Giver (p. 17) has been referred to you by his boss. Various indirect comments and non-verbal cues indicate discomfort at seeing a "shrink," but he proceeds anyway to describe his situation. After detailing his complaints about his fellow workers he asks, "What do I do, Doc?" You do not believe it appropriate in this situation to give the kind of advice he seems to be seeking. You respond instead by saying, "What have _you_ thought of doing?", and later, "How do you explain what happened?" You say nothing about your observations of his discomfort.

2. _Explicit Statement of Therapists' Preferences, Expectations:_ Another method is for the therapist or counselor to simply state what he prefers or expects in given situations. There is no explanation or discussion of client expectations; if they are mentioned at all it is only for the purpose of confirming or denying them. It is hoped that clients will recognize whatever discrepancies exist between their expectations and those stated by the counselor or therapist and adjust accordingly.

Example: With Don and Kay, the married couple, you could say, "I prefer you to talk directly to each other and not expect me to intervene. I believe I can be of more help by observing and then commenting on your interaction than by acting as a go-between."

Example: With the mill worker you might say, "I don't see my role as offering advice as to what you might do to resolve the difficulties you are having in these relationships; rather I see my job as helping you to understand what happened so that you can figure out for yourself what to do differently. We might start by . . . ."

3. _Exploration, Discussion of Client and Therapist Expectations:_ In this third method, therapists and counselors deliberately check out their understanding of client expectations, thus making them quite explicit to all parties, before attempting to correct them.

Example: To Don and Kay the counselor might say, "It seems you expect that I will act as a referee or a go-between. I say that because I have noticed that both of you talk to me rather than to each other, am I correct?" Supposing the couple answers in the affirmative, you might go on to say, "I believe I can be of more assistance as a commentator on how I perceive the two of you interacting, and as a facilitator of changes in that communication process. Would you be willing to try it my way?"

Example: To the mill worker you might say, "It appears that you expect me to give you specific advice regarding your relationship with your co-workers--to tell you what to do and how to do it. Am I right?" If the mill worker gives an affirmative reply, you might then go on to say, "I can see why you might think that since this is the role likely to be assumed by other professionals you have seen, such as physicians or lawyers. I also suspect it has been hard for you to get yourself to see someone about this problem, especially a "shrink," and that you are therefore doubly eager to resolve it quickly--or am I wrong about that?" Supposing the mill worker confirms your suspicions, you might continue, "Well it might be hard for you at first, but I hope you will be willing to try out a different mode of interaction with me. I perceive my role as that of a facilitator, not that of an advisor. What I do primarily is to help you understand what happened, so you can figure out for yourself what to do differently. It may seem like the long way around but I think it will prove to be more efficient and effective in the long run. Would you be willing to try it my way?"

As is clear from the above examples the third approach is more comprehensive, takes longer, and could easily precipitate abstract discussions of appropriate reciprocal roles, rather than directly attacking the problem that has been posed. It could also require more participation than many clients are prepared to give. However, it is the approach that gives all parties the maximum opportunity to identify and correct faulty or mis-matched expectations and to negotiate appropriate ones. Thus, from an ethical point of view it most nearly fits the principle of informed consent on the part of the client. The client is invited to be an active, informed participant in the therapy or counseling process, rather than a mere recipient or subject of it. It has the added therapeutic value of helping raise clients' level of awareness of their expectations, which may be crucial if such expectations are also the source of difficulties outside of the therapy situation.

The second method also provides relatively full information about the counselor's expectations and preferred procedures, and could be used by the assertive client as an opportunity to express contrary preferences. However, the counselor's deciphering of client expectations is treated more as facts than as hypotheses, and the client is not invited to correct such assumptions. Hence, there is no real invitation to discussion and negotiation of future procedures, but rather more of a "this it how it is (will be)"statement on the part of the counselor. This method has the advantage of being efficient, at least within the immediate time period, and of reducing the opportunity for the clients to get side-tracked or confused by abstract discussions. It is appropriately invoked when the therapist's or counselor's intentions are essentially non-negotiable, or when it is abundantly clear that the client is not, at the moment, prepared to discuss and negotiate reciprocal roles.

The first method, subtle shaping, is really more of an on-going process than a method. We all respond consciously and unconsciously to subtle cues of what others expect and want of us. However, trained therapists and counselors can deliberately utilize these mostly non-verbal cues to communicate what they consider to be appropriate behavior on the part of the clients. As a pragmatic matter, such cues will either support or sabotage explicit, stated expectations; thus it is essential that they be monitored. The exclusive use of this method of communication would violate the principle of informed consent, but the use of it to supplement explicit agreements and intentions is necessary to maintain the integrity of such statements.

Let us now review all three illustrative cases described in this chapter (pp. 16-19) and see how these methods, especially the third one, could be used to handle the potentially unrealistic expectations of each of the clients.

In the case of Joan who apparently expects her therapist to become her friend, the therapist could invite Joan to make such expectations fully explicit. Then, depending on the therapist's own theoretical orientation, the therapist could point out the appropriateness/inappropriateness of these expectations and clarify his own stance in such matters. Should they agree as to the nature of their future relationship, it is then up to the therapist to monitor his own future behavior, as well as Joan's, to be sure that their actions conform to the explicit agreement.

In the case of the mill worker, the issue of deliberate deception is of primary concern--is it okay to provide worthless advice in order to retain the client until such time as the client is amenable to self-exploration? Or perhaps, as the strategic therapist would claim (Watzlawick, Beavin and Jackson, 1967), good advice could be found which would break the vicious interpersonal cycle between the mill worker and his co-workers.

However, even purely behavioral intervention approaches will have to cope with the client's apparent expectation that good advice can be given after only one session. Thus regardless of how explicit the therapist chooses to make her own expectations, diagnosis, and prognosis, it may be well to clarify the client's expectations about length and nature of therapy, preparatory to countering or accommodating them.

Finally, in the case of the woman with tension headaches, the therapist must decide how willing she is to admit to her lack of experience with the treatment methods the client wants before she can fully discuss these expectations with the client. However, it would be possible for the therapist to first explore the degree of interest the client has to having biofeedback and/or hypnosis before clarifying her own attitude about the necessity to use these particular approaches.

We have reviewed issues that are most closely associated with the onset of therapy. The next two chapters will be concerned with the nature of the therapist-client relationship that develops once therapy is initiated.

> In essence the contractual mode of psychotherapy is an equalitarian partnership... The therapist enables the client to become what he intends to be (i.e. self-actualized) by respecting his potential for autonomy and self-development. He does so by not trying to protect the other from having to make choices. [1]

CHAPTER III

DEPENDENCY VERSUS AUTONOMY

It would be difficult to find a psychotherapist, regardless of therapeutic persuasion, who would not agree that one of the essential goals of psychotherapy, and perhaps the central goal, is the development of the fullest potential of clients to be autonomous, competent individuals. [2] Paradoxically, in order to achieve this goal it is thought necessary for the client to first come to trust the therapist's judgement and good will and to accept her guidance, albeit conditionally--i.e., become dependent on the therapist. Thus dependency per se is not an ethical issue--what is disputable is whether the dependency of the client on the therapist has been unnecessarily broadened or extended to the client's detriment, and what is clearly unethical is for therapists to deliberately encourage unnecessary dependence for their own financial gain, or to satisfy their own desires to feel needed or powerful. The would-be ethical therapist must not only wish to avoid such unnecessary client dependence but also have the awareness of practices that are apt to affect client dependency.

Dependency, or the potential for it, is so rampant in psychotherapy, that it is almost impossible to find a situation which does not illustrate some aspect of it. Every time a therapist does something for a client which the client presumably could do for himself, the therapist is promoting the client's dependency on her--

---

[1] From Therapeutic Partnership by Goldberg, 1977, p. 97

[2] Being autonomous is not to be confused with being "fiercely independent." An autonomous individual is goal-directed and not fear-controlled, and thus can freely choose to enter relationships.

whether it is to think through a problem, offer a hypothesis, prescribe a course of action, make a decision, or act as the client's agent in dealing with some third party. Dependency is also promoted indirectly insofar as the client-therapist relationship substitutes for, rather than encourages, close relationships outside of therapy. From this abundance of possibilities I have selected but a few to illustrate ethical dilemmas involving dependency: The first, The Would-Be Helper, depicts the all-too-common situation in which the client's mother volunteers to be a behind-the-scene helper, with the therapist providing the instructions. The Obstinate Client, depicts a situation in which the client resists any dependency relationship with the therapist, with the result that therapy cannot proceed. The ethicality of various ways of overcoming or bypassing this resistance is at issue. The Crisis-Time Client, illustrates another way in which clients may resist therapy, and the ethicality of how much pressure to put on the client to participate in on-going therapy is at issue. Finally, The Institutionalized Client, poses another familiar problem--how to ethically "evict" a mental hospital patient who is afraid to leave and sees no good reason for doing so.

The commentary sections which follow focus on the multitude of ways in which therapists, intentionally or unintentionally, promote dependency, and on how autonomy can be fostered. The autonomy-promoting elements of Mahoney's "personal scientist" model (1974) are described. Several of the illustrative cases are then analyzed in terms of dependency- and autonomy-promoting elements. The final section reviews some of the special problems posed by institutionalization.

Illustrative Cases

The Would-Be Helper: A parent of one of your college student clients calls you and expresses her willingness to be helpful. Her daughter, Gloria Parker, had told her she was seeing you. The mother knows Gloria is having a tough time adjusting to her first year in college, feeling both alienated and incompetent. Mrs. Parker wants to know if she should encourage Gloria to go out more, stay home and study, or what. She is willing to do whatever you say, but doesn't want Gloria to know that she called. What should you do?

1. Should you simply give the asked-for advice and agree to Mrs. Parker's request to keep the phone call confidential?

2. Should you tell the mother thanks for the offer, but it would be best for her simply to use her own judgment?

3. Should you tell her you will have to inform Gloria of her concern and then ask Gloria what kind of support, if any, she might want from her mother?

4. Should you tell her to simply ask Gloria how she can help?

<u>The Obstinate Client</u>: Tom is a very difficult client. He is fiercely independent and thus quite ambivalent about seeking therapy in the first place. He exhibits this independence in the therapy sessions by resisting any suggestions you make and argues with you at the slightest excuse. You are convinced that if you were to tell him to do anything he would do the exact opposite, if that were possible. He complains of worrying incessantly about his health--he is sure he has some undiagnosed malady which makes him tired and have sudden, inexplicable pains. Recent medical consultation to the contrary has done nothing to alleviate this suspicion. You believe it is time for some sort of intervention on your part. Which of the following actions seems most appropriate?

1. Take advantage of Tom's resistance. Tell him to spend the whole next week thoroughly charting all his symptoms so the two of you can later analyze them. If there appears to be a pattern he can then show it to a number of physicians until he can find one which will recognize it as the symptomatology of an illness. You anticipate Tom will either resist your suggestion entirely, or he will soon despair of the task. You hope this might start him to focusing on more productive matters.

2. Express your helplessness in dealing with him--your inability to have him respect your opinions, to even give you a chance to be of any value to him. Tell him of your frustration, your despair. You hope this sharing of your actual emotional reactions will lead to his lowering of his defensive resistance to you and to any suggestion anything non-

physical is wrong with him.

3. Seek to find parallels in Tom's reactions to you to those he had to one or more significant figures in the past. Point out to Tom how he is projecting on you the characteristics of these persons from his past. You hope this will help him accept you as you are and allow you to more effectively work with him.

The Crisis-Time Client: John is a long-term client of the University Counseling Center, long-term in that he has been in and out, seeing a variety of practicum, intern and staff counselors for the last two years. He always comes in on an emergency basis, claiming to be in a crisis situation and "needing to see someone right away." It is almost always recommended that he continue with counseling on a regular basis since some of the participating factors appear to be long-term problems in his behavior and thinking. He typically agrees, makes one or two appointments and then fails to show for the next. When followed-up he apologizes, claims things are going better and may even agree to another appointment but fails again to make it. You are the lucky counselor whom he has just seen for his last emergency and you now are seeing him for a second interview. What should you do?

1. Review his history at the counseling center and ask him what, if anything, he is willing to do--in essence, leave it to him to decide.

2. Invite the director in, review the history, and say that it appears he is not serious in seeking help, only in alleviating some immediate distress; again on an emergency basis, but he can choose to come in to see you on a regular basis. Should he fail to show up or cancel without satisfactory reason he will be terminated.

3. Review his history and point out that it reveals a fear of really finding out about himself. Reassure him that the process, albeit sometimes painful, is well worth it in the long run and that you will support him every step of the way.

The Institutionalized Client: John has been in the mental hospital for most of the last ten years. He is diagnosed as a chronic schizophrenic but has not shown any aberrant behavior for some months. A halfway house has been found that will accept him and in the staff's opinion he is ready to leave. However, John has visited the house and doesn't like it and refuses to go. If he doesn't take this opening within the next few days it will be offered to someone else and it will probably be a long time before John will have another chance, since there is a long waiting list for halfway house placements and he has no friends or relatives who will put him up. In view of his long hospitalization you do not consider it likely he would last very long on his own in the community, although he expresses more willingness to try that than to go in the halfway house. Assuming you can decide his fate, what should you do?

1. Should you take the easy course and simply let John remain indefinitely in the hospital?

2. Should you tell him he has no choice, he no longer needs hospitalization and must go to the halfway house?

3. Should you give him a choice between the halfway house and helping him get settled in the community?

Commentary

Although recognized as a general ethical concern for psychotherapists, neither the Ethical Principles, nor the Specialty Guidelines specifically warns against creating client dependency, only against exploiting it (Principle 6a of Ethical Principles).[3] I believe this reflects the profession's recognition of the diversity of ways in which client depencency may be intentionally or unintentionally promoted in therapist-client interactions and the impossibility of clearly identifying any but the most extreme examples as being unethical. It also reflects the fact that clients often enter therapy and counseling in extremely dependent states and

---

[3] The Ethical Standards of the American Personnel and Guidance Association (1981, Section E. 4) does caution against creating "a future dependency" but only in consulting situations.

to treat them as if they were fully capable of deciding for themselves may result in their feeling rejected and alienated. Nevertheless, this aspect of the client-therapist relationship is too essential to the process of psychotherapy to be ignored or scantily treated in a book of this sort. What follows then is an attempt to sort out some of the factors and techniques which restrict client choices and thus promote dependency, and conversely some of those that provide choices and thus promote autonomy.

Dependency-Promoting Practices

Mystification: As a general rule, the less the client understands of what is going on and why, the less autonomous the client can choose to be. Thus dependency is enhanced by any technique or approach which incorporates mystification (Hare-Mustin, et al., 1979). For many clients or potential clients there is a certain attractiveness about little understood techniques or therapies, especially those which promise to release untapped powers or break through to long repressed parts of ourselves. There is a corresponding temptation for the therapist who is seeking fame or fortune to "cash in" on such tendencies, and it is hard for even the most ethical therapist to resist the shaman-like role that corresponds to the use of such techniques.

Since its origin as "animal magnetism," hypnotism has enjoyed such a reputation by the layman of being a "magical" cure. Freud experimented with its use and discarded it as being too inconsistent and sometimes counterproductive in its effectiveness. Today it has made a comeback, albeit the emphasis has changed from that of achieving deep trance-like states, which many people are unwilling or incapable of achieving, to that of relaxed passivity and receptivity. Regardless of its depth, the desired state is one of increased suggestibility to whatever doctrine or instructions the therapist wishes to communicate--i.e., a state of high dependency. This is not to say that the subject completely relinquishes self-control, only that the control of the therapist relative to the client is increased, and with this increase comes greater responsibility.

There are a number of ways of enhancing client control and reducing mystification in hypnosis. One is to thoroughly explain what is to be expected and correct misapprehensions of the client. It can be pointed out, for example, that hypnosis is a self-initiated process and that it can be utilized as a means of learning a self-control technique (Katz, 1979; Redd, Andresen & Minagawa, 1982). Clients can pre-approve the basic hypnotic suggestions and be taught to induce hypnosis in themselves via audio-tape recordings which they take home with them. Finally each session can be debriefed to clarify exactly what happened and why, and to give the client opportunity to choose whether or not to repeat the experience. Similar precautions can be taken with any other technique which has especial potential for misuse.

Ambiguity: Both ends of the structured-unstructured dimension are antithetical to autonomous functioning. Any method characterized by a deliberately induced, high degree of ambiguity can promote dependency, since it places the client in the position of not knowing what is being expected or asked-for with the result that the client, in his anxiety, may search out subtle cues from the therapist as to what is a "right" response. The psychoanalytic techniques of free association and dream interpretation, in conjunction with the relatively unresponsive and perhaps out-of-sight therapist clearly utilize ambiguity. The frequency of the sessions and the length of the overall therapy in classical psychoanalysis also contribute to the possibility that the client will become dependent upon the therapist in many ways during the course of the therapy.

High Structure: Highly structured techniques such as hypnosis and authoritarian approaches also promote dependency. Behavior modification therapy, Gestalt therapy, or any step by step procedure that is completely therapist directed, once initiated, greatly reduces the opportunity for the client to exercise choice. This is alleviated somewhat when the proposed techniques are accompanied by full description, explanation of purpose and anticipated results, and provision of alternatives. Advice-giving is always conducive to dependency on the advice-giver, but especially so, when the supporting rationale is omitted.

"Hard Sell" Approaches: Cognitive re-structuring therapies such as Ellis's Rational-Emotive-Therapy (RET) can also be practiced in such a way as to promote dependence on therapist judgment as to what is "rational" and thus "right" as opposed to what is "irrational." This occurs when the therapist, secure in his belief that he knows what is best for the client to believe, engages in a "hard sell" approach for substituting his beliefs for the client's. RET implicitly assumes that it is always irrational to be extremely upset--yet Mahoney (1974, p. 184) points out, there is nothing self-evident about this premise.

Reassurance: Offering of assurance and other forms of evaluation also tend to promote dependency, because the therapist assumes the role of knowing what is true, or what will happen with respect to the client, thus leaving the client with the choice of either ignoring or denying his own feelings or judgments. If the therapist says, "You will soon feel better," or, "You'll get over it," and the client disagrees, it is considered a bad sign and not an indication of independent judgment based on the client's own past experience. Evaluations, whether based on tests or simply on the therapist's experience tend to promote a dependent state. Thus even such congratulatory statements as, "You handled that much better than last time," and, "You have really made progress," tend to accentuate the therapist's position as expert and substitute his perspective for the client's.

Friendship: Still another way in which dependency is promoted is incorporation of elements of friendship, such as therapist self-disclosure and physical expressions of affection and comfort in the client-therapist relationship. We shall explore the ramifications of such practices in the next chapter and only note for now that insofar as the client's relationship with his therapist is a substitute for another relationship, rather than an incentive to form new ones, the client is dependent on that relationship.

Client Advocacy: Intercession on behalf of individual clients with third parties, when it may be presumed that the client could have accomplished much the same by herself, albeit with some skills training and support, is also obviously dependency-building. Intercession or political activity on behalf of clients as a group or as an unfairly treated class is advocated by many psychologists as being a social and ethical responsibility of the profession.

Deception: The final collection of practices which promote dependency are those which involve deliberate deception of the client by the therapist. Acting as a behind the scenes manipulator of the client's social or physical environment as in the case of The Would-Be Helper (p. 34) is one of such practices. "Accidental" encounters are arranged and relatives or friends are instructed how to respond to the unsuspecting client.[4]

A technique that enjoys especial popularity with the "stategic" therapists (Watzlawick, et al., 1967) is the "paradoxical command." The client is commanded to do something as if it were good for her, but the therapist fully expects that the client will find it impossible to actually carry out the command and will end up renouncing an unhealthy way of acting. The illustrative case, The Obstinate Client (p. 35), contains an example of this technique. Obviously the client's autonomy in both environmental manipulation and in the use of paradoxical commands is severely restricted.

When is Dependency Illegal?

Generally speaking the law has not concerned itself much with regard to creation or maintenance of dependency in clients of psychotherapists. As we shall see in Chapter VIII, unless there are some tangible consequences which are clearly deleterious and clearly traceable to the psychotherapy itself, there is little basis for suit. However, there are some types of cases in which "undue influence" by a therapist has been alleged. The Schwitzgebels (1980, p. 257) report that this allegation has been made when therapists were left estates by older clients. There have also been claims of alienation of affection by spouses. Finally, parents have charged child enticement or undue influence when their children were estranged from them and they suspected the therapist had a role in the process.

Re-Assertion: Dependency per se is not Bad

Before we continue on to the next section which will describe practices that emphasize and encourage client autonomy I wish to remind the reader of my statement at the outset--that client dependency is not in and of itself a bad feature in psychotherapy; on the contrary, some dependency is thought to be necessary as

---

[4] Milton Erikson's method of finding a friend for a lonely client fits this mode, as described in Haley's book on him (Haley, 1973)

a transitional phase which enables clients to relinquish old dependencies and automated thought-feeling-action patterns that have proved detrimental. It follows then that methods and techniques that promoted dependency are also not in themselves bad--it is their over-utilization that needs to be guarded against. My purpose has been to identify some of these practices, or rather the dependency-promoting aspects of them, and thus enable the would-be ethical therapist to better choose when and if to invoke such methods and techniques, and, in some instances, to suggest modifications which promote more of an egalitarian partnership in the application of the techniques.

Autonomy-Promoting Techniques

There are several methods which solicit active involvement of clients in the decision-making aspects of therapy. Two of them, client-therapist contracts (p. 7) and explicit clarification and correction of client expectations and therapist intentions (p. 27), were described in the immediately preceding chapters. Both methods may be seen as means of obtaining the informed consent of clients to therapeutic procedures.

Who speaks? About what? This process of obtaining informed consent is not limited to the beginning of therapy, but can be conscientiously extended throughout therapy in several ways. It is theoretically possible to provide the client with information regarding practically every option considered by the therapist. To illustrate: Suppose a client comes in and sits down wordlessly and then looks expectantly at the therapist. The therapist could elect to either "wait the client out" and thus pressure the client to speak first, or could pick some topic with which to begin, or could throw the choice open to the client in the following fashion: "It seems you want me to speak first, am I right?" In doing so the therapist has, of course, already spoken first, but she has also done something else--she has opened for negotiation that which could have been unilaterally decided.

It is not only at the beginning of sessions that the topic and the speaker are a potential matter of negotiation. This occurs at any point of discontinuity. For example, suppose a client briefly refers to a topic and then apparently is ready to leave it. If the therapist thought it was important she might say, "Tell me more about that." Or she could say she would like to know more about the topic and provide her rationale for believing that the topic is important, thus giving the client the option of deciding whether, in his opinion, her reasons are appropriate and sufficient before deciding to continue.[4]

Obviously, such thorough-going application of the principle of informed consent threatens to make therapy an impossibly cumbersome activity. It is not possible and certainly not desirable for therapists to articulate every intuitive notion they have as to the most fruitful procedure to follow at every decision point in therapy. On the other hand, not to do so on at least some occasions effectively leaves all but the most assertive clients with only two choices--to compliantly follow the therapist's lead, or to resist doing so. When, in addition, the latter course is interpreted to the client as being evidence of "resistance" then it is difficult indeed for the client to continue without adopting a dependent role.

<u>Introduction of a new Technique</u>: Commonly accepted junctures for informing clients of options are whenever a new technique is to be introduced, especially if the technique is considered experimental in the profession itself (cf. Section B.12 of the <u>Ethical Standards</u> of the American Personnel and Guidance Association). Also, as pointed out in Chapter I, "techniques that might be at odds with the client's values should be specified." (Hare-Mustin, 1979, p. 8)

Certain techniques, however, cannot be explained beforehand without destroying their value. Paradoxical commands (p. 41) are an example. Another one is the mode of interaction adopted by the therapist in Provocative Therapy (Farrely and Brandsma, 1974) in which the therapist deliberately provokes the client to angry outbursts which reveal the client's true feelings and attitudes. Many other techniques also hope to "surprise" the client and can only be described beforehand in

---

[4] This is not to say that the explicit negotiation option is not also constraining to some degree. There is no completely neutral behavior for the therapist in this or in any other instance. There is only less or more pressure upon the client to respond in certain ways, and less or more information provided to help him make an informed choice.

general, if at all, to be effective. It can, of course, be argued that the naively dependent state of the client in such situations is only temporary or is restricted only to these limited therapist-client interactions and in no way contributes to any more generalized dependency.

The Client as a Personal Scientist

A therapeutic approach which incorporates a number of autonomy-promoting techniques has been recently described by Mahoney (1974). In his approach the client is taught to become his own personal scientist--"individuals who are skillful in the functional analysis and systematic improvement of their own behavior" (p. 274). The basic premises of the model come from cognitive behaviorism and thus adoption of the whole model would be out of the question for most therapists. However, it may be instructive to look at some of its components in terms of their transferability to and incorporation into other types of therapy.

The Therapist as "Technical Consultant": The therapist portrays herself as a "technical consultant," thus implying that she is but an assistant, albeit an expert assistant, to the client's own endeavors to achieve certain changes. The client is trained to delineate representative problems in his personal adjustment--the idea being that the process of learning how to analyze problems into their essential components is, in the long run, more important for the client to know than it is for the client simply to identify specific current problems, since it enables the client to function without a therapist the next time he gets into difficulty.

Socratic Dialogue: Socrates developed a style of questioning which prompted the person being questioned to discover his beliefs and to examine their coherence and rationality. Mahoney recommends this mode of dialogue for therapy. My own attempt at a portrayal of an excerpt of such a dialogue follows:

Client: "Well, I got rejected again."

Therapist: "What do you mean, 'rejected'?"

Client: "I asked a girl out and she said, 'No'."

Therapist: "Did you ask her out to someplace in particular?"

Client:	"Not exactly, I just asked if she liked to ski."
Therapist:	"Did you tell her you wanted to take her skiing?"
Client:	"No, I thought she would know that without my asking."
Therapist:	"So you neither clearly stated your interest in doing anything with her nor did you ask her to do anything in particular?"
Client:	"Yeah, you're right. I can see where you are leading to. I didn't put myself on the line in any way."

Hypotheses, not Interpretations: Another aspect of Mahoney's model is the conversion of therapist interpretations into hypotheses. Hypotheses are by definition speculative attempts to make sense of certain data, and hence open to challenge and change by the client, rather than "objective truths" which the therapist is privy to and the client will accept if they are properly timed. Clients are encouraged to develop their own hypotheses, both with regard to understanding the data and with regard to ways of solving their problems.

Multiple Solutions and Experimentation: Multiple solutions are encouraged, thus further emphasizing that there is not apt to be only one "correct" solution, and that only the therapist knows it. These various solutions are then experimentally evaluated by the client in order to determine their relative efficacy, but more fundamentally to teach the client how to repeat this process when on his own.

Faded Contacts: Abrupt termination is discouraged; rather "faded contacts" are continued for at least one year following resolution of the first set of concerns, as a sort of preventative measure and as a transition to full independent functioning.

Analysis of several Illustrative Cases in terms of Dependency- and Autonomy-Promoting Techniques

The Would-Be Helper (p. 34): If the therapist accedes to Gloria's mother's request to instruct her how to interact with Gloria without Gloria's knowledge, this would constitute deception of or, at least, concealment from Gloria of part of her overall treatment program, and thus would be dependency-promoting.

If, on the other hand, the therapist informs Gloria of her mother's request he would be violating her mother's "confidentiality," assuming the mother wanted her phone call to be kept confidential. However, only by sharing her mother's concern with Gloria is Gloria in a position of maximum information and thus maximum opportunity to decide what is best for herself. Gloria can then choose to have the therapist involve her mother as an assistant, or not, as she sees fit.

The Obstinate Client (p. 35): The issue highlighted in this case is when, and to what degree, is it ethical for you, the therapist, to deliberately choose to deceive your clients by concealing your intentions or convictions? If you are convinced that there is a strong psychological basis for Tom's physical symptoms then you can choose to hide or reveal such a conviction in any of the three optional approaches. If you choose to hide the conviction, the justification will be that it is necessary to do so in order to avoid losing, and thus not helping the client.

Use of the paradoxical command involves a different deception--namely, the concealment that your intention is not truly to aid in the diagnosis of Tom's physical disease, but rather to get Tom to quit searching for such a "solution." The justification would be to make therapy more effective and efficient.

The risk of any kind of concealment is that the client will either suspect or discover it and this will result in his feeling manipulated and considering you as not trustworthy.

One way that may circumvent the impasse is for both you and Tom to treat the possibility of psychogenic illness as a hypothesis to be tested, and not as something for you to know and the client to discover. Persuading the client to take an experimental attitude with regard to the basis for his symptoms, however, is not likely to be an easy task.

The Crisis-Time Client (p. 36): The issue raised in this case is how much coercion is it ethical to use in order to get a client to work through his problems rather than to seek help in coping with them only when he is in a crisis situation. Option one, that of reviewing John's history and asking him what he wants to do, affords him the greatest latitude of unpressured choice. The second option of having the director threaten to refuse future service unless he cooperates and the third option of reassuring him that the exploration process will be bearable are alternative ways of trying to get the client to do what appears to be best for him, to commit himself to making a sustained effort to change his crisis-producing behavior.

One way of combining the best of all three options makes use of Socratic dialogue and presentation of interpretations as hypotheses for John to consider, rather than as "truths." After reviewing the history of crisis counseling and aborted follow-through with John, you could pose several hypotheses for his behavior as illustrated in the following dialogue:

You: "It appears that you might be afraid of discovering something unpleasant about yourself if you were to really commit yourself to counseling." (Option three) "Or perhaps you are just afraid of the stigma of being a regular client--you believe that it is 'okay' to come in at times of crisis, but only really screwed-up people come in on a regular basis. Do you think either one of these explanations for your behavior has any validity? Or is there some other reason that you know of and could tell me?"

John: "No, I think you are right--probably both of them are true."

You: "Well, what then do you think we could do about it?"

John: "I don't know. I suppose just commit myself to regular counseling, I guess."

You: "Well, I've thought some about your case and I have a suggestion. It doesn't seem likely that you will change your attitude toward counseling without additional incentive and I wonder if making it an either/or proposition would help. We, by that I mean the whole staff of the counseling center, could refuse to see you anymore on an emergency basis unless you were also being seen on a regular basis." (Option two) "Actually, I suspect any emergencies could be handled in your regular sessions. I mean this as a serious option--if we invoke it we will stick to it. But it is up to you whether you think it would help you do what you think you should." (Option one)

John: "Gee, I don't know. Let me think about it."

Institutionalization

The case of The Institutionalized Client (p. 36) illustrates one of the kinds of practical and ethical dilemmas that occur in institutions for the treatment of mental illness. Psychologists are frequently involved in making decisions for or about inmates (patients) to which the inmates would never agree, if given the choice. Paradoxically, some of these decisions may be made for the purpose of promoting the patient's eventual autonomy apart from the institution. Other times the decision may be to force compliance with the institution's treatment program, whether it be medication, work therapy, group therapy, or what have you.

It is not my intention to thoroughly analyze and discuss the multitude of situations and resultant ethical dilemmas and legal implications that occur within institutions since that would be a major undertaking and has already been the focus of several publications. I am primarily concerned in this book with dilemmas and issues that arise in the course of doing psychotherapy and not with those encountered in acting as a psychiatric ward administrator, institutional program designer, etc. Also this chapter is concerned only with the dependency/autonomy issue. Thus the three phases of institutionalization will be but briefly described in terms of how each represents a constriction of the potential for autonomy of the individual client (inmate). Interested readers are referred to the "Report of the Task Force on the Role of Psychology in the Criminal Justice System" (American Psychological Association, 1978) and to the book containing this report (American Psychological Association, 1980) for fuller discussion of the broad range of ethical issues. An especially valuable review of the legal aspects of behavioral modification techniques in institutional settings is provided by Budd and Baer (1976).

The initial phase of institutionalization, that of considering placing an individual into an institution, is also the first phase in which it is obvious that there is a constriction of the client's autonomy, her range of options, and other people start deciding "what is best," both for the person and for the broader segments of society. Institutionalization, whether in a mental hospital, a psychiatric ward of a regualr medical facility, a rehabilitation treatment center, or a prison is seldom the first choice of potential inmates. More often they would prefer to remain where they are or go to some other environment that is judged infeasible or where their welcome has worn out. Thus, pressure is exerted to get them to "voluntarily" agree to being placed in an institution, and court commitment is imposed if they do not agree to voluntary admission or if it is thought that they would not follow through on such institutionalization, even if they agree to it.

The second phase, that of institutional living, also is markedly characterized by reduced freedom of choice. Practically all major and many minor decisions are made for the inmates, including the kinds of treatment they receive, if any, when to get up and when to go to bed, and when and what to eat. Recently there has been considerable legal furor over the "right to treatment" of inmates who are forcibly detained in institutions whose alleged purpose, at least in part, is rehabilitative or educative. There have also been some major court actions over the "right to refuse treatment," especially medication. These issues are far from being resolved at the present time, but the very fact that they have been raised indicates an increased sensitivity to the dependency-promoting aspects of institutionalization (see, for example, "Judicial Notebook," 1982).

Ethical concern, at least for psychologists, has focused more on the degree to which it is appropriate to pressure inmates into cooperation with treatment programs, especially those which involve behavioral modification, such as token economies or other situations where it is clear that certain designated rewards are contingent upon enactment of pre-selected "appropriate" behaviors. This concern was the focus of an APA commission whose findings were published in the form of a book (Stolz & Associates, 1978). As we shall see in the chapter on research by practitioners the degree to which inmates of institutions can truly give "informed consent" to experimental treatments, and thus the necessity of obtaining it from those who can claim to represent their interests in some way, is a problem of some magnitude.

The third phase of institutionalization, the planning for discharge and placement in the community, is also apt to involve the issue of autonomy/dependency, in that it is rarely the case that the timing of the discharge, the conditions under which discharge will be implemented or denied, or the decision as to which community resources, if any, are to be provided the inmate upon discharge are made with the full knowledge and assent of the inmate. As was illustrated in the case of The Institutionalized Client, it may well be that the inmate's own choice(s) are not considered realistic or in "his best interest."

By the time an inmate is considered ready for release he may have already adapted to a very dependent life style and thus be poorly prepared to take an active role in planning which precedes such release. Ideally, he will have been given increasing responsibility for his own activities prior to discharge, and, in the case of mental hospitals, a number of short visits to the community from which he returned without undue incident. This is often not possible in other institutions, such as prisons, nor is it always possible even with mental hospitals. Nevertheless, there is increasing pressure to evict inmates who might make it "on the outside," given the cost of institutional care and the number of people who are deemed to need such care. Both the ethical and the practical solution, under these circumstances, would seem to be to prevent long-term dependency in the first place, and to create as many out-of-institution treatment options as possible, thus creating "bridges" to the outside for those who are in, and community support systems for those who would otherwise have to be hospitalized. It may well be that given sufficient exposure to such options, and given sufficient options, even the most dependent inmate may voluntarily choose to leave the institution.

This concludes the discussion of the dependency-autonomy dilemma. The next chapter will examine the social and sexual aspects of the client-therapist relationship.

> Psychologists are continually cognizant of their own needs and of their potentially influential position vis-a-vis persons such as clients, students, and subordinates. They avoid exploiting the trust and dependency of such persons. Psychologists make every effort to avoid dual relationships that could impair their professional judgment or increase the risk of exploitation. Examples of such dual relationships include, but are not limited to, research with and treatment of employees, students, supervisees, close friends, or relatives. Sexual intimacies with clients are unethical. (Ethical Principles, 6a)

CHAPTER IV

SOCIAL AND SEXUAL RELATIONS WITH CLIENTS

When is it appropriate to have a cup of coffee with a client? When to accept (refuse) a gift or an invitation to a party from a client? Is it unethical or merely unwise to form a sexual liaison with a recently terminated client? How is one supposed to handle sexual attraction to clients, or respond to sexual overtures? These and other questions are not, and perhaps cannot be explicitly handled in a code of ethics; however, examination of the existing codes and speculation regarding possible meanings of various client-therapist interactions, provide some general criteria for deciding when to do what. This chapter is devoted to this process of examination, speculation and proposal of guidelines. The legal ramifications of client-phychotherapist sexual relations will also be considered.

We shall begin this process by first posing the above questions within specific contexts in our illustrative cases section. The One-Time-Only Client poses the question of whether or not a counselor who fills in for another counselor on an one-time emergency basis is free to then accept dates with the client, since he isn't "really" her client. The Attractive Client poses the question of how therapists should cope with their own feelings of sexual attraction to clients, especially if the attraction seems mutual. In The Cup of Coffee the therapist must decide how to respond to a client's invitation to have a cup of coffee with her at a cafe, as a way of getting better acquainted. In The Gift the therapist must decide whether or not and how to accept/ reject a birthday gift from his client.

In the following commentary sections guidelines will be presented for handling each of the above situations, among others. First, however, there is general discussion over the basic motives for client attempts to socialize the client-therapist relationship and how modern therapeutic practices, such as direct eye contact and therapist self-disclosure, make it easier to transform the professional relationship into a social, or even sexual one. The psychological, social and legal hazards of "socialization" of the psychotherapy relationship will be depicted, with special reference to sexual intimacies between clients or former clients and their therapists. I then present the case for "authenticity," for expansion of the therapist role to include self disclosure. I argue that on some occasions limited social interaction between potential or current clients is appropriate and may even be necessary before a therapeutic relationship can be established. Criteria will be presented by which such situations may be identified.

Finally, I provide a self inventory for therapists to help them decide whether they are inadvertently promoting or allowing themselves to be drawn into a social relationship with a client or a former client.

Illustrative Cases

The One-Time-Only Client: Joan is a graduate student in psychology serving as a practicum counselor in the university's counseling center. She sees a male student, Ralph, on an emergency basis for one interview. Ralph subsequently calls her up and asks for a date. She wants to accept but is not sure it is the right thing to do. She does not expect to see him as a client again since he already has a regular counselor at the center, who wasn't available at the time of the crisis, but who presumably will be available in the future. What should she do?

1. Should she accept the date in view of her interest in him and in view of the fact that he isn't really her client?

2. Should she turn down the date on the basis that their only contact was a counseling situation when

she was in the role of his counselor; thus his request may well reflect false expectations or covert motives?

3. Should she suggest some other sort of arrangement instead that would provide both of them the opportunity to get to know each other in a group situation, rather than in a one to one basis.

The Attractive Client: You have seen Shirley for four interviews and consider her extremely attractive. You find yourself having sexual fantasies and romantic fantasies involving her both within and without the sessions. She seems to welcome any interest you show in her and you suspect the attraction is mutual.

1. Should you ignore and suppress the fantasies as best you can and continue to try to work with this client?

2. Should you simply enjoy the fantasies, say nothing about them, and continue to work with the client?

3. Should you confess your attraction and make it a topic for mutual examination by you and your client and hope to find a mutual resolution which will allow the continuation of psychotherapy, per se?

4. Should you terminate the client with as general an explanation as seems to satisfy her and refer her elsewhere?

How soon after termination would you think it proper to contact this client to pursue an intimate relationship?

The Cup of Coffee: May is a long term client of yours. At the end of your session she asks if you won't have a cup of coffee with her at a nearby cafe during your regular afternoon coffee break. She promises "no business," she says she just would like to get to know you better. What should you do?

1. Should you turn down her request and explain that you don't like to mix business with pleasure, that you are afraid that a purely social relationship might be initiated that would then interfere with the therapy relationship?

2. Should you explore, then and there, "why she would like to know you better," and then decide whether or not to accept?

3. Should you simply accept, see what her intentions appear to be, and act accordingly?

Would it make any difference if May were a new client? If she were an inmate in an institution and if she had not as yet seen you for counseling? Are there any circumstances when you would be sure to say, "Yes"? --to say, "No"? What criteria do you use to decide between the two?

The Gift: Alex overheard the office staff say that it was your birthday and purchased a box of candy which he proudly presents to you at the beginning of the session. He explains that, "Being that you are my favorite therapist, I wanted to give you something for the occasion." Under what conditions would you pursue each of the following options?

1. Accept the gift with a simple, "Thank you," and then refocus on the task at hand? Suppose then that two weeks later Alex makes a point of mentioning his own upcoming birthday?

2. Reject the gift, explaining that, much as you would like to, you would be afraid that accepting it would in some fashion compromise the relationship, that all the thanks you want from him are your fees and for him to make progress in dealing with his concerns?

3. Adopt a compromise stance--such as accepting the gift and also making it clear that you could not do so again in view of the danger it poses to the therapeutic relationship?

What if the gift were a home-crafted item of considerable value? What if it were some "extra" cookies the client made? At what point would the gift be excessive?

Commentary

Striving for Parity

The quality and the nature of the client-therapist relationship are seen by many as the crucial variables in affecting client change, rather than the techniques which are applied or the theoretical approach which the therapist practices. Such a relationship is almost by definition an intimate one, one made so in part by the client's divulgement of intimate, private, perhaps never-before-expressed or admitted thoughts, feelings, and actions. But it is also a one-sided intimacy, since the therapist does not have to, or at least is not expected to reciprocally respond with his own secrets. This places the therapist at a powerful psychological advantage in the relationship. Clients have to trust that their therapist will not misuse their intimate knowledge of them, but the reverse is not true. This inequity, this imbalance in the relationship can be expected to create a desire for some form of countercontrol on the part of clients as well as some testing of the trustworthiness of the therapist. There may also be a desire to establish relationships similar to those in which clients have felt relatively secure in the past.

One form of countercontrol is to socialize the client-therapist relationship--to transform it, at least in part, into a friendship or perhaps even a sexual relationship, or a relationship with sexual overtones. When this desire for parity is met by a complimentary desire on the part of the therapist to alleviate his own sense of isolation or to fulfill his sexual desires, then it is unlikely that a strictly professional relationship will be maintained.

This initial lack of parity of power in the relationship may also, on occasions, result in a similar breakdown of the therapeutic relationship simply by virtue of the therapist's ability to manipulate a trusting, passive-dependent client, even without the client's active assistance. This may be especially true, as we shall see later, with respect to male therapists and female clients.

Erosion of the Distinctiveness of the Psychotherapeutic Relationship

Historically it was thought that client-therapist relations should be as free of social and sexual aspects and connotations as possible, at least on the therapist's part. Social overtures from the client were seen as data to be interpreted, not to be responded to in kind. As we have seen in Chapter I Freud believed the therapist should act as a "mirror," reflecting the client's own behavior so it could be seen in an undeniable way by the client, and not distorting the picture and muddying the interpretation by presenting any of his own personality. This mask-like role of the therapist was facilitated by aligning the therapist and the client in such a way that the therapist could see the client, but not vice versa. The projective role of the client was also enhanced by this arrangement since the client, insofar as she reacted to the therapist in a visual way, was doing so to her image of the therapist, rather than to the actual sight of him.

Eye Contact: Nowadays, at least among those therapists who do not practice psychoanalysis, eye-to-eye contact is allowed and even encouraged. Typically, clients and therapists sit at an oblique angle allowing easy observation of each other. It is considered too formal by many therapists to have a desk in between. This arrangement is common in most social situations as well--it is not distinctive of psychotherapy.

Fees: Another erosion of distinciveness has taken place with respect to the payment of fees. One characteristic of a professional relationship is that one party, the client, pays the other party, the professional, a fee. However, many agencies now offer psychotherapy and counseling without any direct collection of money. The expenses are indirectly assessed through taxes, student fees or third-party payments, rather than being part of a person-to-person transaction which reminds the participants of their respective roles. Even in private practice the client may well pay the major part of the fee through a third party.

Therapist Self-Disclosure: The introduction of therapist self-disclosure as a way of establishing an open, "authentic" relationship between the therapist and the client and of removing client hesitation about discussing some matters, also lessens the distinction between the professional client-therapist relationship and that of friendship.

Touching: Finally, the "hands-off" barrier has been breached. In a recent survey (Holroyd & Brodsky, 1977) approximately half of the psychologist psychotherapists surveyed thought hugging, kissing, or affectionate touching might be beneficial, at least occasionally, to both male and female clients.

Hazards of Socialization in Psychotherapy

Why is it a concern that psychotherapists maintain a distinctive role in the first place? Primarily because it is assumed that professional therapists have something different to offer from that which friends, lovers, mentors, or people on the street can offer. However, unless the parameters of their relationships with clients are kept distinct there is a danger that this distinct portion will get lost in the matrices of expectations and interactions of these other types of relationships.

Less social Risk-Taking by Client: Specifically, one such hazard is that clients who perceive themselves as having found a friend or lover or mentor will not take the risk trying to develop such relationships elsewhere, and thus actually diminish their ability to find such satisfactions in the broader social context in which they live.

Change of Focus: On the therapist's part the risk is enhanced that the focus will change from exclusive concern with the agreed-upon goals of the client to fulfilling the social, sexual, egotistical or financial desires of the therapist. For example, if a friendship develops it is tempting to ask favors of each other--after all, what are friends for? Thus the client who is a financial expert might be asked, "incidentally" of course, for advice regarding the therapist's investments.

Less Openness and increased Fragility of Therapeutic Relationship: Both clients and therapists will have more to lose and thus be less open with each other to the degree that they depend upon each other for social, sexual or financial needs. Therapists are apt to be less confrontative, clients less willing to admit to thoughts, actions, or feelings which they think might threaten or offend their therapists. Thus the whole therapist-client relationship becomes more fragile since a disappointment in any one aspect is apt to sour the whole relationship.

Generalization to other Therapists: Clients who end up being disappointed with the therapist because of conflicts arising from social or sexual aspects will be less willing to try counseling or therapy again, at least with therapists of the same "type" (e.g., female clients may boycott all male therapists because of a single offender).

Sex

Sex deserves special consideration in our review of the hazards that are associated with socialization of the client-psychotherapist relationship. It is a powerful, sometimes dominant interpersonal factor in all kinds of human relationships and has received special mention in recent ethical codes and special attention in malpractice suits. Clients and therapists do think of each other as sexual beings and do, at times, act out some of their feelings. To ignore this fact or to downplay it by mere reference to the relevant statement in the Ethical Principles ("Sexual intimacies with clients are unethical") would be unethical in itself in a book that purports to delve beneath the surface of the existing ethical codes and to examine the various ramifications of these codes for the practicing psychotherapist or counselor.

Accordingly, we will first consider the question of how practitioners should handle their sexual feelings towards clients and former clients. We shall then look at the evidence of actual sexual interchange between clients and therapists. Finally, we will briefly note the legal implications of such interchange.

A colleague of mine has taught human sexuality courses for students in graduate counseling and clinical psychology programs for the past 15 years. One major concern of these students, if not the major concern, is how to handle the sexual feelings they have towards their clients. Fortunately, they have such courses in which they can raise this question, and an instructor who perceives it as important. His answer is summarized below. (Acker, Note 1)

> 1. Enjoy it--it is a natural response of humans to each other. Sex is a highly important aspect of human relationships. Accept, don't reject it out of fear or shame. Remember that feelings do not need to lead to direct expression, and one maintains more control by acceptance than by rejection of them.
>
> 2. Try to understand it--is the desire prompted primarily by flirtatious behavior of the client, or is it primarily a result of your own projections? If the former, then it is appropriate to comment on this

> behavior in the therapy session and to jointly determine its significance for the client. If the latter, then it is appropriate for you to examine how well you are taking care of your own sexual needs outside of your work, and it may behoove you to seek out personal counseling for yourself in this matter.

I heartedly endorse the above statement and would only add that "enjoying" one's sexual response to a client does not necessarily mean unduly focusing on it. After recognizing and accepting such feelings it is appropriate to then suppress further thought of them and return to the task at hand. If such attempts at suppression fail, that becomes a signal to the therapist that he needs to look at his own needs in this area.

On the other hand if the client is the one who seems to be "smitten" with the therapist, it could be that a straightforward provision of information by the therapist such as, "I am committed to my wife and to my profession, and though you are attractive I will not pursue any social or sexual relationship with you," may resolve the situation. At other times a thorough analysis of the underlying dynamics may be required.

The Ethical Principles provide some guidance here also:

> Psychologists recognize that personal problems and conflicts may interfere with professional effectiveness. Accordingly, they refrain from undertaking any activity in which their personal problems are likely to lead to inadequate performance or harm to the client, colleague, student, or research participant. If engaged in such activity when they become aware of their personal problems, they seek competent professional assistance to determine whether they should suspend, terminate, or limit the scope of their professional and/or scientific activities. (Principle 6f)

Application to Case of "The Attractive Client": If we now apply the above reasoning to the case of The Attractive Client (p. 53) we can see that all four options have some part that could be utilized--suppressing your fantasies, enjoying them, confessing your attraction and discussing it, and terminating the client. The first step is to cognitively accept your sexual attraction to the client and not try to immediately ignore or suppress it. To a certain extent these feelings may also be "enjoyed" (Option two). The next step is to try to identify the source of the attraction, to understand it. To the extent that the client appears to be actively contributing to your feelings and fantasies by flirtatious behavior, then that becomes a relevant topic for exploration within the sessions themselves--why is the client behaving this way? What does the client hope to achieve by such behavior? (Option three)

To the extent that your thoughts and feelings represent inadequate, unsatisfying sexual activity in your own life, or that your sexual desires mask desires for dominance, succor, etc. it is appropriate to work through these problems outside of the therapy sessions in order to avoid lessening your competency as a therapist in the sessions. It may be that you can ignore and suppress these interfering thoughts and feelings sufficiently well to warrant continuing working with the client (Option one); or it may be that you may have to terminate working with the client and refer elsewhere (Option four). In either case it may be useful to you to seek professional assistance for yourself.

Another consideration is that malpractice liability coverage usually explicitly exempts "licentious, immoral or sexual behavior intended to lead to or culminating in any sexual act." (Psychologists Professional Liability Policy, American Home Assurance Company).

Social, sexual Relationships with "terminated" Clients: Perhaps a less crucial, but bothersome issue that has as yet to surface in any direct form in the various ethical codes is the appropriateness of sexual relationships with former clients. There is something unsavory about the situation in which a former therapist rushes into bed with his former client immediately after termination of their psychotherapeutic relationship, even if it is not technically unethical or illegal. Even marriages between therapists and former clients are met with some suspiciousness or outright derision from the general public, if not the profession. This is especially true if the sole way in which the two got acquainted and the main portion of their "courtship" relationship appears to have occurred within the psychotherapy, itself.

What are some of the reasons that it may be bad policy, though not exactly unethical, for therapists to engage in sexual relations with former clients? One reason is that it is difficult to say when a client is truly terminated. Some clients are "terminated" many times during the course of their therapy, and entering a sexual or close social relationship with them interferes with subsequent reinstatement as a client.

Another, more important reason is that it is difficult and sometimes impossible for old client-therapist relationships to be transformed to ones in which both partners play relatively equal roles in listening and responding to each other, and assert themselves equally in making joint decisions, rather than one of them being expected to continue to serve as the good listener, only now on a full-time basis, and one expected to defer to the other, more "rational" one in case of differing opinions on some course of action.

APA's handling of a recent case indicates that the profession is now extending its interpretation of Principle 6 to former clients, as well as current clients. In case 80-6-2 (Sanders & Keith-Spiegel, 1980) a woman complained that after two years of therapy, the relationship with her therapist became a sexual one. The therapist did promptly terminate the therapeutic relationship but made no attempt to resolve any of the therapeutic issues still remaining. The sexual relationship continued on a weekly basis for approximately one year before the client finally decided to terminate it because she felt "used." She subsequently refused two more attempts by the therapist to renew the clandestine affair. The therapist eventually admitted that the woman's charges were essentially true and was offered a stipulated resignation from APA for a period of 5 years.

Homosexual Liaisons: Special problems arise when the client-therapist sexual liaison is a homosexual one, either during or after therapy. Our predominantly heterosexually-oriented culture has rather consistently demonstrated its lack of tolerance for and understanding of such relationships. Our profession, by and large, no longer considers homosexuality evidence of psychological disturbance, but its heterosexual members are no more immune to negative "gut feelings" when confronted with manifestations of homosexuality than the general populace from which they come. Our advantage, such as it is, is that our profession forces us to confront such feelings and to try to alter them, and certainly to avoid acting on them. It would be no solution to "bend over backwards" in this situation by assuming a more lenient view of homosexual liaisons between therapists and clients or former clients than we do of heterosexual liaisons. However, there may be a special obligation for us, as a profession, to campaign against laws and customs which put homosexually-oriented persons, clients and otherwise, at a disadvantage in housing, employment, freedom of association, etc.

Psychotherapists as Humans: Does this mean that it is forbidden ever to form friendships or sexual liaisons with former clients? Of course not. Therapists (and clients) are human too. Their role definitions should not be allowed to dominate their whole existence and prohibit the formation of what might be far more important and satisfying relationships. It may be that the relationship was quite circumscribed--consisting of only a few contacts or dealing primarily with information-giving, or testing, such as might occur in vocational counseling. It may be that the relationship, although long-term, did not permanently establish helper-helpee roles, but rather enabled each to get to know and truly respect the other person in a broader sense.

In any case, as long as there is opportunity for a transitional period, a period in which both parties get to know each other as individuals in a number of different settings, there is also the opportunity for a thorough transformation of their relationship to occur, a transformation in which both therapists and former clients are able to escape their previous roles. Thus, in the case of The One-Time-Only Client (p. 52), the third option, that of meeting in a group situation, would seem the most suitable since it does provide a "neutral" setting in which the crisis counselor and the emergency client can observe and get to know each other without the pressure to relate again in an exclusive one-to-one manner. This is not to say that any such "date" would be wise in view of the misconceptions and manipulations that are likely. With The Attractive Client (p. 53), a longer, more tangential and varied transitional period would be appropriate.

Finally, as the Ethical Principles also state:

> . . . psychologists are sensitive to prevailing community standards and to the possible impact that conformity to or deviation from these standards may have upon the

> quality of their performance as psychologists. Psychologists are also aware of the possible impact of their public behavior upon the ability of colleagues to perform their professional duties. (Principle 3)

This guideline does not prescribe conformity to "prevailing community standards," only sensitivity to such standards. If a therapist elects to violate or protest such a standard, it would be important that it be a standard which can be shown to be detrimental to the psychological well-being of the community.

Frequency of sexual Intimacy between Clients and Therapists: There have been a number of studies on the incidence of sexual intimacy of physicians with their patients. Perhaps the largest and most recent one included a random sample of 1000 male physicians, 460 of whom responded, 116 of whom were psychiatrists (Kardener, Fuller & Mensh, 1973). Five percent of the psychiatrists who responded to the question of whether their contacts with patients included sexual intercourse responded in the affirmative. Recently a survey using the same cover letter and a survey instrument was done of 1000 male and female licensed Ph.D. psychologists resulting in 666 usuable questionnaires (Holroyd & Brodsky, 1977). They found almost the identical results for male psychotherapists (5.5%) but only about one ninth as many female therapists (.6%) answered affirmatively to having sexual intercourse with clients.

Similar results were obtained from another questionnaire designed by a task force of the California State Psychological Association and sent to 4,385 licensed psychologists in California who were asked what their clients reported regarding former therapists (Bazar, 1981). Only 16% responded. Again 5% of their clients reported having had sex with former therapists, and that therapy ended immediately for one third of them when sex began. Further questions elicited that:

1. The patient's personality was adversely affected in 34% of the cases.

2. The patient had negative feelings in 29% of the cases.

3. The patient's sexual, marital or intimate relationships worsened in 26% of the cases (some cases are listed in more than one of the above

categories).

4. Only in 9% of the cases was there no reported effect on the patient, and in 16% the patient became healthier or improved emotionally and/or in sexual relations.

Thus, there is at least a modicum of evidence to support the contention that some therapists do engage in sexual intimacies with their clients, that those therapists tend to be male (and their clients female), and that such practices are apt to be detrimental to the clients.

Legal Implications: What are the legal implications of having sex with your clients? Are you automatically liable for malpractice if the client should choose to sue you, especially since professional codes specifically state it is unethical to have such sexual intimacies? As we shall see in Chapter 8, having sex with one's adult clients is not necessarily illegal, even though the profession and most of society would consider it unethical. Among other things the client must prove that "actual injury" was incurred. Originally this was interpreted to refer to only manifest physical injury or consequence, but more recently this requirement has been relaxed somewhat to include demonstrable emotional injury. The client must also prove that such injury was caused by the psychotherapist's actions (or inactions); i.e., by the therapist conducting himself in such a way as to create an unreasonable risk of harm. Of course, if the sexual relationship is one which is illegal for the general public, such as between an adult and an under-aged person, it would also be illegal for the profession.

The Case for Authenticity: The Therapist as a Full Person

Up to now the risks and hazards of socialization of the client-therapist relationship have been presented, but the case for socialization has not. The majority of psychotherapists today do not observe the strict demarcation lines between therapists and clients that were drawn by Freud. They face their clients, at least obliquely; they touch their clients; they frequently engage, especially at the beginning of the session, in some small talk about the weather, prominent events of the day, or other environmental aspects; and they self-disclose, both premeditatedly and spontaneously, in the therapy hour. Many greet their clients when they encounter them on the street or in social gatherings and may engage in casual conversation with them on such occasions. Some think nothing of having a cup of coffee with clients, both within and without their offices, and many are pleased to accept gifts from clients. I knew one licensed psychologist whose office could have been described as decorated in "early client" because it was so filled with various gifts of former clients. He, on his part, treated each client to a cup of specially brewed herbal tea to start off each therapy hour.

What reasons could be advanced to explain such behavior? One that is frequently espoused is that it is "natural" to start off with small talk, greet each other as the acquaintances you are, etc., and it would be "artificial" to restrain from such socialization and place an uncomfortable restraint on both parties, making it more difficult for the client to engage in the self-disclosure necessary for therapy to take place.

To touch or not to touch? It may also be thought artificial not to touch one's clients, not to spontaneously show affection or to physically comfort them, for example. To express a pun, whether, when, and where to touch is a "touchy" subject since being touched and touching are not casual, but very significant activities for many people in our society. Accordingly, it is important for therapists to become sensitive to their client's reactions in such matters, as well as to carefully monitor their own impulses to touch or not to touch their clients. Some discussion on this matter can be found in the two articles by Holroyd & Brodsky, 1977, 1980) in which they found that those therapists who admitted having intercourse with patients advocated and used touching, albeit nonerotic touching with opposite sex clients more often than other therapists. However, to my knowledge, no thorough study has been made with regard to the implications of touching in psychotherapy and counseling.

The "authentic" Therapist: There has been a strong case made for spontaneous behavior in general, and therapist self-disclosure in particular.

Carl Rogers (1970) and Sidney Jourard (1964, 1971), but especially Jourard has argued for therapist "authenticity"--for establishing the therapist as a full-fledged person in the client-therapist relationship.

> If the effective therapists are themselves in the presence of the patient, if they let their patient and themselves be, avoiding compulsions to silence, to reflection, to interpretation, to impersonal technique, and kindred character disorders, but instead striving to know their patient, involving themselves in his situation, and then responding to his utterances with their spontaneous selves, this fosters growth. (Jourard, 1971, p. 139)

However, this is not to be interpreted as carte blanche, as "anything goes" within the therapy sessions. Jourard points out at various points in his book that the therapist's spontaneity is "bound . . . by his ethics and his judgment" (p. 71), "checked by . . . common sense" (p. 146), that he can refuse to answer his client's questions if he chooses (p. 147) and that, "one need not tell the patient about one's life outside the therapy hour" (p. 148).

It is also clear that it is the client and not the therapist who is to be the focus of exploration, that the sessions are not to be devoted to reciprocal sharing of personal concerns such as might be expected in ordinary friendships, but rather to concerns of the patient and responses of the therapist to those concerns.

<u>The Cup of Coffee (p. 53)</u>: This brings us back full circle to the paradigmatic question with which we started the chapter: "When is it appropriate to have a cup of coffee with a client?" The answer has become somewhat more apparent in the meantime. It is appropriate when the situation is such that this social amenity will help focus attention on the client's concerns and how to resolve them, and inappropriate when it threatens to transform the therapeutic relationship into a social or sexual one.

We have, however, concentrated more on the inappropriate occasions or the hazards than on the appropriate occasions. There is one set of circumstances in which shaking hands, inviting the client or potential client to have a cup of coffee, and even joining clients in group games or group outings may be necessary if the practitioner is going to be an effective helper. This occurs whenever there is a strong social barrier between the practioner and the potential clientele, when an administrator-therapist is apt to be perceived as "one of them" and the "them" are generally regarded with suspicion and hostility. This frequently occurs in institutional settings, especially correctional institutions or any place where many if not all of the inmates are there involuntarily. In such settings it is difficult and sometimes impossible to establish a true working relationship with clients, but the task remains especially difficult if the therapist appears to be careful to maintain a superior social position and interpersonal distance. Teaching the client the differences between a client-therapist relationship and an ordinary friendship or other intimate relationship can only occur if the client first agrees to be a client.

Arnold Lazarus carries this type of thinking one step further in his book, Behavior Therapy and Beyond (1971). He advocates that therapists be quite flexible, especially with new patients. Any fixed pattern, such as formal history taking or administering of psychological tests, should be postponed till after the first interview--since this would interfere with establishing rapport. As a result of what is learned about the patient in the first interview the therapist may even decide to change the setting of the second in order to make the patient feel more at ease and facilitate the establishment of a working relationship:

> . . . the second interview should find the therapist immediately applying everything he has gleaned during the initial interview. Personalistic psychotherapy has no preset structure. Thus my second interviews have sometimes been conducted in a restaurant, at the patient's home, or in an outdoor park, rather than in the formal confines of the consulting room. (p. 63)

Criterion for acceptable social Activites

It would seem likely that such occasions would be the exception rather than the rule. However, the main point remains that one cannot make any hard and fast rules regarding participating in social activites with new or potential clients. What I propose instead is a criterion for helping decide when participation in such activities is appropriate/inappropriate:

> Relationships with clients should normally be free of activites with social implications. With new

or prospective clients, however, such activities may be pursued insofar as they appear necessary in order to establish or maintain a therapeutic relationship.

If we now apply this criterion to the case of The Cup of Coffee (p. 53) it becomes apparent that your response to May's request will depend on your perception of the nature of the relationship you already have with her. If you think she already views you as potentially trustworthy and understanding, then you will refuse her request and explain that you are afraid that this sort of out-of-session contact may lead to a social relationship that will interfere with the therapeutic relationship (Option 1). If you think that you have not as yet gained the respect and trust of May and suspect this offer may be her way of exploring whether or not you are to be trusted or could possibly understand her, then you may well accept and later try to sift out any resulting complications (Option 3). If you are basically at loss in understanding the request, it may be well to explore its significance at this time (Option 2).

What about accepting gifts from clients as in the illustrative case of The Gift (p. 54)? It hardly seems likely that a gift could represent a client's effort to break down a social barrier which must be overcome before the client can truly trust the therapist. At best a gift would represent the client's heartfelt appreciation of the therapist's efforts to help him. At worst it would represent a sort of bribe, a way of ingratiating himself with the therapist in expectation that at some time in the future he can expect some special favor in return. It could, of course, also simply be a way of getting rid of something for which the giver has no particular use, something perhaps left over--such as a bunch of cookies.

In view of these various possibilities it seems best, with the exception of the last instance in which you are simply the repository of some leftovers, to find some way of graciously rejecting the gift, at least while therapy is still on-going (Option 2). Perhaps at the end of therapy, or better yet after it is clear therapy has really been terminated, it would be appropriate to accept gifts, since then they are more likely to truly represent the client's heartfelt thanks, rather than a claim on your future services. It would be a special shame if the client suffered from the misapprehension that he needed to "buy" your full concern and attention in some such way, and you did not discover this and correct it.

Therapist Self-Inventory

As a way of summarizing and completing the foregoing discussion I have drafted an inventory which counselors and psychotherapists can use to check whether they are in danger of letting their professional helping role deteriorate into a social or sexual relationship. The following questions are designed to heighten awareness of incipient dual relationships with clients.

1. Do the therapy sessions contain social interactions?
--Examples: Gift-giving, sharing of mutual outside interests, more than incidental small-talk.

2. Do your self-disclosures lead to focusing on your concerns rather than the client's?

3. Does the client expect you to act as a "friend" would outside of the therapy sessions?
--Examples: Ask her how she is if you meet, or be receptive to impromptu progress reports over the phone in between appointments.

4. Are your social contacts truly coincidental? Could it be that one of you is utilizing information gleaned during the therapy hour about outside activities and routines to "run into" each other?

5. Does the client expect you to act on her behalf in other settings? If so, was this expectation ever formally clarified in advance?
--Examples: Write a letter of recommendation for a job; draft and sign a petition excusing her for low grades or unauthorized withdrawal from school because of "psychological reasons"; testify in court.

6. Do you find yourself unclear on the goals of therapy with this individual?

This concludes the attempts to sift out the social and sexual from professional relations with clients. The next chapter shall be concerned with the multifaceted issue of confidentiality.

Whatsoever I shall see or hear in the course of my profession in my intercourse with men, if it be what should not be noised abroad, I will never divulge, holding such things to be holy secrets. (Hippocrates)

CHAPTER V

CONFIDENTIALITY

This chapter is a testimonial to the human capacity of making the simple complex. What appears to be a simple concern, that of keeping a secret, draws us into a maze of legal and ethical considerations. One problem is what is to be kept confidential--is the fact that you have or have not seen a client to be kept as secret as what a client tells you? What if there is more than one client, a family for example--when can one keep the secrets of one family member from another? When, and to whom is it advisable, or perhaps legally required to breach confidentiality? Is confidentiality a necessary component of modern therapeutic practice? Is it even a desirable component? The answers, or lack thereof, to all these questions and many others are to be found in this chapter. But before we start that process, let us first begin our discussion in the customary way--by sampling some specific situations in which therapists may find themselves.

The Latent Homosexual poses the problem of client access to therapist notes. The Incestuous Father concerns the legal and ethical obligations of the therapist to report a form of child abuse to the authorities. The Revengeful Suitor raises the question of whether or not to breach the confidentiality of a potentially homicidal client, and to whom. In The CIA Inquiry the counselor must define the confidentiality of information regarding the general problem of the client and the duration of the therapy. In The Informal Opinion the obligation of the counselor to provide her informal opinion to her employer as to the appropriateness of promotion for a fellow employee, who is a client of hers, is at issue.

The first commentary section analyzes the provision of confidentiality by depicting its positive and negative functions. It is argued that modern therapeutic practice, to a large degree, no longer needs or benefits from the provision of confidentiality. The following section defines the basic legal terms of confidentiality, privilege, and privacy, which translate the ethical concept of confidentiality into legally protected categories. These ethical and legal distinctions are given more concrete form in the following section on the parameters of confidentiality, which points out the different degrees of confidentiality of different kinds of data, such as appointment book data, informal versus formal opinions, and nonverbal behavior. Also some of the implications of the Tarasoff case for confidentiality are depicted in the section on situations of "clear danger"--murder and suicide. A section is devoted to child abuse, how it is defined and what the ethical and legal obligations of reporting it are. Advice for handling requests for information from legal authorities is provided in another section. Release of information to third parties--supervisors, team members, referral sources, etc. is analyzed. How to protect the confidentiality and promote the best interests of under-age and mentally incapacitated clients is also discussed. The practical, ethical and legal aspects of keeping confidential records, client access to such records, protecting client identity in publications through disguise, and recommendations for record keeping are presented in the closing sections.

Illustrative Cases

The Latent Homosexual: Meg comes in for her first interview with you. She was seen by an intake counselor about six weeks ago and placed on the agency waiting list and has just now been taken off. As is your custom, you decide to review the summary of the intake counselor with her to determine its accuracy in light of changes since then. Meg notices you reading from the summary before paraphrasing and asking for an update. She demands to see the record herself. You notice belatedly that the intake counselor has hazarded a guess that Meg is "a latent homosexual--with paranoid tendencies." What should you do?

1. Should you simply turn over the record to her to read for herself and then discuss her reactions with her and provide alternative interpretations as necessary?

2. Should you refuse to turn over the record, saying it was meant for interpretation by a fellow professional and was not written in a manner or at a level untrained clients could understand?

3. What is the legal situation--does she have a legal right to reading the unvarnished, unedited text?

The Incestuous Father: Ben, the father of three daughters, comes to you for treatment of alcoholism. In the course of the treatment Ben confesses that he has had incestuous relations with his oldest daughter, now aged 15, for the past two years and is now finding himself attracted to the next oldest daughter, aged 13. He claims he engages in such contacts only when intoxicated, and then only rarely, but is quite ashamed of himself and wishes he could quit. You check with a lawyer friend, being careful not to identify your client in any way, and he informs you that the state law is not clear regarding your obligation to report child abuse. In any case it is your "right" to report, i.e., you will not be liable in any way if you do as long as you have not previously promised the client that you would not divulge such information. What should you do?

1. Should you report it immediately and inform your client you are doing so?

2. Should you formally incorporate this element into the therapy and wait to see how the therapy goes before considering reporting. If so, what do you tell the client? Would it make any difference if Ben had admitted to regular or frequent incest as opposed to very infrequent?

3. Should you share your dilemma with Ben and ask him to decide, on the assumption he is asking for your intervention by revealing this situation to you?

4. Should you suggest the whole family be brought in for therapy and try to work it out in this way?

The Revengeful Suitor: Prorosenjit, a graduate student from India, met Tanya at a folk dancing class. They saw each other weekly during Fall term, and on last New Year's Eve she kissed him. He interpreted this as signalizing a formal engagement, as it might have been in India according to the customs of his caste. However, Tanya told him she was involved with other men and did not want to become intimate with him. Prorosenjit became depressed as a result of the rebuff, but continued to pursue the relationship and even tape recorded some of their conversations in an effort to understand why she didn't love him. Tanya left for the Summer, and Prorosenjit followed a friend's advice and went to the Student Health Center where he has been seeing you for therapy. In this session he expresses a desire to revenge his loss of pride by killing Tanya when she returns and states he intends to purchase a gun to do so. You fear both the taking of her life and of his own. What should you do?

1. Should you inform the campus police and ask them to observe Prorosenjit for possible hospitalization as a person who is "dangerous to himself or others"? If so, do you inform Prorosenjit of your action?

2. Should you inform Tanya of the threat when she returns?

3. Should you make no disclosure, but instead try to intensify your therapeutic efforts and persuade Prorosenjit not to pursue his plan? If these efforts meet with questionable success, what then?

4. Suppose you have informed the campus police and apparently as a result Prorosenjit terminated therapy. Do you have any further responsibility in the matter?

The CIA Inquiry: You receive a phone call from a person who identifies himself as a CIA agent. He states that he is conducting a "routine security clearance" on one of the applicants for employment in the CIA. This individual, Matt Buskin, has disclosed that he saw you for individual counseling two years prior. The agent does not want any confidential information about the contents or the course of the counseling. He says he merely wants to confirm the general nature of the problem that was dealt with, and the number of counseling sessions. He intimates that this information is necessary before further processing of Matt's application can take place. How should you answer?

1. Should you look up Matt's file and provide the requested information on the basis that such data are not strictly confidential and that not to do so might arouse unwarranted suspicions and thwart Matt's chances for employment?

2. Should you refuse to release any information, including confirming whether or not Matt was a client, unless you receive a written request to do so from Matt, himself?

3. Should you temporize by claiming the file is not immediately at hand but ask for a number to call later when you can obtain the file, and then spend the intervening time attempting to locate Matt and see what he wants you to do? If you do so and can't find Matt, what then will you do?

The "Informal Opinion" Request: You are a psychologist in the personnel office of a large firm. One of your duties is to do psychotherapy with employees of the firm who are sometimes referred to you and sometimes come in voluntarily. Jennifer has come to you voluntarily over a problem she has with some of her co-workers. This proves to be rather involved and you have been seeing her for several months. One day you get a call from the executive to whom both of your supervisors report. He tells you that Jennifer is being considered for promotion and that he knows that you have been seeing her for counseling. What he would like is an "informal opinion" whether this might be the right thing for Jennifer at this time. He emphasizes he does not want to know anything about the nature of the counseling she has received; he is simply interested, as he knows you are, in doing the right thing for Jennifer and for the firm, and, in any case your opinion is but one of many that he will be considering. How should you respond?

1. Should you simply provide the asked-for opinion, being careful not to be induced into justifying it by giving any details learned from your contacts with Jennifer? Would you then inform Jennifer of this act, regardless of whether your opinion was negative or positive? Would you give the opinion in the first place if it were negative?

2. Should you claim such an opinion would breach confidentiality and politely decline to give it? If so, how would you justify this claim in view of the fact no specific disclosures of Jennifer's were asked for?

3. Should you respond by offering to provide the opinion only if Jennifer gives you her explicit permission to do so? How then counter a reminder to the effect that you don't work for Jennifer, you work for the firm?

Commentary

Functions served by Confidentiality

Before dealing with any of the questions raised by the illustrative cases in this chapter I ask what I consider even more fundamental questions: namely, what are the main functions of confidentiality, and, is confidentiality always an essential or a desirable condition of psychotherapy.

Positive Functions:

1. Provision of confidentiality facilitates disclosure of certain subject matters: intimate details, shameful thoughts, emotions and acts, and illegal intentions or acts--things which people are afraid may be used to discredit them or will lead to retaliation if known more generally.

2. It facilitates traditional therapy. The state of the art is such that therapists are often not sure what may or may not be important for them to know about their clients in order to help them. The knowledge thus acquired may help therapists make better decisions when decisions are called for. It may also be useful in the development of theories of psychological functioning.

3. It facilitates clients' own clarification of thoughts and feelings when they expose these matters to others.

4. It facilitates clients' acceptance of themselves when their therapists do not react negatively to "shameful" disclosures.

Negative Functions:

1. It promotes a sense of intimacy between the client and the therapist. Since the sharing is one-sided, this in turn facilitates forming dependent relationships, including social and sexual ones, which can be easily manipulated by the therapist.

2. It may contribute to a sense of mysticism and add an esoteric dimension to therapy, which may make the transition to everyday life more difficult.

3. It indirectly supports cultural attitudes towards recipients of psychotherapy as people who are unable to cope and who have shameful secrets. The strength of such attitudes was evidenced in the 1972 presidential campaign when the democratic contender, George McGovern, replaced Thomas Eagleton as his running mate when Eagleton was found to have received psychotherapy and electric convulsive treatment for depression several years previously.

4. It may be used as a manipulative device by clients--as a means of testing their therapist's limits, as a way of arousing the therapist's sexual interest (by revealing intimate sexual episodes and desires), as a way of claiming tacit approval for acts they would not otherwise commit, etc.

5. It can be used as a protective screen by therapists for hiding their misjudgments in therapy. They can avoid answering questions that interested and concerned parties might ask regarding how they are handling any particular client on the basis that it would violate their client's confidentiality. It can also be used to obstruct research into what actually happens in their sessions, as opposed to what they say happens. As Slovenko (1975, p. 381) said with respect to law students who have attempted to investigate client experience of psychotherapy, "It is a foregone conclusion that the researcher will receive no cooperation from the private practitioner. Follow-up studies might focus on the allegation that psychotherapists go merrily along from failure to failure."

Thus the provision of confidentiality, even when the therapist is under no pressure to breach it, does not always have a beneficial effect in psychotherapy. Even the necessity of providing it in the first place has been challenged by recent developments. Do-it-yourself manuals, self-help groups, classroom formats for teaching people how to cope with anxiety, with stress, with depression, etc., as well as the traditional and modern forms of group therapy, some even on TV, demonstrate alternatives to the giving and keeping of "holy secrets." This is not to say such alternatives are equivalent forms of treatment or will be effective with the same clients. Rather it is to suggest that as we learn more about the processes involved in faulty psychological functioning we may be able to move away from the in-depth explorations that characterized earlier forms of treatment, which explorations were facilitated by the provision of confidentiality. Therapists may be able to directly invoke instructional and behavioral interventions on the basis of general knowledge, rather than needing to know specific, intimate details of each client's life.

Basic Terms

Let us now adopt a more traditional approach by examining the core terms, "confidentiality," "privilege," or "privileged communication," and "privacy."

Confidentiality: Put most simply, "Confidentiality indicates an explicit promise or contract to reveal nothing about an individual except under conditions agreed to by the source or subject" (Siegel, 1979, p. 251). In psychotherapy, the promise is made by the therapist to the client(s).

Although confidentiality has long been part of professional ethics it has only recently been formally recognized in law. Two primary areas of law apply: one is termed "confidentiality," and "prohibits any disclosure of communications made to a professional by a client during the course of professional employment. Thus disclosure of a client's communications may not only subject the psychologist to professional (ethical) reprimand but also the civil or criminal liability" (Dekraii & Sales, 1982, p. 372).

Privilege: The other primary area of law is that of "privilege" or "privileged communication" and is designed to protect confidential material from disclosure specially in the arena of legal proceedings, an area not covered under the "confidentiality" statutes which the courts have held are designed as antigossip legislation and do not constitute a testimonial privilege (Dekraii & Sales, 1982, p. 372).

Whether or not information that is considered confidential by therapists and clients is protected from disclosure in legal proceedings varies from state to state. The psychologist-client privilege exists, either separately or under the cover of, or in conjunction with other privileges, such as the psychotherapist-client or physician-patient privilege in all but four states: Iowa, South Carolina, Vermont and West Virginia. The psychiatrist privilege (as distinct from the physician privilege) exists in 17 states and the social worker privilege in 18 states (Dekraii & Sales, 1982).

The privilege of withholding certain information from the court may seem contradictory to the interests of justice, but in context it can be seen as serving the same general function that all law is supposed to serve: namely, the furtherance of the public interest. It is argued that the protection of disclosures made within certain relations is more likely to benefit society than the lack of a safe outlet. There are four requisites that have been recommended for the establishment of the privilege (Wigmore: Cited in Schwitzgebel, et al., 1980):

> (a) The communications must originate in a confidence that they will not be disclosed.
>
> (b) This element of confidentiality must be essential to the full and satisfactory maintenance of the relationship between the parties.
>
> (c) The relation must be one which in the opinion of the community ought to be sedulously fostered; and
>
> (d) The injury that would inure to the relation by the disclosure of the communication must be greater than the benefit gained for the correct disposal of litigation. (p. 201).

Privacy: "Privacy" is another term that has consequences for the confidentiality of information about clients. Privacy has a statutory basis stemming from the prohibition of unlawful "search and seizure" provision of the 4th Amendment of the Constitution. Its modern importance was signalized by the creation of the Privacy Protection Study Commission by Congress in 1974. This commission is charged with recommending legislation to protect privacy and introduced over 60 bills on privacy and related issues into the 94th Congress (Siegel, 1979). The confidentiality of records, in particular educational records, was affected by passage of the Family Educational Rights and Privacy Act of 1974, which gave "students 18 or older (or those attending an institution of post-secondary education) and [in some cases] their parents the right to inspect relevant school records" (Schwitzgebel, et al., 1980, p. 211). Later in the chapter we will discuss this right as it applies to psychological records. Public law 94-63 is also important in that it applied the guidelines first developed for alcoholism and drug abuse programs for protecting confidentiality to the community mental health center system of quality assurance.

Parameters of Confidentiality

A number of issues were raised in the "Illustrative Cases": accessibility to the client of records about the client, breach of confidentiality in cases of child abuse, breach in cases of potential murder or suicide, dual allegiances (client versus employer) and the relative confidentiality of various parameters of therapy such as: client status, number of interviews, and general opinions about clients as opposed to specific judgments. I will first clarify the ethical and legal aspects of these parameters before turning to the other issues. The reader may find it helpful to read Principle 5 of the Ethical Principles (Appendix A) and sections 2.3.3 through 2.3.5 of the Specialty Guidelines (Appendix B) as a prelude to the following comments.

It is clear that if anything is to be treated as confidential it is the actual utterances made by the client to the therapist in the individual psychotherapeutic session. It is not so clear that the therapist's remarks in that context are to be treated in the same way. Both the Ethical Principles (Principle 5) and the Specialty Guidelines (2.3.3 through 2.3.5) refer to information gathered from the client, and make no explicit remarks about therapist replies. However, since therapist replies could scarcely be interpreted without knowing the stimuli, it may be safely assumed that it is the therapeutic exchange that is to be protected, and not just the client's disclosures.

Legal descriptions of prileged information tend to be more exact--for example, Section 33 of the Oregon Rule of Evidence (Oregon Revised Statutes 40.230, Rule 504) states:

> A patient has a privilege to refuse to disclose and to prevent any other person from disclosing confidential communications made for the purposes of diagnosis or treatment of the patient's mental or emotional condition among the patient, the patient's psychotherapist or persons who are participating in the diagnosis or treatment under the direction of the psychotherapist, including members of the patient's family. (Subsection 2)

This was modeled after the proposed Rule 504 of the Federal Rules of Evidence which was prescribed by the United States Supreme Court and submitted to Congress, but not enacted. As you can see, only "confidential communications made for the purpose of diagnosis and treatment" are included. Oregon's previous rule, also common to other states, applied to "any communication made . . . in the course of professional employment."

Nonverbal communication can also be assumed to be included as part of the core of the confidential material, since it, too, cannot be separated in any realistic sense from the accompanying oral utterances. This is also considered true of privileged communication in the courtroom: "The privilege, where it exists, does cover, however, nonverbal as well as verbal communication, including information obtained from observation of the patient's appearance and symptoms" (Foster, 1976, p. 398).

Opinions and judgments regarding clients which are based on confidential therapeutic exchanges would also seem to be intrinsically related to the client's disclosures and thus to be treated as confidential unless explicit permission to provide such judgments to specific others is obtained from the client. As we shall see later, this is clearly true of such opinions when they are part of a written record, and this would indicate the same should be true of oral communications.

Does this mean that answering general questions, such as, "Is she doing okay?" or responding to other requests for "informal opinions" is prohibited? There can be no definite answer to this issue since it can be argued that there exist circumstances where not to answer would almost surely convey a false impression, whereas giving a general positive reply would not. These instances, however, would seem to be the exception, and not the rule.

> Unless the requesting party has some specific right to such information, and this right was previously explained to and accepted by the client, then the guiding principle would be not to provide such opinions without first getting specific permission from the client to do so.

In the case of the well-meaning relatives and friends of the client, it can be pointed out to them that they could ask such questions directly of the client and it would be best for them to do so.

Finally, what about the external facts of the therapeutic relationship--whether or not the client actually showed up, and if so, for how long, how many times, and when was the client seen. It is clear that a person who is referred for counseling or therapy and who fails to show up is not a client, and thus to reveal such information would hardly seem to constitute a breach of confidentiality. And yet if the person does make initial contact and formally becomes a client, is it ethical to reveal that fact to other parties? If you only refuse to divulge the client/non-client status of those who are clients, and openly reveal the non-client status of non-clients, then it soon becomes obvious who is or is not a client. Thus, if such matters are to be confidential, the status of both non-clients and clients must be kept secret. A similar argument could be made regarding whether or not a person still is a client, or has terminated and thus is no longer a client.

In an ideal world such matters would be of no consequence. But as a matter of practical reality it is considered a real risk to be known to have had personal counseling or psychotherapy.

> Acknowledging to present or potential employers and insurers that one is or has been a participant in psychotherapy may have fateful consequences for one's life opportunity. . . . The data obtained by Weinstock and Haft (1974) is of particular relevance. They found that regardless of type of position--executive, clerical, or maintenance--the hiring policies of those industries sampled would lead to rejection rates of up to 77% for applicants who were in psychotherapy. (Noll, 1981, p. 915)

Inferences about the severity of the client's problem can be drawn, rightly or wrongly, on the basis of the number of times the client was seen and on how long the therapy lasted. Thus release of this information also poses potential risk to the client, perhaps as much as disclosure of the actual client-therapist exchanges. Insofar as such information is contained in case records it it considered as part of the confidential files of the client according to the Specialty Guidelines (sections 2.3.3 through 2.3.5).

Legally, a distinction has been made between client-therapist exchanges and appointment book information.

> Privileged communications when authorized by statute may be narrowly interpreted to exclude information the client did not communicate (e.g. therapist's appointment book). This information can be subpoenaed if there is litigation. (Schwitzgebel et al., 1980, p. 202)

Situations of "Clear Danger"--Murder and Suicide

In certain situations the therapist is ethically required to breach confidentiality on the basis that the client's present or predictable future behavior constitutes a definite threat to his own life or the lives of others.

> They [psychologists] reveal such information to others only with the consent of the person or the person's legal representative, except in those unusual circumstances in which not to do so would result in clear danger to the person or to others. (Ethical Principles, Principle 6)

A major difficulty is determining what constitutes "clear danger." Some rules of thumb do exist, such as clients who have the motive (e.g., revenge, despair), the means (e.g., gun, pills) and the plan (e.g., will take overdose, just before retiring at night) are more apt to be serious than those who only express some vague intention to harm themselves or others. However, some clients may be in such a state that they will do something impulsively, such as throw themselves before a moving vehicle, or drive a car into a tree or into an on-coming car.

Even if the therapist does decide to breach confidentiality the question remains, to whom? Some of you may have recognized The Revengeful Suitor case (p. 73) as the famous Tarasoff case (Schwitzgebel, et al., 1980; Everstine, Everstine, Heymann, True, Frey, Johnson, and Seiden, 1980). Here the treating psychologist did inform the campus police, both orally and in writing, that Prorosenjit Poddar was dangerous and should be taken to a community health center for psychiatric commitment. However, the police released Poddar after interviewing him and informed the health service. Subsequently, Poddar went to Tanya's home and shot and repeatedly stabbed her when she refused to speak to him and attempted to run away. He was found guilty of voluntary manslaughter, was imprisoned, and upon release returned to India.

The parents of Tanya Tarasoff filed suit against the Board of Regents of the University of California, several members of the campus hospital facility, including the psychologist who served as psychotherapist, and the chief of the campus police, plus four of his officers. A lower court dismissed the suit, the parents appealed, and the California Supreme Court upheld the appeal in 1974 and reaffirmed its decision in 1976.

This case has been widely cited as imperiling the confidentiality of psychotherapist-client relations, as demonstrating that therapists run legal risks in protecting the confidentiality of those clients who might be dangerous to others or themselves.[1] But more closely read, the issue is more that of failure to follow through on an already executed breach of confidentiality, than that of making the breach in the first place. The therapist had already decided the client was dangerous and informed the campus police, the problem was that he did not inform the intended victim or her parents.

Thus the Tarasoff case sheds little light on the usual psychotherapeutic situation in which the therapist struggles with the issue, "Is this client really apt to commit a dangerous act in the near future, and if so, can I best reduce the risk by maintaining the psychotherapeutic relationship and not revealing his intentions to others, or by revealing these intentions without his permission and thus risking the relationship?" In fact, it could be argued that Poddar's therapist could better have protected Tanya by not informing the campus police, since by doing so his working relationship with Poddar was severed, and Poddar's tendency to perceive himself as a victim of injustice was strength-

---

[1] In this connection the Court's decision is oft-cited. "The public policy favoring protection of the confidential character of patient-psychotherapist communications must yield to the extent to which disclosure is essential to avert danger to others. The protective privilege ends where the public peril begins," (Tarasoff v. Board of Regents of the University of California, Cal Rptr. 14, No. S.F. 23042 (Cal, Sup. Ct., July 1, 1976) 131).

ened. I am not hereby suggesting this would have been the "right" course of action in this case; indeed none may exist. I merely wish to point out that the case may be instructive in ways which have not received emphasis.

A legal commentator points out the narrowness of the set of circumstances to which the case is apt to be applied (Slovenko, 1975):

> It may be predicted that Tarasoff, modified or unmodified, will not bring in a parade of horribles . . . the decision will make little or no difference . . . since the court would have to be convinced that the therapist believed that danger was imminent and then did nothing. This would be difficult to estimate. The facts of Tarasoff, where the therapist actually reported the danger to the police . . . is a most unusual set of facts. (p. 392)

Further analysis of the implications of this case is found in Chapter IX.

Reporting of Child Abuse

The issue of whether or not to breach confidentiality in order to report child abuse is another difficult one to resolve in most instances. The image of a young, innocent child being psychologically crippled and physically endangered by the actions of a relatively powerful adult is one which few people, including psychotherapists, can portray without arousal of turbulent emotions. Obviously, if the criterion of "clear danger" found in Principle 6 is met the psychologist is ethically required to report it. However, it is not at all clear what "clear danger" is in cases of child abuse. Does it extend to danger of lifelong psychological maladjustment which might result from sexual molestation and incest or from other treatment, which although not life-endangering is usually thought to result in both current and later-life problems? If we do define "clear danger" to include danger of psychological maladjustment, where are our data for such a stance? Could we really make a strong case based on post-hoc and anecdotal historical research? These quesitions are largely unanswered. In his review of the area Starr (1979, p. 872) states:

Physical and sexual abuse that leave obvious injury are relatively easy to define, but many forms of abuse leave no such evidence. Professionals are therefore reluctant to deal with emotional abuse. They need guidelines to govern their involvement in new areas.

But even with cases of obvious injury or inadequate physical care it is not always obvious what is truly dangerous. Since intent to murder is not typically the issue, we are dealing as much with medical prognosis as with psychological. Most psychologists are not equipped to decide with any assurance at what point parental neglect may precipitate an irreversible physical deficiency, or how many blows of what kind are apt to result in brain concussion. Clearly, medical consultation is advisable here.

A third complicating factor is whether the client is the abusing parent or relative, or the abused child. If the client is the adult then it becomes feasible to frankly discuss the option of reporting the abuse to the authorities and the possible consequences thereof. It may be that the child will be allowed to stay in the home and the parents will then become eligible for certain kinds of home assistance programs, such as the help of parental aides and crisis nurseries--i.e., the consequences may be more desirable than noxious, even to the offender. But in order to have such an open discussion, the treating professional will have to have acquainted himself in advance of the possible options. Such knowledge of community resources is, in itself, an ethical responsibility (Specialty Guidelines, Section 2.2.5).

If, however, the client is not persuaded that it would be best to inform the authorities, and if so doing would jeopardize the on-going therapy, the therapist has no choice but to decide what constitutes "clear danger" and if this criterion applies. Consultation with peers may prove quite helpful in such situations and serves as a legal safeguard as well.

If the client is the child any discussion of the options must be tempered by the child's presumed capacity to understand them. This is also true of obtaining the client's permission to disclose this information to the authorities. Since the offender would also probably be one of the legal representatives of the child it makes little sense in most cases to ask this person for permission to report. At best some family therapy could be instituted, or this element could be introduced in such on-going family therapy that exists. Should the child already be court-referred or agency-referred then it would be the unusual situation when it would not be appropriate to report child abuse, since the referral, itself, would mandate reporting of pertinent factors of the case.

Admittedly this is an involved and difficult issue. Accordingly, the following questions are suggested as a means of clarifying the situation.

1. Is the abuse mainly or wholly a matter of the past, as opposed to a current phenomenon? If so, no "clear danger" seems to be involved and there is no ethical requirement to report it. The only exception might be if local regulations or state laws require it.

2. Is it reasonably clear what actually happened and if that constitutes abuse? Although it is currently thought children seldom lie about abuse it may be difficult to decipher exactly what occurred, when, and how frequently. With a very young child one way to check to see if sexual molestation has occurred is to ask the child to put his or her hands on the part of the body that the adult touched. We are not suggesting here that the therapist conduct any kind of home investigation, that is the duty of the authorities; simply that she do as careful a job of verifying this information as with any other client statements.

3. Is the "abuse" that is described or alluded to a matter of cultural differences in child rearing, or truly a physical danger to the child?

4. Are you familiar both with the state statutes that apply and with the treatment programs that are available? If so, make yourself so.

5. Have you recourse to medical and to peer consultation on such matters? If not, develop such resources.

<u>Child Abuse: Legal Aspects</u>

It is always tempting in areas with clear legal implications to look to the law and its interpreters, the legal profession, to tell us what we, as psychologists, should do--especially when the ethical issues are so complicated. As was expressed in the foreword to this book, I believe this approach to be a mistake for any profession that claims to be an independent profession. It is also a mistake to be unaware of the law, and in this case, as in most, it varies considerably from state to state. A summary of the legal situation is provided below (Schwitzgebel, et al., 1980).

> "Child abuse"--the intentional use of force resulting in physical injury serious enough to endanger the health or life of the child--is a criminal offense in all states. "Neglect" is a less certain concept but generally refers to persistently inadequate child care of a physical nature, and sometimes to the failure to insure conditions for positive social-psychological development. Statutes typically prohibit cruel corporal punishment, physical neglect, and sexual exploitation. Some states include emotional abuse. Idaho has one of the broadest and most psychologically-oriented negligence statutes. It gives the court jurisdiction over any child whose behavior indicates social or emotional maladjustment. Criminal negligence has been found even where there are no physical signs of abuse. The Federal Child Abuse Prevention and Treatment Act refers generally to situations of "physical or mental injury, sexual abuse, negligent treatment or maltreatment of a child." (pp. 165-166)

Thus it is apparent that in order to know if emotional abuse or social-psychological neglect are included, and also possibly sexual exploitation, you will have to check with your state's statutes. This is also true of reporting requirements (Schwitzgebel, et al., 1980).

> All states require physicians to report suspected cases of child abuse, and the majority of states have expanded this requirement to nurses, school teachers, social workers, and mental health professionals . . .
> Every state provides some form of immunity for the reporter against possible defamation of character, invasions of privacy and breach of confidence, although, even without such statutes, a person acting in good faith and with-

out malice would probably have a successful defense. (p. 167)

Penalties for failure to report, when the law requires it, are provided in most states. "Violation of the reporting statute may, in itself, constitute negligence and therefore support a civil suit against the professional" (Schwitzgebel, et al., 1980, p. 167). Thus the overall effect of the law is to encourage reporting; it protects the reporter and penalizes failure to report by those required to do so.

Loss of Privilege: Even though you may choose not to report and may be legally exempted from doing so by virtue of being the recipient of privileged communications, the privilege may not carry over to certain legal proceedings which are instigated by someone else's report. To determine whether or not you have such an exemption, and whether or not it carries over to specific legal proceedings it is necessary to ascertain the current state statutes on these matters. This is true, of course, of all other legal issues as well.

This brings us to the general issue of how to respond to requests from legal authorities regarding any material we consider confidential information.

Subpoenas and Waiving of Privilege

Forensic psychology, sometimes described as, "how not to appear more of a fool in court than you already are," has become an involved subject matter in itself. It is not our intention to delve deeply into this specialty area in this book, but only insofar as it touches on the topics of confidentiality and malpractice. A general discussion of the difficulties of fulfilling your ethical obligation to provide impartial and objective assessment within a courtroom setting may be found in an article by Anderton, Staulrup and Grisso in *Professional Psychology* (1980).

With regard to confidentiality the legal system impinges directly on the therapist when she receives a subpoena. A general guide of how to respond (not a legal opinion appropriate to any and all particular situations) follows (Schwitzgebel, et al., 1980, pp. 203-204; Swanson, Note 2).

How to Respond when Served with a Subpoena

1. Determine the nature of the subpoena. Some governmental agencies or commissions may have subpoena power, others do not but use a subpoena-like form hoping to produce information. If issued by a court and titled a subpoena it should be assumed valid and should not be ignored if properly delivered. Some subpoenas compel the production of records, others only require attendance. If the subpoena has the words "duces tecum" plainly on its face it requires records and may or may not require attendance.

2. Whether the request is for records of for oral testimony, initially assert the privilege not to reveal any material pertaining to the client unless or until the client or her attorney explicitly grants permission to do so, or the court orders you to do so. Failure to initially assert the privilege may result in legal action against you by the client. If the subpoena requires attendance at a legal proceeding, it is important to show up at the hearing in order to assert the privilege.

3. Alternatively, if an attorney was responsible for having the subpoena issued, he can be contacted and informed of your intention to assert the privilege and may as a result, dismiss the subpoena.

4. If employed by an institution, notify the appropriate administrator. Do not destroy or tamper records to prevent disclosure. Tampering constitutes a misdemeanor or a felony.

5. Contact the client and/or the client's attorney. Explain the probable impact on the client of public exposure. If the impact might be detrimental, put this in writing and send a copy to the client's attorney and possibly to the client. If the client wants you to testify, request written authorization to release confidential information from the client, or the client's representative if the client is presumed incapable of making this judgment.

6. If the client does not give you written authorization or is not specific enough, or if the authorization is otherwise inadequate, two remaining options are:

(a) Request a private conference with the appropriate judge. Seek clarification from the judge so that the information you provide will be limited to that essential to the court proceedings.

(b) Provide only the information that the court requires you to produce. Subpoenaed records should be sealed and labeled "confidential" when submitted to the court, agency, or person that has subpoenaed the records.

Advice from the Specialty Guidelines

The *Specialty Guidelines* also caution therapists against immediate compliance with legally processed requests for confidential information.

> The clinical psychologist does not release confidential information, except with the written consent of the user directly involved or his or her legal representative. Even after consent for release has been obtained, the clinical psychologist clearly identifies such information as confidential to the recipient of the information. If directed by statute or regulations with the force of law or by court order, the psychologist may seek a resolution to the conflict that is both ethically and legally feasible and appropriate. (Section 2.3.5)

The *Guidelines* go even one step further in proposing that therapists act on their own independent judgment of whether or not confidential information should be released, even if the client requests such release.

> When the user's intention to waive confidentiality is judged by the professional clinical psychologist to be contrary to the user's best interests or to be in conflict with the user's civil and legal rights, it is the responsibility of the clinical psychologist to discuss the implications of releasing psychological information and to assist the user in limiting disclosure only to information required by the present circumstance. (Section 2.3.5)

It is only a short step from there to the position argued by Everstine, et al. (1980):

> . . . the privilege should be held independently by the professional as well as by the client. If we are to be responsible for helping our clients and protecting them from harm, we need the legal sanction to refrain from revealing that which, in our judgment, is likely to be harmful to the client. (pp. 837-838)

At least one reader of this suggestion reacted quite negatively to it: "To think that the client cannot make an informal judgment about whether or not to waive the testimonial privilege for the therapist is the grossest form of paternalism" (Hays, 1981).

<u>When Privilege does not Apply</u>

Regardless, as of this time at least, the privilege belongs to the client and not to the therapist. Clients may release the therapist from confidentiality by providing a written, signed statement to that effect. They may also automatically waive their privilege within the courtroom in at least three situations (The [federal] Uniform Rules; cited in Cleary, 1972):

> 1. <u>Proceedings for Hospitalization</u>. There is no privilege . . . if the psychotherapist in the course of diagnosis or treatment has determined that the patient is in need of hospitalization for mental illness.
>
> 2. <u>Examination by Order of Court</u>. If the court orders an examination of the physical, mental, or emotional condition of the patient . . . communications made in the course thereof are not privileged . . . with respect to the particular purpose for which the examination is ordered unless the court orders otherwise.
>
> 3. <u>Condition an Element of Claim or Defense</u>. There is no privilege . . . as to a communication relevant to an issue of the physical, mental, or emotional condition of the patient in any proceeding in which he relies upon the condition as an element of his claim or defense . . .

An example of "3" would be in child custody cases "in which either party raises the mental condition of the other party as part of claim or defense . . ." (Schwitzgebel, et al., 1982, p. 207).

Release of Information to a Third Party

Consultation, Supervision: In many, perhaps in most cases, there is a good reason for the treating psychotherapist to share part of the confidential communications with some third party. Some of these "breaches" are not even considered as such by the profession, although this does not obviate the therapist from getting the client's permission to do so. This is the case when the third party is another professional psychotherapist bound by the same or very similar code of ethics, and is acting in the role of a consultant or a supervisor to the treating therapist. In such instances, not only is it not unethical to discuss the client with the third party, but it would be unethical not to do so, especially if you feel the need for consultation on the case. A possible exception would be if the client, for some reason, did not want you to discuss his case with your particular supervisor or some other specific therapist. In that case you should arrange for alternative supervision.

> To consider confidentiality as an absolute . . . would impede the "quality control" of care. "Quality control" necessitates a review of individual patients and therapists and involves, not indiscriminate, but discriminate disclosure. The therapist in training must "breach" the confidence of his patient in order to discuss the cases with his supervisor. (Slovenko, 1975, p. 380)

Treatment Teams: Another instance in which sharing of confidential information within a larger confidential framework is expected occurs when the treating unit is a team, perhaps a multi-disciplinary one. Such teams are common features of many psychiatric wards and community health centers. The client or patient really has no choice in the matter, or at best a very limited one. Nevertheless, it is incumbent to explain the arrangements for confidentiality to him.

Groups: It is tempting to consider group therapy as such a team situation since in many groups all members are asked to commit themselves to helping each other--i.e. act as therapists, at least part of the time. They are also typically asked to maintain confidentiality regarding each other's disclosures, and may even sign a contract to do so.[2] However, they are not members of a profession which obligates them to such confidentiality, nor is their fundamental role in the group that of fellow therapist, but rather that of fellow client. As a practical matter it is unrealistic to expect a high degree of confidentiality in most groups, but especially short-term or open-ended ones. In fact, group members will frequently openly admit that they plan to discuss what happened with non-present spouses or other living partners. As was discussed in the introductory part of this chapter, this lack of confidentiality is not necessarily a bad thing.

Marital and Family Counseling: Even more complexities arise in marital and family situations due to the possible involvement of children and the likelihood that one or more of the family members will have already been seen in individual counseling or will be seen also in individual counseling during the course of the family counseling. Whether or not the counselor agrees to keep some confidences, such as an ongoing affair, from the spouse or other family members will be, in part, a result of the personal preferences and the theoretical orientation of the counselor. What is important is that the counselor make clear whatever policy he plans to adopt, and if possible, do this as a precondition to any family or marital counseling.

In family counseling, it is also important to recognize that children should share whatever rights other family members have to confidentiality, and in view of their vulnerability may have more need for such protection. Also their rights may have to be protected by the therapist to the degree that the children are unable to understand or guard their own rights. The reader is referred to a recent article by Margolin (1982) for further discussion of these issues.

The legal situation also reflects the difficulties associated with keeping confidentiality in a multi-client situation. Slovenko (1977, p. 415) concludes:

> Thus, present-day privilege laws offer a modicum of assurance that communications in psychotherapy are shielded from disclosure in litigation of family matters, but they

---

[2] For an example of a particularly binding contract see Appendix M in Schwitzgebel, et al. (1980).

offer no assurance whatever in personal injury litigation where a group member makes his health a matter of issue. Likewise, should one group member assault another in the course of therapy, and suit ensue, the occurrence would not be shielded."

An exception to this general statement is to be found in an amendment to a Colorado statute. It "prohibits the questioning of any persons who have participated in group therapy sessions 'concerning any knowledge gained during the course of such therapy without the consent of the person or persons to whom the testimony sought relates'" (Schwitzgebel, et al., 1980, p. 209).

Referred Clients: When a client is referred for counseling or psychotherapy by another agency or a person, perhaps a physician or some other professional, it is not unusual for the referring party to expect a report of the outcome of the referral. Sometimes the referral is not for treatment, but only for assessment, in which case a formal report is almost always expected. There is no problem in either of these situations as long as all three parties--the referring party, the therapist, and the client have an explicit understanding regarding what information is to be shared, and what not shared. Difficulties arise when reliance is placed upon implicit understanding of the limits of communication. Therefore it behooves the in-between party, the therapist, to clarify at the time of the referral exactly what information is expected by the referring party, to correct any obviously false expectations at that time, and then to approach the client and explain what has been tentatively agreed upon. Should the client not be agreeable to releasing some or all of the information this fact is relayed to the referral source and further negotiations are made as necessary to reach an agreement, or until such point as it is clear that no agreement can be made.

> When a psychologist agrees to provide services to a client at the request of a third party, the psychologist assumes the responsibility of clarifying the nature of the relationships to all parties concerned. (Ethical Principles, Section 6.6)

This sounds more complicated than it usually is since often both parties already know fairly well what is reasonable to expect and the client's presence is indication of agreement to the referral source's desires. In other instances, such as when the referral source is a relative or friend, all that the therapist need do is to point out to the referral source that there is nothing to prevent her from asking the client directly about the outcome of the referral. With teachers, clerks, and others who have only a short-term, perhaps incidental relationship with the client, a simple statement by the therapist as to the confidentiality of psychotherapy or counseling usually suffices.

If as a result of these negotiations it is determined that some confidential information is to be released, then that needs to be put in writing. The nature of the information, as precisely defined as possible, the party to whom the information is to be released, and the purpose for which the information is to be used should all be specified. This statement is then signed by the client and dated. In some instances it may be best to also have the signature of one or more witnesses and/or have the statement notarized.

Other precautions specified in the Specialty Guidelines (Section 2.3.5) include, as mentioned before, that the psychologist makes sure that the client understands the possible implications of the disclosure and assists the client "in limiting disclosure only to information required by the present circumstance." Also such information should be "released only to a person recognized by the clinical psychologist as qualified and competent to use the data," and should be identified as confidential to the recipient of the information.

If a client has been referred by an agency to which the therapist is acting as a consultant, then the client often has already signed such a release of information as part of the procedures of being helped by or employed by that agency. In such cases the therapist needs to have a copy of the standard release form in order to determine the precise nature of the requested information. If the disclosure requests seem broader than necessary or desirable he should attempt to negotiate more appropriate limits with the referring agency.

Intrainstitutional Referrals: Perhaps the most ticklish situations occur when the psychologist works in an agency or institution and has as clients either inmates or fellow employees. In the employer-employee situation the psychologist may have already formed a separate relationship with the individual, thus compromising his ability to work objectively with the individual either in assessment or in therapy. In the employee-inmate situation the psychologist may have lost sensitivity to the dimension of institutionally induced helplessness of inmates. But in both situations the psychologist is especially vulnerable to pressures from administrative superiors who can affect his salary and status. A request for confidential information from such a source is more apt to be viewed as a command than an inquiry which is only to be satisfied if the client agrees.

A special task force, the Task Force on the Role of Psychology in the Criminal Justice System, was created by APA's Board of Social and Ethical Responsibility for Psychology to examine such ethical dilemmas. Albeit their concern was with the relationship of psychologists to the police, court, correctional and juvenile justice agencies, the guidelines they developed can be more broadly applied. Their report delineates two types of intra-agency situations (American Psychological Association, 1978, p. 1103):

> 1. The client, whether inmate or employee, wants to change his behavior. In such instances, "Therapy should only be given on a truly voluntary basis and . . . it should not be used as a means to pursue administrative ends, such as release or promotion decisions."
>
> 2. Clients referred for assessment or for treatment of a job-related problem. In such situations, "The psychologist takes the agency as his primary client. Further, the psychologist clearly informs the officer when each of these contingencies apply."

Application to the Case of "The Informal Opinion Request": If we apply these recommendations to the illustrative case in which your administrator requests an "informal opinion" (p. 75) it is apparent that since Jennifer is a self-referred client whatever she discloses to you should be kept confidential. According to our previous analysis of the parameters of confidentiality, any opinions you have formed as a result of these disclosures should also be considered confidential. However, the overall definition of your job must also be considered. If you were hired to treat only job-related concerns (such as Jennifer's), and if it were previously specified that you are to provide general reports about your clients upon request, then the agency is the primary client, and as such is entitled to your "informal opinion." Of course, in such cases the client should be informed of this in advance of making any disclosures. Perhaps the single guideline to follow that covers all such circumstances is, "Information should not be used for purposes that were not intended when it was revealed within the professional relationship" (Everstine, et al., 1980, p. 837).

Underage and Mentally Incapacitated Clients: Another set of concerns arises with clients who are presumed not to have the maturity or capacity to determine their own best interests, including what information should be kept confidential. We are primarily concerned here with people who fit into such legal or quasi-legal categories as minors, mentally retarded, and otherwise mentally incompetent. In such cases it is important to identify the person's guardian or legal representative --the person to whom information may be released for purposes of implementing various treatment plans or other actions on behalf of the client, or who may expect certain information to be released to him upon request. In most cases the parents are the legal guardians; but under certain circumstances, the client may be a ward of the court or have some other legally appointed guardian or representative.

In some instances it is recognized that mandatory disclosure to guardians would serve as an obstacle to the minor seeking useful information or cooperating with treatment programs. Thus, parent permission may not be required for adolescents to receive birth control or drug abuse information or counseling, depending on the regulations and statutes under which the agency operates. Then there are those who are obviously too young or too mentally incapacitated to make intelligent choices regarding their future. With such cients, "talking therapy" has limited applicability, but other forms of therapy, such as play therapy, and nonverbal forms of communication become more dominant. But even very young children have a concept of secrets and of keeping secrets, and will, in some instances, be able to discern that what they revealed in interaction with their therapists resulted in being treated differently by their parents or teachers. Regardless, there is no point of maturity or immaturity at which full disclosure of therapeutic interactions to a third party can automatically be assumed by the therapist to be the ethical course of action. It thus behooves the therapist to make some judgment as to the effect of such disclosures upon the client, i.e., the therapist should decide how the client's guardian is apt to use the disclosed information before deciding whether or not to release it. Principle 5d of *Ethical Principles* states:

> When working with minors or other persons who are unable to give voluntary, informed consent, psychologists take special care to protect these person's best interests.

Since children and the mentally incapacitated are typically referred clients, rather than voluntary, all that was stated about referred clients applies here as well; in particular, it is important to determine in advance exactly what the referring party expects in terms of return information, what the claim of that party is to such information, and to negotiate changes in expectations when necessary or desirable, including suggesting the referring party seek some information from other sources if providing this information might threaten the therapeutic alliance. Finally, insofar as it is possible to inform the client beforehand as to the limits of the confidentiality, this is done and consent is obtained.

Recordkeeping and Publication

Confidential information exists not only in the memory of the psychotherapist who is privy to it, but also in records of confidential activities and transactions. Such records include agency intake information, diagnoses, case notes, observation notes by agency and institutional personnel, test protocols, and results of research. All such information should be protected from unnecessary and unwanted disclosure.

In general, there are three ways in which to protect confidential records: to prohibit release altogether; to release only to authorized persons; and to disguise the identity of the client.

Complete confidentiality of records is not a practical possibility except in those instances where the therapist has her own secret files. Even then, these files may inadvertently be exposed to others in the advent of the therapist's death or severe incapacitation. Thus it is recommended that therapists specify in their wills what is to be done with their private client records (Siegel, 1979, p. 259). If no will exists the

Specialty Guidelines (2.3.5) recommend that:

> Following approval by the affected user, it is appropriate for another clinical psychologist, acting under the auspices of the local standards review committee (LSRC), to review the records with the user and recommend a course of action for continuing professional service, if needed. . . . the reviewing psychologist may also recommend appropriate arrangements for the balance of record retention and disposition period.

In most instances a therapist either works with an agency which has a central filing system or has a receptionist-secretary who keeps track of the files. Thus it is incumbent that these individuals receive special instructions regarding care of such records, instructions designed to keep all unauthorized persons, including themselves, from reviewing the contents. "All persons supervised by clinical psychologists, including nonprofessional personnel and students, who have access to the records of psychological services are required to maintain confidentiality as a condition of employment" (*Specialty Guidelines*, section 2.3.5). As mentioned before, this would include keeping confidential the status of the client, and appointment book information.

More than one person may contribute to and have access to agency records, and the client should be informed of this. "For instance, clinical psychologists in hospital, clinic, or agency settings inform their patients that psychological information in a patient's clinical records may be available without the patient's written consent to other members of the professional staff associated with the patient's treatment or rehabilitation" (*Specialty Guidelines*, section 2.3.5).

Client Access to Records

Paradoxically, clients have less right to records about themselves than agency personnel:

> Users have the right to obtain information from their psychological records. However, the records are the property of the psychologist or the facility in which the psychologist works and are, therefore, the responsibility of the psychologist and subject to

> his or her control" (Specialty Guidelines, section 2.3.5).

Thus in the case of The Latent Homosexual (p. 72) the counselor was ethically entitled to deny the client direct access to the intake counselor's notes--albeit, admittedly, there was no graceful way to exit from this situation once enmeshed in it.

The major argument for this policy is that some of the material found in client records, such as formal or informal diagnoses, test results, and speculative hypotheses regarding psychodynamics might lend themselves to misinterpretation by the client and result in unnecessary psychological distress. Also, the records may contain information transmitted in confidence to the therapist by others about the client, and release of this information would violate these confidences. Accordingly, the client is entitled to an edited, interpreted version of his record, but not to a photocopy or other visual inspection.

There are those, however, that argue that such a policy may temporarily serve to protect the profession, but is inimical to the interests of the client. A report by the federally appointed Privacy Protection Study Commission states (Plotkin, 1978):

> . . . after conducting extensive inquiries and holding hearings on this issue, [the commission] reported that "not one witness was able to identify an instance where access to [one's own] records had an untoward effect on a patient's condition. . . . In fact, several officials . . . believed that clients' potential access to the files actually improved the quality of the notes, because their personnel were striving to enhance accuracy and exclude irrelevancies.

The law is variable and largely untested in this area, but generally favors limiting client access to their own records (Schwitzgebel, et al., 1980).

> States and private organizations may not be required by the Freedom of Information Act or the Privacy Act [federal laws] to disclose information. . . . Several states give statutory permission to . . . mental patients to examine and copy . . . their

> medical records. Most states with access statutes explicitly prohibit disclosure of records of patients in mental hospitals . . . except . . . upon request of the patient's attorney. Access may be further limited to a professional intermediary, such as an independent psychiatrist or psychologist retained by the patient to examine the record and report relevant conclusion.
>
> In states without statutes granting mental patients access to their medical records, a review of the record by the patient is likely to be difficult unless the institution or practitioner voluntarily agrees. In case law, patient access is the exception rather than the rule. . . .
>
> Finally, some distinction may be made between records such as transcripts or test protocols, in which the patient has a proprietary interest, and the more informal professional products such as technical notes, comments, or uninterpreted data, which are meaningful only to the practitioner. Those informal products are usually in the sole possession of the practitioner or assistants and are not accessible to or transmitted to other persons. (pp. 212-213)

A similar distinction is made with respect to educational records (Schwitzgebel, et al., 1980):

> The revised Family Education Rights and Privacy Act of 1974 . . . gives students 18 or older (or those attending an institution of post-secondary education) and in some instances their parents the right to inspect relevant school records. . . .
>
> Some "education records" may not be available to students over 18 or to their parents. Among such records are those "created or maintained by a physician, psychiatrist, psychologist, or other recognized professional or paraprofessional acting in his or her professional capacity, or assisting in that capacity" and those records "created, maintained, or used only in connection with the provision of treatment to the student.". . . However, if the student requests that a physician or other appropriate treatment

> professional of the student's choice be allowed to see the treatment record, that record must be disclosed. Finally, it may be noted that those regulations apply to students 18 and over. Thus the records of those students under 18 in secondary or elementary schools may need to be made available to the parents of the students. (pp. 211-212)

Release to Non-Agency Third Parties

We have already covered the ethical code provisions (Specialty Guidelines, 2.3.5 and Ethical Principles, 5) relevant to release of information to third parties other than co-workers and supervisors in the previous sections, so I shall just briefly summarize them at this point. First of all, written consent of the client or his legal representative should be obtained prior to any release of confidential information to such parties. This information is to be identified as confidential to the recipient. Exceptions include instances in which "clear danger" to the client or others exists and when statutes, regulations with the force of law, or court order require otherwise. When ethics and law appear to conflict the psychologist may seek an appropriate compromise with the authorities. In any case, "Written and oral reports present only data germane to the purposes of the evaluation, and every effort is made to avoid undue invasion of privacy" (Principle 5a).

Case and statutory law is "sparse and ambiguous" with regard to release of records of state and private organizations. According to some state statutes hospital records of mental patients may be legally released without the consent of the patient or his attorney if the hospital director deems it necessary to do so for the treatment of the patient or "as a court may direct upon determination that disclosure is necessary for the conduct of proceedings before it, and if failure to disclose would be contrary to the public interest" (Schwitzgebel, et al., 1980, p. 212). The routine release of information to insurance carriers will be examined in the following chapter.

Publication and Classroom Presentations

The final way in which to protect confidentiality is by disguising the client's identity. This is typically done whenever a case is presented to a general audience for purposes of illustration and instruction, whether in a classroom or in a book or an article. The intent is not to seek consultation that can be expected to benefit the client, but rather to demonstrate some principle, or to determine policies designed to benefit future clients. The danger is that, in order to make a case vivid and interesting, certain particulars will be divulged that will enable some members of the audience to recognize the client who is being described, even though name, age, when seen, and exact educational or employment status are deliberately altered or not mentioned. As Slovenko points out (1975, p. 383), "the skill of Sherlock Holmes is not required to identify the subject of an article by a psychiatrist living in the same community, the large metropolis excepted." Even if the disguise is successful it may be that audience members may think they know who is being described and thus alter their perceptions and actions toward innocent third parties.

The Principles clearly identify this concern as an ethical issue:

> Psychologists who present personal information obtained during the course of professional work in writings, lectures, or other public forums either obtain adequate prior consent to do so or adequately disguise all identifying information. (Section 5b)

What constitutes "adequate disguise" is left to the judgment of the psychologist. Slovenko (1975, p. 383) reports that one gynecologist resolved the issue by writing under a pseudonym--an ingenious, if limited solution.

Recommendations for Record Keeping

Adoption of the following procedures may simplify the problems associated with confidentiality:

1. Keep only essential records. With the advent of computerized data banks it has become apparent that the more information there is on file the more administrative and research questions can theoretically be answered. Therefore the number of "bits" of information that are preserved in the anticipation that they will sometime prove useful has geometrically expanded. The "can't throw anything away" mentality that

characterizes many of our homes and leads to overflowing closets, garages, attics, and even the rental of additional storage units has spread to our offices. As a result more and more file cabinets are purchased, and the chances something will be lost or misfiled also have increased geometrically. Periodic reviews of files to determine that which is truly functional need to be made, and instead of garage sales periodic paper-shredding parties should be held.

2. Write behavior description, not speculations, in your case notes. It is just as simple and more useful in the long run to write down the basic facts of client-therapist interchanges than it is to write down the derivative speculations. For example, instead of writing, "Client appears to have paranoid delusions," write, "Client reports frequent suspicions of being followed by strangers and of being talked about behind his back." The behavioral report will probably evoke the speculative diagnosis at any given future date, whereas the reverse is far less apt to hold true--i.e., it is harder to reconstruct the facts than the general speculations. More important from the point of view of confidentiality, one can readily share the behavior descriptions with the client upon the client's request since it is the interpretation of these descriptions, and not the descriptions themselves, which are apt to be threatening or misinterpreted by the client. This in turn helps maintain or create a more cooperative relationship with clients.

3. Document the important decisions. There are certain decisions, such as to inform/not to inform the authorities of suicidal or homicidal tendencies of your clients, that should be justified at the time of their being made in order to ensure that this material will be maximally accurate and available in the event of some future request for such justification. This documentation would consist of the description of the behavior and the basis for your interpretation, including a report of any consultation you received. It is appropriate here to record your speculative interpretation since it constitutes a primary part of the basis for your decision. But most important are the facts you used in arriving at your interpretations and conclusions, including the presence/absence of environmental controls. For example, if you know the client lives with others who can readily observe her behavior and intervene in any crisis situation you would be less apt to worry about her committing suicide than if she lived alone. Knapp (1980) states:

> Careful documentation of the treatment and the treatment plan reduces the likelihood of a successful malpractice suit. Complete records can aid the psychologist in court. Records should include detailed notes of symptomatology, a diagnosis, treatment, all aspects of consent, relevant consultations and their outcomes, and descriptions of significant sessions.
> Psychologists should seek professional consultation with difficult or life-threatening clients. (p. 611)

4. <u>Follow the official policy on record retention that applies to your situation.</u> If you work in a governmental agency, either local, state or federal, the policy for record retention is probably already fixed by the relevant governmental authority. If you are in private practice or work for an independent private agency the <u>Specialty Guidelines</u> recommend:

> (a) that the full record be retained intact for 3 years after the completion of planned services or after the date of last contact with the user, whichever is later; (b) that a full record or summary of the record be maintained for an additional 12 years; and (c) that the record may be disposed of no sooner than 15 years after the completion of planned services or after the date of last contact, whichever is later. These temporal guides are consistent with procedures currently in use by federal record centers. (Section 2.3.5)

This ends the discussion of the complex area of confidentiality with the exception of the impact of third-party payments on confidentiality and other aspects of psychological practice. This will be the theme of the next chapter.

"He who pays the piper calls the tune."

CHAPTER VI

EFFECTS OF THIRD-PARTY PAYMENTS ON PRACTICE AND THEORY

From a practitioner's point of view, one of the benefits accruing from being a recognized mental health professional is that one's clients become eligible for partial reimbursement of the expenses they incur while receiving services from you. Many medical insurance policies pay for psychotherapy and assessment of psychological-physiological functioning under the rubric "mental health." In many cases this means people are able to afford services of this nature that they otherwise would forego, and this in turn means more income for licensed psychologists and other mental health professionals. One survey reports 22% of psychiatrists and 13% of psychologists received over 30% of their income from Blue Shield--just one of the medical insurance carriers, albeit a major one ("Reimbursement: How get along with Blue Shield," 1980).

Another survey, conducted by the Council for the National Register of Health Providers in Psychology (1982), found that 79% of the registrants receive third-party payments from an average of 44% of their patients for about one third of their income.

Thus, it seems safe to assume that a substantial portion of the income of licensed psychotherapists consists of insurance money. It seems reasonable to also assume that the recipient psychotherapists would be loath to jeopardize this portion of their incomes. This assumption would also apply to the organizations which represent the interests of these practitioners. One of the more successful political-legal battles fought in recent years by the American Psychological Association, for example, has been for licensed psychologists to gain parity with psychiatrists as recipients of third-party payments ("Historic Agreement on Parity Signals End of Psychologist-Psychiatrist War," 1980). Given this "stake" in this source of income it becomes relevant to inquire what psychotherapists are willing or tempted to do in order to protect their financial interests. This chapter is devoted to pursuit of this inquiry.

To better understand the interaction between psychotherapists and insurance carriers we must acknowledge that both parties have ethical obligations--the carriers to their stockholders and the psychotherapists to their clients. The carriers are obliged to make sure that monies they provide for mental health are properly utilized. In order to do so a certain amount of investigation and inquiry is necessary, and some form of quality control must be instituted--that is, not every form of treatment by every practitioner can be accepted as appropriate. Otherwise the monies available would risk early depletion, and the insurance premiums would become infeasibly high. To use a medical model analogy: applying psychoanalysis to what appears to be a simple case of test anxiety would be like performing extensive cosmetic surgery in order to correct a small facial blemish. It might prove to be necessary in the long run, but it certainly would seem appropriate for less extensive and less expensive measures to be tried first.

It should also be acknowledged that the field of "mental health" is much less clearly defined than that of physical health; neither the "diseases" nor the "treatments" can be readily defined, except in isolated instances, and there is considerable conflict between opposing diagnostic systems and overlap between diagnostic categories. Thus, the need for information as to exactly what is done for what reason is greater than in regular medical insurance if the insurance carrier is to be a proper steward of the money of its members.

One can argue, as many have, that the medical model is at fault or rather that it is the application of the medical model to psychological phenomena that is the basic problem. I do not pretend to be able to resolve that issue in this chapter or in this book. My focus is on the present situation, including its medical and quasi-medical aspects, and the ethical issues that arise out of it. Before approaching these general issues, let us first look at how they might arise in particular situations.

The Married Man and His Mistress raises the issue of how much responsibility a psychotherapist should assume for preventing a client from using his medical insurance to cover the expenses of a non-family member. The Short-/Long-Term Client poses the dilemma of providing long-term therapy when short-term might do, under the assumption that the insurance carrier would pay for either; The Indigent Client poses the issue of "stretching" a diagnosis to fit into a reimbursable category versus offering free service to indigent clients.

The following commentary sections review the positive and negative effects of such reimbursements upon the practice and theory of psychotherapy and are followed by a short report of some of the actual abuses by psychologist-psychotherapists of third-party reimbursements. The last section describes different approaches for resolving some of the continuing ethical and legal dilemmas. Included are a brief review of the ethics code proposed by the Oklahoma Psychological Association Insurance Committee, a description of recently developed quality assurance peer review programs, and a look at Health Maintenance Organizations as a way of reducing the rewards for excessive, unnecessary treatment and emphasizing preventive care.

Illustrative Cases

The Married Man and his Mistress: Chodoff (1972) reports the following incident:

A recent issue of the Journal of the American Medical Association [1971, 218, 1443] contained a letter from a psychiatrist asking for guidance about a sticky situation with which he had been confronted. He was treating the mistress of a married man who asked the psychiatrist to make out the bill in his name as if he were the patient. It had occurred to the psychiatrist that the married man's purpose was not only to keep the relationship secret, but also to collect insurance payment for the services. What, dear editor, the psychiatrist prayed, was his duty in the face of this thorny ethical and legal conundrum? (p. 540)

Suppose you were the editor--how would you answer?

1. Would you advise him to do as the married man requested? After all, if the client wishes to pay the bill, that's up to him how he does it. It is not up to the therapist to impose his ethics on the man, especially since the therapist is not sure his assumption about the man using his medical insurance is correct.

2. Would you advise the psychiatrist to refuse the request on the basis that, if the married man simply wanted to pay the bill, this could be arranged without making it appear that he was the recipient of the treatment and that to make out the bill in his name would be deceptive, hence unethical and possibly illegal?

3. Would you advise the psychiatrist to discuss his qualms with the married man and see if some mutually acceptable course of action can be found? If none can--what then?

The Short-/Long-Term Client: A young woman comes to see you for help regarding a long-term problem with anxiety. She claims that she has been tense and anxious, usually without any obvious or sufficient reason, for most of the past ten years, i.e., since she was an adolescent. She has been seen in therapy by several different therapists for varying lengths of time, from a few weeks to a year. The year's therapy seemed to help at the time, but there seemed to be no lasting value to it, and she discontinued when she decided to move to another city. Medication was also only of temporary assistance, and she does not want to go back to it.

You spend the first two sessions exploring the dimensions of her problem and ascertaining her present situation. It is apparent that she is able to function well in spite of her anxiety and that she is articulate and quick to grasp difficult concepts, i.e., she is an "ideal" client. Also it is apparent that her previous therapists were psychoanalytically or psychodynamically oriented, and she is prepared to spend a great deal of time exploring her past in the belief that this is the best way to understand and resolve her chronic problem.

Your training has been a mixture of both long-term investigative therapy and a brief "here and now" type of therapy. The latter you learned in order to cope with the requirements of your last position as a therapist in a community mental health clinic where psychotherapy was limited to ten sessions. To your surprise at the time, you found that you seemed to accomplish in ten sessions what previously took much longer using the more historically and relationship oriented approach. However, you prefer the relaxed pace of the more open-ended long-term approach.

In your experience the client's insurance policy will cover most of the expense of the psychotherapy, whether long- or short-term. You presume she is prepared to see you for up to 40 or 60 sessions and is not aware that her goals might be achieved in a much shorter period of time. What would you do?

1. Would you describe both the long-term and the short-term treatment options as fairly as you can and leave it to the client to decide which she prefers?

2. Would you take the most "natural" course--namely, follow your own preference and meet the expectations of the client by taking the leisurely, more lengthy therapy option?

3. Would you try some in-between approach, such as starting with the short-term therapy but without setting any hard and fast limit to the number of sessions, and being prepared to transit to the other approach if it seems useful or desirable? How then would you describe this in your treatment plan for the insurance company? (You suspect they will turn the claim down if it appears that you are trying an experimental mix of treatments.)

The Indigent Client: Pete is referred to you by his former therapist at a mental health clinic in another city. Pete has moved to your city, and his former therapist thought it would be advisable for him to receive some follow-up therapy. He is described as having had a number of acute depression episodes over the past ten years, and at one point had attempted suicide.

When you first interview Pete it is several weeks since his last appointment with his previous therapist, and there is no evidence that he is or has been depressed. He reports that he feels fine, reasonably optimistic, and believes he has finally gotten a handle on his depression; in fact, the last episode was quite brief and relatively minor. He has come in with hopes of receiving vocational counseling, and not for any additional therapy for depression. You consider yourself qualified to provide vocational counseling since that was at one time a specialty of yours and you have made some efforts to keep abreast of recent developments in the field. Pete is currently living off unemployment compensation, and he could not pay for your services at this time. Also, you know that such services are virtually non-existent in the community, at least at the level of sophistication that Pete seems to require.

Your choice seems to be either to provide vocational counseling and hope you will eventually be paid for it by Pete, or to provide such counseling under the guise of treating him for depression, and thus receive reimbursement under Pete's health insurance plan. What should you do?

1. Should you approach Pete with the proposal that the vocational counseling be treated as a follow through on his recent bout with depression, rather than a separate new activity? Thus, he could be made eligible for insurance benefits in view of the fact that his referral was evidence his previous therapist did not think the therapy was finished.

2. Should you tell Pete that his insurance unfortunately will not cover vocational counseling and that, unless he can somehow cover the costs of the counseling sessions himself, he will simply have to forego such counseling for now, or at least forego the level of analysis and expertise that you can provide as compared to the free services at the State Employment Office?

3. Should you offer to provide him such counseling at your own expense, or at least until such time as he can reimburse you? Note in this connection Principle 6d of the Ethical Principles states in part: "They [psychologists] contribute a portion of their services to work for which they receive little or no financial return."

Commentary

As can be seen by the foregoing cases the availability of third-party reimbursement can tempt both the client and the therapist to utilize such money for services that might otherwise not be considered. This may not necessarily be bad, but when actual deception is involved in obtaining the money, it is not just a matter of ethics but a matter of fraud. As we shall see later, such practices are not just theoretically possible, but there is evidence of their occurrence. But first let us sketch the more general picture by reviewing the broad range of effects of third-party payments, real and potential, positive and negative, on the practices and theory of psychotherapy.

Positive Effects of Third-Party Payments

If we view psychotherapy as a beneficial treatment for certain disorders then we must view the greater availability of this treatment as a positive effect of third-party payments. As said earlier, many people can afford this service with the aid of their insurance policies who could not otherwise avail themselves of it. Also, clients are better able to afford longer term therapy, and for some clients this may be necessary or especially important. This, in turn, provides employment to psychotherapists and funding support for mental health agencies.

The other major positive effect of third-party payment is pressure for greater accountability within the profession that provides the services. As Paul Chodoff (1972) clearly foresaw:

> Insurance officials and their actuaries are going to want to know what they are paying for . . . they expect this kind of accountability from surgeons . . . and are not likely to regard psychiatrists as any more sacrosanct or immune from questioning than other medical specialists . . . thus, we see that an already troublesome problem--the criteria for various forms of psychotherapy and evaluation of their effectiveness--has been given a new urgency by the increase in third-party payment. (p. 544)

Negative Effects of Third-Party Payments

The list of negative and potentially negative effects is long, but this should not be viewed as a judgment by the author that they weigh heavier in the balance.

Perhaps the most serious criticism is that, since the tendency is to reimburse only standard diagnoses (i.e., the DSM III categories) and "proven" (i.e., traditional) treatments, the net effect is to stiffle creative change, both in theory and in practice. For example, one major insurance organization specifically excludes from reimbursement such services as "therapies for weight reduction, sexual dysfunction or 'inadequacy,' treatments for organic brain syndrome, dyslexia and enuresis. Additionally excluded are biofeedback services and . . . 'mind expansion' programs such as transactional analysis, gestalt therapy, EST, Rolfing, transcendental meditation, and Z-therapy" (Foltz, 1979, p. 9).

Such a reward system may have a "backwards" effect. If only standard diagnoses and treatments are to be reimbursed, why strive to develop and teach new, better diagnostic systems or forms of therapeutic intervention? In particular, the proactive role for professionals and non-professionals in developing a broad range of psychological prevention-intervention strategies is neglected in favor of a return to the reactive medical or social welfare model (Danish & Smyer, 1981). The use of paraprofessionals and self-help peer groups, for example, is not encouraged when only licensed professionals administering standard therapies receive reimbursement for mental health services.

Also endangered is the recent thrust towards brief forms of therapy. One of the positive effects was the increased availability of psychotherapy to members of the public who would not otherwise be able to afford it. A possible corollary negative effect is that more therapy will be provided than is necessary or even desirable. Thus, as in the case of <u>The Short-/Long-Term Client</u> (p. 110) the tendency may exist for the client to "get her money's worth" or for the therapist to do a "thorough" job, since the insurance company is paying for most of it anyway, or perhaps even for the therapist to encourage the client to doubt her capacities for working through her problems without long-term assistance.

Another effect of supporting the status quo in diagnosis is that the required labels and the general impact of such a labeling process may precipitate further problems (Danish & Smyer, 1981).

> One consequence of being labeled "mentally ill" is that . . . it may relieve the individual's family and support network of their responsibility. . . . If mental illness is labeled a <u>disease</u>, and not an interpersonal or competency deficiency, the causes are assumed to be biochemical or physiological. . . . Family and friends may feel they should not interfere in an area they know nothing about. . . . However, it is not just the loss of social support that adversely affects the patient. If individuals become convinced that they are victims of mental illness, they may feel less able to master the problems themselves and therefore, less able to help themselves. (pp. 18-19)

Another potential problem arises at the time of peer review of claims for past or for further treatment. The peer review forms (see Appendix D for a sample) require that treatment goals, treatment procedures, and estimates of the number of sessions needed to effect the goals be established early in the therapy. A number of clinicians find that "such requirements simply don't fit all current modes of therapy and tend to create rigidly programmed expectations of third-party insurers. . . ." (Foltz, 1981b, p. 12).

In order to better appreciate the dimensions of the diagnostic issues and later of the issue of confidentiality, it may be helpful to contrast the procedures that are mandated by the intervention of third-party payments to those that are required when the client pays directly for his own therapy, especially if he is an outpatient of a therapist in private practice. In such cases it is not necessary for the therapist to assign a diagnosis at all, much less early in the sessions. Neither is it ever necessary to formally or even explicitly set any goals for treatment, much less estimate the number of sessions required to reach them. Therapists of the client-centered persuasion, among others, can be presumed to resist assigning diagnostic labels, especially traditional ones, and would see such constraints as being detrimental to the actual therapy. On the other hand, it can be argued that these requirements, especially the setting of goals, promote accountability. This is essentially the argument presented in previous chapters with regard to the desirability of establishing contractual agreements with clients as consumers. Finally it is thought by many therapists that the client who pays directly for services is more involved, more committed to getting something from these services, and thus will do better.

The other major allegedly negative effect of third-party payments is the reduction of confidentiality. Again it can be argued, as we have seen in Chapter V, that confidentiality is more apt to protect the therapist from disclosure of her mistakes than it is to protect the client, but this is decidedly a minority opinion in the profession. Perhaps the greatest risk to a client is that a prospective employer may somehow gain access to his mental health claim forms and reject him on that basis or that the client's social status and reputation may be damaged. Insurance companies promise to protect the confidentiality of such records. The federally established CHAMPUS, for example, has pledged to keep its files from outside employer and unlawful government access and separates psychiatric and psychological treatment claims from other medical claims (Foltz, 1979, p. 9). However, the value of this pledge has been questioned. "The Daniel Ellsberg case should at least have taught us that if the government wants information on its citizens, it will stop at nothing to get it. This would be especially true if that information were resting innocently in the computers of its own agencies" (Roskam, 1979, p. 18).

Several psychologists have reported trying to exclude progress notes from communications to the insurance carriers and to provide only diagnosis, prognosis, and a brief description of the methods of treatment. In one case it is argued that providing such information would make second class citizens out of Medicaid recipients since the files of consumers in the private sector have more protection (Herbert, 1979). In another case the psychologist objected that the insurance carrier, a Blue Cross-Blue Shield company, was "requiring a proof of effectiveness from psychotherapy that is required from no other professional, at least for insurance purposes" (Roskam, 1979, p. 3). In both cases the insurance carrier disallowed the claims.

In Hawaii, a licensed clinical psychologist had somewhat more success when he went to court to protest the seizure of his client's records by the Attorney General, who had obtained a warrant to do so on the basis of a Medicaid fraud law (Psychotherapy Finances, 1980). The Hawaii Psychiatric Association provided lawyers who fought the case to the federal court, which held that the Ninth Amendment--equal protection under the law--outweighs the state's right to ferret out cheaters. However, the judge did not completely rule out inspection of the full record. "He held that if the state first audited the 'non-confidential' portions of the therapist's records--treatment given, dates, fees, etc.--and determined that a reasonable suspicion existed that there was fraud, a warrant to inspect the more sensitive records might be available" (p. 2).

Evidence of Unethical, Incompetent, and Fraudulent Behavior by Psychologists

This brings up the question of how much fraud does exist in the billing practices of psychotherapists, and the corollary questions of the prevalence of unethical and incompetent behavior. Unfortunately, most of the data on these matters are informally derived, especially with regard to unethical or incompetent behavior that falls short of provable fraud. Based upon his contacts in the insurance industry Claiborn (1982) makes a claim:

> The working definition of <u>abuse</u> for third-party payers is <u>fraud</u> rather than <u>incompetence</u>. . . . Even when utilization review leads to the conclusion that incompetent treatment has occurred, the usual disposition is to deny reimbursement for the individual case alone and to take no further action against the incompetent provider. (p. 154)

Sheldon Morton (1982), who served as a consultant to Blue Shield of California, has disclosed some of his experience and the experience of fellow consultants with unethical practices of psychologist-psychotherapists. He noted that a number of psychologists, many of whom were not psychoanalytically trained, billed daily sessions of individual psychotherapy (5-6 hours per week). "In some instances each session was billed for two or more hours; in some instances several members of the same family were seen individually on a daily basis" (p. 142). There were even examples of fraud--for example, "billing for 42 individual 50-minute sessions in one day by a single provider, seeing a family group but billing for each member at individual rates, billing for psychological tests not administered, using Medi-stickers for members of families who have not been provided services, etc., etc." (pp. 142-143). Morton also provides a number of examples of increases in fees to levels at which it is doubtful non-insured private clients could or would pay. As he states in his foreword:

> The general opinion of professional advisors in the Provider Review Department at Blue Shield is that fees and types of services billed . . . tend to rise with the passage of time to the maximum that the traffic will bear . . ." (p. 141).

<u>Proposed "Solutions" to the Ethical, Legal Problems</u>

Despite the lack of formal evidence of abusive and exploitative practices by psychologist-psychotherapists, it does appear that there is good reason to believe that such practices do occur, and it would be appropriate for the profession to develop ways of policing itself in this respect. One such attempt was made by the insurance committee of the Oklahoma Psychological Association (1981) which developed a code of ethics for interacting with third-party reimbursers. According to the code it is unethical to "change the diagnosis to fit the coverage, or to treat the patient in a hospital, when outpatient treatment would suffice, because insurance coverage provides treatment only when hospitalized." It is also considered unethical to charge a patient a higher than usual fee simply because the patient has insurance coverage. It is unethical "to seek insurance reimbursement for services for which one is not competent to provide" or to claim that a Ph.D. did the therapy when he only acted as supervisor. A number of other provisions clearly spell out other unethical, but financially rewarding practices.

Supposing this code were adopted by the APA--how could it be enforced? Psychologists would have to know more about what other psychologists do in practicing psychotherapy. They would also have to be willing to report unethical and illegal practices. Finally, the profession, itself, would have to employ sanctions powerful enough to discourage such practices. The ultimate sanctions would be expulsion from the official membership bodies (state and national associations), recommendation of revocation of licensure, and reporting of illegal actions to the proper legal authorities. None of these latter actions should be attempted without firm evidence and adequate grounds, and they would normally be employed only if there is no indication that lesser actions would suffice. (See the chapter, "Policing the Profession," for a more complete discussion of the procedures that would be applied.)

Quality Assurance through Peer Review[1]

One methodology that has been already adopted as a means of controlling abuse of the third-party reimbursement system by unethical or incompetent practitioners and yet promises a certain degree of privacy for the client is referred to as peer review. There have been

---

[1] For more detailed information on this topic the reader is referred to the February, 1982 issue of Professional Psychology, which entire issue is devoted to peer review and quality assurance.

a number of different kinds of peer review programs that have and are being developed and tested, but they all share the common feature that panels of peers, fellow practitioners, are formally established to review information provided by psychotherapists about their clients and the proposed and ongoing treatment programs for these clients. They use this information to judge the appropriateness of the treatment for the client and the competency of the psychotherapist to administer such treatment.

The first such national health care review program was established by Congress in 1972. Professional Standards Review Organizations (PSROs) were to operate at state and federal levels with federal aid to monitor Medicare, Medicaid, and Child Health Programs. They were asked to establish their own criteria with the aid of national guidelines. Unfortunately, it took several years to get the groups organized, and "private insurance carriers have been reluctant to contract with the PSROs, as originally conceived, because net cost savings have not been demonstrated and proof of improved quality has not been forthcoming" (Young, 1982, p. 12).

Subsequently another effort, spearheaded by the Department of Defense through the Office of the Civilian Health and Medical Plan of the Uniformed Services (CHAMPUS), has proven more attractive. The motivation for institution of this type of quality assurance program came not so much from the profession for ethical reasons, but rather from the reimbursing agency for monetary reasons. CHAMPUS, which insures dependents of military personnel and military retirees, had found that its mental care services had grown from about one fourth in 1972 to one third in 1977 of what it paid out in benefits (Foltz, 1979). The Department of Defense reacted by requesting a credible, quality-conscious scheme for insuring that mental health care underwritten by CHAMPUS live up to professional standards. This request was made of both the American Psychological Association and the American Psychiatric Association. As a result of the subsequent negotiations the two APAs set up panels of three professional practitioners who independently review insurance claims (with names of therapist and client omitted) at specified points in the therapy (8, 24, 40, and 60 sessions) and recommend in favor of or against their reimbursement. The reviewers are paid $40/hour for their services, and general requirements suggest that they spend no more than 20 minutes on each case. They, themselves, are eligible CHAMPUS service providers and should reasonably spend no more than 20 percent or so of their professional time with claims work. This restriction of 20 percent is intended as a protection against therapists becoming too closely identified with the insurance industry. Each profession provides its own reviewers for its own practitioners and has developed (in conjunction with CHAMPUS) different, albeit similar forms to be completed by the practitioners, which forms serve as the basis for the reviews.

The forms for psychologists contain a narrative description of the current functional impairment(s), an outline of the goals between now and the next review point, and a listing of the planned services (procedures, techniques, strategies for attaining goals). Psychiatry's forms emphasize classical diagnostic labels and require less specific description of each patient's problems. (See Appendix D for CHAMPUS psychologist form).

The initial results have led to a reduction of mental health costs to CHAMPUS from about one third to one sixth according to Department of Defense figures (Foltz, 1981b). AEtna Life and Casualty of Hartford has also been using some aspects of PRP for the past two years, and the American Psychological Association has agreed to apply the system to a pilot study by Prudential Insurance. APA's Board of Directors voted recently to negotiate with still more third-party carriers regarding providing peer review services (Abeles, 1982, p. 657).

Criticism of Peer Review Programs (PRPs): Ideally PRPs would serve three purposes: one, protect the profession from undue control by the insurance industry over its choice of treatment modes and procedures; two, provide a comprehensive and effective quality control mechanism for the insurers; and three, protect clients from undue invasion of their privacy. In other words, PRPs would serve as a buffer between the industry and the private practitioner. Critics claim none of the above is being accomplished.

An article in the APA Monitor reports the following criticisms (Foltz, 1981b, p. 12):

> 1. . . . architects of psychology's review program . . . have handed insurance companies discretion over clinical routine that tradi-

tionally and properly belongs to the practitioner. . . . Critics . . . protest strongly that APA designers of the review and treatment reporting requirements have made a "narrow and arbitrary" attempt to define "proper practice.". . .
Possibly the most frequent complaint raised against the system by psychologists has been the guidelines recommending a ban on payments to practitioners for individual treatment for multiple members of a single family.

2. Many critics say that the peer review system . . . promises little in the way of cost effectiveness and better care, but it does generate a lot of paperwork with much of the burden on providers. . . .
Psychology providers are wary of the frequency with which third-level review by their peers can be brought into the treatment process at the discretion of fiscal intermediaries.
"There is no evidence . . . that indicates such frequent intervention increases the quality or effectiveness of services provided." [Rogers Wright, former member of APA's Board of Directors]

3. Disgruntled clinicians add that psychology's guidelines for CHAMPUS providers have made it an unprecedented "ethical responsibility" of psychologists to cooperate with third-party insurers in providing information some psychologists feel is unnecessary and which threatens confidentiality.

Are such criticisms simply the result of clinicians chafing against ethical bindings that they previously were able to disregard with relative impunity? For example, with regard to the ban on payments for individual treatment for multiple members of a single family, it is argued that this practice "has been an embarrassing source of abuse by clinicians cashing in on entire families and one which . . . research has shown to be an unsound practice. . ." (Foltz, 1981b, p. 12).

Or do the criticisms represent valid observations that the profession has capitulated to the insurance industry's concerns at the expense of professional integrity? There can be no question that the APA involvement in designing and implementing PRPs has legitimated inquiries and restrictions that have been considered presumptious, demeaning and unethical by some psychologists, from the very outset. However, there is also no question that such features would obtain in any transaction with insurance carriers and are not unique to PRPs. PRPs provide the profession with some buffer, some protection against direct control by the insurance carriers. At least psychologists, and not regular employees of the industry, are telling psychologists what is allowable or unallowable treatment in order to get reimbursement.

It may be that methods for assuring both quality control and development of professional practice can be developed, or it may be that insurance for "mental health" will be discarded as being too difficult to administer and police properly. What seems more likely, at least in the near future, is that further refinement of the peer-review approach will be attempted.

Health Maintenance Organizations

Another type of health coverage that offers potential resolution to some ethical problems but poses others is offered by Health Maintenance Organizations (HMOs). The Kaiser-Permanente Health Plan is the acknowledged prototype of such organizations. It was founded by Henry J. Kaiser just before World War II as a benefit for employees. Due to the tremendous expense associated with the establishment of any comprehensive health care plan the national government was persuaded to provide seed money for such organizations under a bill enacted in 1977. At the present time there are about 200 HMOs in the USA with about two million subscribers. Much of the following information is provided by the director of Selectcare, a HMO located in Lane County, Oregon (Spero, Note 3).

Although the scene is changing and threatens to change even more drastically on almost a daily basis, as of this writing certain features distinguish the health care plans and delivery of services of insurance carriers from those of HMOs. There are two basic distinctions: designation of health care providers, and degree of local control.

HMOs designate certain health care personnel--physicians, psychologists, clinical social workers, physical therapists, etc.--as health care providers.

Subscribers, those who have purchased an HMO health care plan, must choose among these providers. Exceptions are made under certain conditions, such as traveling outside of the area served by the local HMO, or when a specialist is needed who is not a designated provider.

In order to be listed as a provider, the health care professional must agree to certain conditions, such as setting fees at a certain level for specified services and making available certain records to the HMO for quality assurance inspection. Thus, HMOs exercise a greater measure of control over the amount, type, and cost of services available to their subscribers than regular insurance carriers.

This control is enhanced by the fact that HMOs are locally based, that is, they operate only within a particular company, community, or region. This permits arrangements to be made that reflect local conditions and preferences, many of which arrangements can be negotiated on a face-to-face basis.

One relatively new contractual model is for a certain collection of services, such as mental health services, to be provided by an Independent Practitioners Association, an IPA. The IPA agrees to provide mental health services, such as psychotherapy, to all the subscribers that are referred to them by the "primary care providers," the physicians. In return, the IPA is paid a set amount of money per month, which amount is based on the total number of subscribers in the system, and not just on those who are actually referred for mental health services. It is up to the IPA to select its own members, to establish a fee structure, to designate reimbursable services, etc. Members may be paid less for interviews after a certain limit than for those prior to that limit, less per family member when whole families are seen than if each member were treated as a separate client, less for group members than for individuals, etc. It is also the prerogative of the IPA to establish its own diagnostic categories and measures for protection of confidentiality--with the proviso that sufficient, readily interpretable information be communicated to the HMO to allow for quality assurance review. Theoretically, the IPA could conduct its own preventive treatment programs to be offered to all subscribers, if it so wanted, and its own evaluation of services research, which data could be offered the HMO in lieu of individual client data for purposes of quality assurance. Exactly what the contractual arrangements are between each IPA and its HMO will vary from IPA to IPA and from HMO to HMO.

This type of arrangement appears promising in that it provides more internal autonomy and flexibility for the practitioners. However, if the portion of the subscribers' fees assigned to the IPA is too small the practitioners will be tempted to cut back on necessary or desirable services instead of merely pruning the unnecessary ones, and will leave the monitoring to the HMO.

In conclusion, the HMO type of third-party payment system appears to have both some advantages and some disadvantages from an ethical point of view, at least at the present time. There is less reward for prolonged, unnecessary, or expensive modes of treatment and more support, in some localities at least, for innovative treatment methods and diagnostic systems. Also there may be more opportunity for quality assurance methods that are less intrusive of confidentiality. Traditional insurance carriers are experimenting with similar mental health care delivery plans, so it would be presumptious to judge one system as being more promising than the other, or to predict that the distinctions that now obtain between the two systems will hold up in the future.

> The public and most professionals believe that occupational licensing protects service consumers against charlatans and incompetence. This review . . . reveals licensing to be a mystifying arrangement that promises protection of the public but that actually institutionalizes a lack of accountability to the public. The collusion between the state and the professions is maintained by myth.
>
> (S.J. Gross, 1978)

CHAPTER VII

LICENSURE

Licensure of psychotherapists and counselors is truly an idea whose time has come. Recent statistics indicate that there are forty-nine statutory boards of psychologist examiners in the United States which monitor 36,000 licensed psychologists, and that about 4000 persons take the EPPP (Examination for Professional Practice in Psychology) each year (Wiens & Menne, 1981). In addition three states (Arkansas, Alabama and Virginia) have licensure of counselors, and twenty more have drafted counselor licensure bills (Swanson, Note 4). When three states (Florida, South Dakota and Alaska) recently sunsetted their licensing laws for psychologists strenuous efforts were made by organized psychology to re-establish licensure, with at least partial success (Foltz, 1981c).

Why all this effort and activity? Why do psychologists in particular, and psychotherapists and counselors in general want to impose licensing on themselves? Since licensure is granted through state legislation its ostensible purpose must be to protect the public from charlatans and incompetent practitioners: "A group proposing that it be licensed must usually convince a legislative body that the public is being harmed by the absence of regulation" (Shimberg, 1981, p. 1138). However, critics have suggested that a strong self-serving motive may be more basic. It has been noted that licensing has rarely been sought by the public and imposed upon a group; rather, it has been sought by the professionals who wished to be licensed (Ozanne, 1977; Gross, S.J., 1978). And those who do seek licensure laws make sure they are not thereby disenfranchised:

> If it is in the public interest, and if it is really to raise the standards and protect the public, why is it that in every licensing situation there's a grandfather clause. In other words, why is it that when the licensing statute is created, everybody who is already a lawyer or doctor or Indian chief or whatever it is, gets in without having to take the test, but everybody after that has to take the test. (Ozanne, 1977)

This question of whether or not licensing truly benefits the public or whether it is actually detrimental by virtue of restricting access, raising costs, etc. is an ethical issue of some magnitude and of considerable debate both within and without the profession. It may be that both the public and the profession are being served by licensure. It may be neither is. This chapter is devoted to presenting this debate, as well as alternatives and reforms of licensure.

First some situations are presented which highlight certain aspects of this broad issue in concrete ways. In We too should be Licensed--help Us! the issue is raised of whether licensed psychologists should support the efforts of other organized groups of professional psychotherapists, in this case marriage and family therapists, to gain licensure. Is he or is he not a "Psychologist"? raises the awkward problem of the in-between status of Ph.D.s in psychology who have lost their licensure by transferring from a state in which they had been licensed to one where their license isn't accepted. Disqualified because of Training raises the question of whether or not graduate students in counseling and clinical programs should be allowed to continue with their private practices as "counselors" while getting training to become "psychologists."

In the following commentary sections licensure of psychologists and other psychotherapists will be compared to that of other professions whose functions are more definitive and less apt to overlap with those of people in general or those of other professions. The four stages of licensure of psychologists are described and then the effects of licensure--disputable and nondisputable, negative and positive. Methods for correcting the defects of the present system are presented, as well as a revolutionary proposal by Dan Hogan, author of a four volume study on the regulation of psychotherapy (Hogan, 1979). Finally some comments are offered on the "Illustrative Cases."

Illustrative Cases

We too should be Licensed--help Us! You are a member of the local county psychological association which provides full membership only to licensed psychologists. Your association receives a request from its local counterpart of the American Association for Marriage and Family Therapists (AAMFT) to officially and unofficially lend it support in its attempt to establish a state licensing procedure for its members, i.e., to support its bill before the state legislature. A spokeswoman for the group is invited, at her request, to present its case. She points out that members of this association are already licensed to practice in several states, including California, Michigan, New Jersey and Georgia, and that their qualifications are arguably every bit as high as yours, although a Ph.D. is not required, and in any case they restrict their practice to marriage and family therapy. She further points out that some of your members know some of their members, know how qualified and ethical they are, and even refer clients to them. What would your response be?

1. Vote against supporting their request. You feel no obligation to support their request, especially since they did not support your organization's attempts at licensure. Also, you think a Ph.D. degree from an accredited program is important for practitioners and does add some depth and breadth of perspective, albeit our crude performance measures may not as yet demonstrate any real advantage to the consumer.

2. Vote for their request and perhaps personally support their attempt to achieve this legal status. You believe that they are deserving of such status and licensure will help them regulate their profession, even as it has helped yours.

3. Vote against it on strictly economic grounds. Why should you assist your competitors?

4. Vote to refer their request to the state organization without recommendation from your local group and wait for its decision.

Is he or is he not a "Psychologist"? Jerry Reed has recently moved here from another state. He has his Ph.D. in psychology from an APA-endorsed clinical psychology program, but this was many years ago, and to his dismay he discovers that his license (he "grandfathered in") is not transferrable. He is ambivalent about taking the EPPP exam, recognizing it represents a lot of work and some expense with no guarantee of success--all of which time he will be without employment as a psychologist. What he would like to do is to establish a local weight reduction program, something he has had considerable experience and success with in the past. However, he wishes to be able to refer to himself as a "psychologist," which, indeed, he believes himself to be, but has heard this would be against the law. He knows that you are a licensed psychologist in the state and asks what the legal/ethical situation is. Do you know the official position? If not, where could he (or you) obtain such information? What do you personally believe to be right in this situation?

Disqualified because of Training: You are a member of the faculty of a doctoral program in clinical psychology. A motion is before this faculty to require that all candidates for master's and doctor's degrees should be discouraged from engaging in any private practice while working towards a graduate degree in the program. Specifically, they risk removal from the program unless they desist from such practice. The rationale is that they should not be practicing that which they are still in training to learn how to do, except through the regular practicum and internship arrangements where it can be assured that they are receiving the proper supervision. One of the graduate students, a representative of the graduate students' association in the department, points out that many of the students have been in private practice for some time before returning to school, and some of them depend on this source of income, on a part-time basis, in order to afford to go to school. Your program caters to older, experienced applicants, many of whom have families to support, and this is the natural result of such selection. She asks, if they were "good enough" to be accepted in the first place, why are they suddenly not "good enough" to be allowed to continue with what they had been doing to earn a living, as long as they don't advertise themselves as being bona-fide psychologists? What would your response be?

1. State that some temporary exceptions may have to be made, but that in general the policy is a good one since the fact that these people are now in the program changes their status and they in some sense "represent" the program?

2. Vote for the motion with the amendment that the students make arrangements to be supervised in their private practice by licensed psychologists or other licensed psychotherapists?

3. Vote against the motion and the amendment on the grounds that it unfairly restricts competition (some of the faculty members are in part-time private practice) and that it can be assumed that the students will apply whatever they learn from the program to their work outside of the program without any special supervision?

Commentary

Licensure of psychotherapists is somewhat different from licensure of physicians and other professional and occupational groups. A pure licensing statute contains scope of practice statements that define what a licensed practitioner may do and makes it illegal for unlicensed persons to engage in any of the activities defined by the scope of practice (Shimberg, 1981). However, what psychotherapists do in general, or psychologists in particular, may not be distinctive enough from what many other professionals or even people on the street do to make such an exclusory definition possible. For example, the Oregon Licensing Statute (ORS 675.010), which is modeled after the national guidelines (APA Committee on Legislation, 1967) states:

> "Practice of psychology" means the rendering or offering to render to individuals, groups, organizations or the public any psychological service while representing himself to be a psychologist, involving the application of principles, methods and procedures of understanding, predicting and influencing behavior, such as principles pertaining to learning, perception, motivation, thinking, emotions and interpersonal relationship. . . . (Subsection 4)

It would be difficult and probably impossible to find a person who did <u>not</u> apply principles of learning, perception, etc., and did <u>not</u> predict and influence behavior while engaging in everyday life, albeit without being able to formally identify the components in these processes. There is no activity mentioned in the listing that is so distinctive that one could prohibit others from performing it without substantially interfering with their freedom. For example, how could one prevent parents from applying principles of predicting or influencing behavior to their children. This is not true of most other licensed occupations. One can, for example, reasonably limit such things as prescription of drugs and performance of surgery to physicians.

The key phrase in such a scope of practice statement is the "while representing himself to be a psychologist." Essentially, we have a "protection of title" statute, otherwise known as a certification statute. Further in the statute (ORS.020) the title of "psychologist" is expanded as follows:

> A person represents himself to be a psychologist when he holds himself out to the public by or uses any title or any description of services which incorporates one or more of the following terms: "psychology," "psychological," "psychologist," or any term of like import, "psychometry," "psychometrics," "psychometrist," "psychotherapy," "psychotherapist," "psychoanalysis," "psychoanalyst," or variants thereof or when he holds himself out to be trained, experienced or an expert in the field of psychology.

Exemptions are then made from the provisions of this chapter for persons "licensed to practice one or more of the other arts" as long as they don't specifically refer to themselves as "psychologists," "psychometrists," etc., and also for teachers of psychology, school psychologists, and numerous others in certain circumstances. Thus, even the protection of the title is a complicated matter, so much so that two past chairs of state boards of psychological examiners, who have also been active in the American Association of State Psychology Boards, recently commented (Wiens & Menne, 1981):

> How can licensed psychologists deny others this "title" [psychologist] when schools and state agencies authorize "psychologist" positions? Really, only the "licensed

psychologist" title can or should be defended. (p. 392)[1]

Accordingly, the essential thrust of certification and licensing statutes is to certify that certain people have successfully negotiated certain academic and training programs and have demonstrated in exams the knowledge thought relevant to ethical and competent practice. To this end regulatory agencies, referred to as state boards of psychologist examiners, are set up and are typically empowered to establish standards of training and service and to institute procedures to enjoin unlawful practice. Qualifications and procedures for licensure or certification, fees, and penalties are all prescribed by statute.

The Four-Stage Licensing Process

In order to establish a common reference for the critical analysis of the effects of licensure that follows I will first describe the various stages in the licensing process.

1. The first stage consists of the graduate training program which must be successfully completed before admission to the actual licensing process can be gained. The state boards have the power to reject applicants on the basis that the graduate program of the candidate's educational institution was of insufficient quality or that the candidate's own personally chosen degree program and course work was of insufficient breadth and depth.

The state boards also review the one or two years of supervised employment as an intern or "psychologist resident" that is typically required. The boards determine the actual length of employment, its appropriateness and the adequacy of the supervision. The American Association of State Psychology Boards has prepared

---

[1] The restrictive power of one of the scope of practice statements defining the practice of psychology is now being tested in court. The District of Columbia's licensing statute for psychologists is being used as the basis for a suit against Lifespring, an organization that promises "self-improvement trainings," by two former members who claim they suffered "severe emotional and physical trauma" as a result of Lifespring's programs ("Lifespring suit cites D.C. law," 1982).

guidelines for the employment and supervision of uncredentialed persons providing psychological services (1980). These guidelines serve as a basis for many of the states' licensing statutes. Two guidelines with pervasive implications are as follows:

> Persons providing psychological services who are not credentialed by the Board of Psychological Examiners must be under the direct and continuing administrative and professional direction of a psychologist licensed or certified by the Board. (Section C:2)
>
> The credentialed psychologist shall have sufficient knowledge of all clients, including face-to-face contact when necessary, in order to plan effective service delivery procedures. The progress of the work shall be monitored through such means as will insure that full legal and professional responsibility can be accepted by the supervisor for all services rendered. Supervisors shall also be available for emergency consultation and intervention. (Section C:4)

2. Those applicants whose graduate training programs are approved proceed to stage two: The EPPP (Examination for Professional Practice in Psychology). This exam is designed to "verify acquisition of basic knowledge in psychology, that is, the minimum amount of knowledge which defines the generic discipline of psychology and which all psychologists are expected to possess" (Wiens & Menne, 1981). It is a national multiple choice exam whose items vary from testing to testing. The passing score also varies from state to state and may be based on the national mean for each testing or on some fixed percentage of items passed or on some fixed number of items passed. Sub-doctoral or master's level licensure, where available, typically requires a lower passing score. The chart on the following page describes the situation in the U.S. and Canada as of March, 1980 (Note 5). It is obvious that this wide degree of variation contributes to difficulties in determining reciprocity of licensure from state to state.

3. Those candidates who met their state's standard for passing the EPPP then advance to the third stage which typically consists of an essay and/or an oral examination designed to identify the applicant's

SURVEY OF CUT-OFF POINTS ON THE EXAMINATION FOR PROFESSIONAL PRACTICE IN PSYCHOLOGY (EPPP) UTILIZED BY STATE & PROVINCIAL LINCENSURE BOARDS

March 20, 1980

STATE/PROVINCE	*DOCTORAL*	*SUB-DOCTORAL*
Alabama	Mean (all doctoral candidates)	---
Alaska	Mean - 1 S.D. (all candidates)	Mean - 1 S.D. (all candidates)
Arizona	Mean (all doctoral candidates)	---
Arkansas	Mean - 2/3 S.D. all candidates	Mean - 1 S.D. (all candidates)
British Columbia	Mean - ½ S.D. (M.A. first timers)	Mean - ½ S.D. (M.A. first timers)
California	Mean (all candidates)	---
Colorado	75% of the "highest score nationwide"	----
Connecticut	Raw score of 142	---
Delaware	Mean - 1 S.D. (all doctoral candidates)	---
District of Columbia	Mean - 1 S.D. (all candidates)	Mean - 1 S.D. (all candidates)
Florida UNSETTED	35th percentile (as of 4/79)	---
Georgia	75% questions correct (raw score of 150)	---
Hawaii	Mean (all doctoral candidates)	---
Idaho	Mean - 1 S.D. (all candidates)	---
llinois	Mean - 1 S.D. (all first timers)	---
ndiana	Mean - 1 S.D. (all doctoral candidates)	---
owa	75% questions correct (raw score of 150)	---
ansas	Mean (Ph.D. first timers)	---
entucky	Mean - ¾ S.D. (all candidates)	Mean - 1 S.D. (all M.A. candidates)
ouisiana	25th percentile	---
Maine	65% questions correct	60% questions correct
Manitoba	Mean - 1 S.D. (all candidates) or 65% questions correct	---
aryland	Mean - ¾ of S.d. (all candidates)	---
Massachusetts	Mean - 1 S.D. (all candidates)	---
Michigan - did ot test	Mean (as of 4/79) (all candidates)	Mean - 1 S.D. (all candidates)
innesota	Mean - 1 S.D. (all candidates)	Mean - 1½ S.D. (all candidates)
ississippi	Mean - 2/3 S.D. (all doctoral candidates)	---
issouri	Mean (all candidates)	Mean (all candidates)

STATE/PROVINCE	*DOCTORAL*	*SUB-DOCTORAL*
Montana	65% questions correct	---
Nebraska	Mean - ¾ S.D. (all doctoral candidates)	---
Nevada	75% questions correct	---
New Brunswick not testing	---	
New Hampshire	Mean - 1 S.D. (all candidates)	---
New Jersey	Mean - 1 S.D. (all candidates)	---
New Mexico	75% correct	---
New York	Mean - ½ S.D. (all first timers) (as of 10/79)	---
North Carolina	Mean - 1 S.D. (all first timers)	Mean - 1½ S.D. (all first timers)
North Dakota	Mean - ½ S.D. (all doctoral candidates	---
Ohio	70% questions correct or (raw score of 140)	---
Oklahoma	Mean - ¾ S.D. (all candidates)	---
Ontario	65% questions correct	---
Oregon	Mean (all candidates)	Mean - 1 S.D. (all candidates)
Pennsylvania	65% questions correct	---
Quebec	50% questions correct	---
Rhode Island	Mean - 1 S.D. (all first timers)	---
Saskatchewan	Mean - 1 S.D. (all doctoral candidates)	---
South Carolina	Mean - ½ S.D. (Ph.D. first timers)	---
South Dakota SUNSETTED	Mean - 1 S.D.	---
Tennessee	Mean - ¾ S.D. (all candidates)	---
Texas	70% questions correct	Mean - 1 ½ S.D. (all candidates)
Utah	70% questions correct	---
Vermont	Mean - ½ S.D. (all candidates)	---
Virginia	Mean - ½ S.D. (all first timers)	Mean - 1 S.D. (all candidates)
Washington	Mean (doctoral first timers)	Mean (doctoral first timers)
West Virginia	Mean - 1 S.D. Ph.D. first timers)	---
Wisconsin	Mean (all doctoral candidates)	---
Wyoming	Mean (all candidates)	---

professional competencies in the area in which she is expected to practice. This exam is usually conducted by licensed psychologists, some of whom are in the same specialty area and who pose potential practical situations for the applicant to consider (Wiens & Menne, 1981). This is the last hurdle to initial licensure.

4. The last stage consists of the monitoring of the licensed psychologist's performance to assure competency. Typically, this involves processing of complaints received by the state boards about licensed practitioners. Various state boards also have recently instituted continuing education requirements. In Oregon, for example, each licensed psychologist must file an annual report with the state board of psychologist examiners listing the number of actual hours of "formally organized educational experiences." The instructional personnel "must be recognized professionals in their domain of study", and the activities "must be designed for professional level participants." It is also possible to count hours spent in "formally organized ongoing study groups" with appropriate objectives and "whose regular participants are recognized professionals in their domain of study" (ORS 858-10-050). Licensed psychologists must earn at least 25 continuing education credits in each calendar year.

Should a licensed practitioner's behavior be found delinquent in any respect the boards are authorized to warn, admonish, prescribe remediary action, and ultimately to remove the license of the offender.

Post-Licensure Certification

Certification of additional experience or competencies beyond those required for licensure is available. Two accrediting agencies are the National Register of Health Service Providers in Psychology and the American Board of Professional Psychology (ABPP). The Register has three requirements for listing:

- Currently licensed or certified by the state board of examiners of psychology at the independent practice level of psychology.

- A doctorate degree in psychology from a regionally accredited educational institution.

- Two years of supervised experience in health service, of which one year is postdoctoral and one year (may be postdoctoral year) is in an organized health service training program (Council for the National Register of Health Providers in Psychology, 1981).

Somewhat more stringent criteria must be met before a diplomate in clinical, counseling, industrial and organizational, or school psychology is awarded by the ABPP. The administrative structure, staffing and content of the candidate's graduate education program are reviewed to determine its adequacy. The breadth, quality and amount of professional experience are determined, including five years of "acceptable qualifying experience," four of which must be postdoctoral. The candidate must provide the names of three sponsors, preferably fellows of APA or ABPP diplomates, who can attest to professional competence, personal character and ethical standing in the profession. A work sample must be provided by the candidate, and if all other criteria have been met the candidate is given a four hour examination by a three person committee. The exam determines: (a) ability to assess and effectively intervene in a problem situation; (b) awareness of relevant theory and research; and (c) ethical sensitivity (American Board of Professional Psychology, 1979).

Alleged Effects of Licensure

There are a number of alleged effects of licensure of psychologists both on the profession and on the public, some of which are less disputable than others. We shall begin with the generally agreed-upon effects.

Increased Status of the Profession: One consequence of licensure has been to increase the status of the profession, at least in terms of making licensed psychologists eligible for third-party payments to psychotherapists. Previously psychologists, along with clinical social workers, family and marital counselors, etc. were essentially dependent upon referral from physicians, and often had to be under the nominal supervision of physicians as well, in order to receive such reimbursement. Now, as a result of licensure and a variety of legal and political battles, medical insurance policy holders of most insurance companies and in most states are free to choose licensed psychologists as psychotherapists without risking their coverage. This war is far from over, but for now at least, psychologists have achieved near-parity with psychiatrists in this respect. It is only to be expected, then, that other groups of professional psychotherapists will seek licensure.

Increased Cost to Practitioner: A second consequence is the increase in costs for the entire process of obtaining and maintaining a license. One of the newer contributors to these costs is the heightened importance of the EPPP and the burgeoning industry that has developed for preparing applicants for the exam. Full back page ads in the APA Monitor have been devoted to descriptions of one such entrepreneur group. The January 1983 ad describes a five day workshop for $515 plus an independent study program for $220 as well as 30 "professionally recorded cassette tapes" for additional money.

In addition to such non-mandatory, but apparently ever more necessary workshops there are costs of administration of the oral and written exams, and the cost of administration of the state boards themselves. As a result there is an ever-increasing expenditure of money for licensure renewal and application fees. Whether or how much of this cost is eventually borne by the consumer is, as we shall see, a debatable issue. In the case of nonsuccessful applicants for licensure who subsequently change career goals it would seem they, or their parents or families, are apt to be the primary cost-bearers. In the case of successful applicants, those who live in states which have established formal, continuing education requirements may well end up spending more for officially sanctioned workshop experiences than they would if freer to decide what constitutes adequate continuing education for themselves.

Political Divisiveness among Psychotherapists: A third effect is to promote an in-group/out-group social-political split among those who hold themselves to be psychotherapists. The innermost "in" group of licensed psychologists, for example, consists of the members of the state boards of psychologist examiners since they have the responsibility and the authority to judge the adequacy of the qualifications of those who aspire to licensure, and also the adequacy of the graduate programs. The outermost out-group consists of those whose hope for licensure is unrealistic, in view of their life situation and the barriers that would have to be overcome. As is illustrated in We too should be Licensed--help Us! (p. 127) a division is created between those professional groups whom the state "recognizes" by conferring on them the opportunity to be licensed and those whom the state does not license.

Increased liability of the Practitioner: The final relatively uncontested effect is that the increased legal status conferred by licensure increases the legal liability of the practitioner. The public is apt to expect more in the way of confidentiality, expert opinion, and beneficial outcomes from therapeutic contacts and to be less tolerant of apparent lapses. But apart from that the courts are more apt to support such expectations should they get involved in such client-therapist disputes. This is not to say that there will be any increase in successful malpractice suits against licensed practitioners; indeed the evidence is not very supportive of such a contention, at least with psychologists. It may be that the obstacles to establishing proof of negligence and of harm in psychotherapy (as detailed in Chapter VIII) are sufficient to discourage such suits, even with the increased legal status of the profession. Hogan (1979) notes the exponential increase in suits against psychotherapists, hospitals and others responsible for the treatment and care of the mentally ill, but then adds:

> It is still the case that virtually no reported decisions exist in which a psychotherapist has been successfully sued for negligence in what was said to a client during the therapeutic process. As long as therapists restrict their practice to talk, interpretations, and advice, they will remain nearly immune from suit. (p. 27, Vol. III)

Public Protection through Licensure? The major purported effect of licensure is, as was stated before, to protect the public from charlatans and incompetents. It is also a major area of contention whether in fact this occurs. Although the guidelines of the American Association of State Psychology Boards recommend that scientific and professional ethics and standards be one of the core areas of study in graduate programs there is, of course, no guarantee that studying ethics will make one ethical. It can be argued that incompetent and unethical behavior is apt to be detected during the course of the supervised practicum and intern experiences, but this would apply to doctoral degree and also to some extent to master's degree holders, whether or not they continue on for licensure.

It is perhaps because of this that Wiens and Menne state:

> The competency assurance that licensing boards can provide consumers of psychological services is directly proportional to the vigor and dispatch with which a licensing board remediates, disciplines, or removes the license of an incompetent, unethical, negligent, dishonest, or unprofessional practitioner. (1981, p. 391)

It could be added that the "vigor and dispatch" is, at least partially, a function of the funds provided the board for investigatory procedures. The budgets of many boards do not allow for much more than processing of applications for licensure.

Whatever the reasons, whether it be inadequate funding or lack of zeal for seeking out incompetent or unethical colleagues, or something else, critics of licensure have pointed out that there seems to be very little policing of licensed professions by the professions, themselves. This may be partially an effect of the lack of lay representation on the licensing boards. The most complete comparable statistics that have been compiled have been on the medical profession, and during one 16 month period only 16 out of 1000 complaints of medical incompetence originated from licensed health practitioners (Danish & Smyer, 1981). Hogan (1979, vol. III) found only 306 legal actions against psychologists and psychiatrists since 1850. The inference is that far more complaints and legal actions would have occurred if the professions were more concerned with protecting the public against unprofessional conduct than in protecting fellow professionals from public exposure of incompetence and unethical practices. After reviewing the relevant historical, economic, and sociological research S.J. Gross (1978) concludes: "Of the evidence found, some is inconclusive or insufficient on some points, but mainly the research refutes the claim that licensing protects the public" (p. 1009).

<u>The EPPP--a Predictor of Incompetency and Unethicality?</u> The EPPP is the focus of much criticism, both formal (i.e., published in articles) and informal. One of the bitterest complaints of those who have failed the test one or more time is the floating cutoff score. As the writer of a letter to the editor noted, her score, although six points below the cutoff point at the time of her testing, was above this point on both the immediately prior testing and the following testing (Allender, 1982). Another letter states, "First we

dumped the MA/MS psychologists and now we 'clean house' of older psychologists naive enough to move to another state five or more years from original licensure (MacHovec, 1982)."

One reason for the cutoff score varying from testing to testing in some states is that a different form of the test is developed for each administration of the test. Nevertheless, the point remains that, since the passing score does "float," the tendency would be for it to become higher over the years if the difficulty of the items does not increase, since those who didn't pass the first time will probably study more and take it a second time, presumably do better and thus force out some more first-time testees, who then re-study, re-take the test, etc.[2] Also the introduction of speccially designed workshops and the possible redesigning of graduate school courses to optimize students' chances of passage of the test are likely to result in more and more test sophistication and higher and higher scores, which makes it unlikely for psychologists five or more years from original licensure to do as well on a new re-testing without considerable studying.

Does this mean that such "older psychologists" have become less competent in the interval? Or is it that we have erected a standard which has little or no relevance to competency? As Flexner (1910) observed:

> There is only one sort of licensing test that is significant, viz., a test that ascertains the practical ability of the student confronting a concrete case to collect all relevant data and to suggest the positive procedure applicable to the conditions disclosed. A written examination may have some incidental value; it does not touch the heart of the matter. (p. 169)

On the other hand, it does seem quite reasonable that some sort of demonstration of basic knowledge of the field should be made independent of the graduate training, since there are so many educational institutions and programs from which candidates come. There

---

[2] This will not occur if states are careful to specify that the comparison is only to those who take the exam for the first time, such as Virginia and Washington.

can be no competency without knowledge of the "relevant data" and "positive procedures." As Wiens and Menne (1981) argue:

> We believe that passing this exam is a necessary but certainly not a sufficient condition for licensing. . . . The examination is only a check to see that the candidate has some knowledge of that basic corpus of knowledge which is the science of psychology. A passing grade on the exam does not necessarily tell us how much someone knows, but failure indicates that something is wrong, either with the candidate or with the institution from which the candidate graduated. (p. 394)

In any case the investment in the EPPP is sufficient at this point in time as to preclude any sudden decision to drop it as one of the necessary hurdles in the licensing process. More alterable, perhaps, is the definition of "failure," the cutoff score, and how it is determined.

What is lacking in this theoretical debate over the value of a compulsory written exam is any empirical evidence of its relationship to competency or ethical behavior. In fact, critics claim that what empirical evidence exists is contrary to the claim that licensing protects the public (Gross, S.J., 1978; Kocher, 1979; Danish & Smyer, 1981). What is also lacking is an empirically validated alternative method for assessing competency.

The EPPP-- a Source of Discrimination? Some empirical data do exist that minorities and older applicants fare less well on the EPPP than whites and younger applicants. State employment officials in California examined the test form and the results of one administration of the EPPP in San Francisco in April 1980 and found that 57.4% of all whites passed the test, compared to 25% of the blacks, and 16% of other minorities (Foltz, 1981a). Grouped according to age, applicants performed best in their twenties, and their performance uniformly declined through the succeeding decades. Review of two exam forms by a consumer affairs analyst found that only 6% of the items were concerned with treatment intervention, planning, implementing and evaluation. Consequently the California Department of Fair Employment and Housing filed a complaint against the state's psychological examining committee. Obviously one study does not a fact make, but a troublesome ethical issue of unfair discrimination in connection with the general issue of the relationship of the EPPP to competency of practice has been raised by the study.

Higher Cost to Consumer? As pointed out earlier a number of costs are assumed by practitioners who acquire licenses, and it also costs money to maintain licensure. It is easy then to assume that those costs are passed on to the consumer. However, other factors also operate, especially in a field where essentially only the use of the professional title can be protected. A major source of variation is the level of competition --the more practitioners there are who offer comparable services, presumably the greater the chance of a "price war." However, that may not be true either. The amount of demand may rise to meet the number of providers, as seems to be the case with physicians (Danish & Smyer, 1981). The growing effect of third-party reimbursement is also to be considered, as well as the potential effect of consumer education. S.J. Gross (1978) reports only two inconclusive studies in this area.

Licensure--a Hindrance to Innovation and Experimentation? Two major unanticipated consequences of credentialing and third-party reimbursement claimed by Danish & Smyer (1981) are:

> (a) a restriction of the self-direction of graduate education and (b) a return to a medical or social welfare model, in contrast with recent concepts of proactive roles for professionals and nonprofessionals. (p. 15)

As discussed earlier, state boards of psychologist examiners have the authority to decide the adequacy of the graduate training program of an applicant. Graduates of APA-approved graduate programs in counseling or clinical psychology have a greater chance of meeting the criteria. Graduates of relatively new or innovative programs or graduates whose individual programs contain many nonstandard courses, courses that do not readily fit into established "core areas" may well have difficulty gaining the board's approval. At the institutional level it is not infrequent that representatives of the professional schools and even of APA-approved graduate programs in psychology will "explore" with their respective state boards the possibility that certain courses would be found acceptable, then designate such courses as required courses in their own programs, and create additional courses as suggested. Otherwise they risk that their graduates will be disadvantaged relative to graduates of other programs and institutions when they apply for licensure.

The state boards, on their part, have little choice but to set and insist on such standards. They would be irresponsible if they were to accept any and every new course or group of courses as contributing to a solid understanding of psychology. Whether, in fact, this scrutiny of the novel, the relatively unknown, and non-accredited is helpful or harmful to the development of the science of psychology and the art of psychotherapeutic practice is not clear at this time and may never be.

The threat that innovative, proactive treatment procedures and programs would be stifled and that psychology would return to a medical or social welfare model is seen by Danish and Smyer (1981) as a consequence of licensing and also as a result of third-party reimbursement. I concur with this concern about the effects of such reimbursement and have devoted Chapter VI to an analysis of the full range of such effects.

Private Practice at the Cost of Public Service and Accountability? Another unintended consequence of licensure claimed by Danish and Smyer (1981) is the movement of psychologists out of public agencies into private practice. This is made possible by the third-party reimbursement of licensed psychotherapists. It is further claimed: "In the private sector, consultation, training, and psychoeducational programming may be used less frequently, since they are less likely to be profitable to the provider" (p. 18). Furthermore, the protection provided by the professional administrators of public agencies "who are in a position to evaluate the providers' backgrounds and assess their competency to perform in this situation" (p. 18) is lacking to the consumer who sees someone in private practice.

Reduction in Consumer Choice? It is sometimes asserted or assumed that non-licensed psychologists and psychotherapists of other disciplines who haven't gained licensure status are less able to compete for the consumer dollar and eventually become fewer and fewer in number. This then results in less consumer choice. Such is the background for the following statement by Slovenko in his foreward to Hogan's four volume work on the regulation of psychotherapists (1979):

> A regulated trade is a guarantee against unwanted competition, a closed shop sanctioned by the state . . . thus, the American Psychological Association and the National Association of Social Workers have urged the enactment of licensing laws granting them the nearly exclusive right to practice psychotherapy. At the same time, the American Psychiatric Association urges that even these groups, should only be allowed to practice psychotherapy under appropriate medical supervision. (p. XV)

This would certainly seem to be true if third-party reimbursers continue to reimburse directly only licensed professional psychotherapists, to the extent that such coverage is available to and used by consumers of the service of psychotherapy, and to the extent that such consumers have, or are labeled as having reimbursable "illnesses" or disorders.

It would also be true to the extent that employers of psychotherapists demand that applicants and job holders have such credentials.

At the present time it is debatable that third-party coverage of psychological complaints will expand much more than it has, unless some breakthrough in quality assurance is achieved and costs are stabilized rather than continuing to increase at a rapid rate. It is also debatable that in the foreseeable future consumers will desert non-licensed private practitioners, unless additional laws are enacted which limit the claims made by therapists regarding the benefits of their services. However, sufficient concern was aroused by the passage of Florida's new licensing statute (the old one was sunsetted) to provoke an "anti-trust" $700 million suit by the disenfranchised mental health professionals. ("APA sued," 1982). The new law not only sets minimum standards for psychologists but also for clinical social workers, marriage and family therapists, and mental health counselors. The American Psychological Association, among others, was charged with conspiracy to deprive the plaintiffs of their right to practice psychology in order to reduce competition. The suit did not prove successful ("APA cleared in Florida," 1982).

Alternatives and Reforms

The question raised in this chapter is not so much whether or not to regulate psychotherapy, especially as practiced by psychologists, but how to do it. Licensure has been seen by many as an inappropriate means, one that causes more problems than it purports to alleviate. Because of this some critics of licensure have proposed alternative ways in which the profession can be regulated and the public protected. I will first present some of the minor, somewhat piecemeal reforms and then the revolutionary system proposed by Hogan (1979).

Competency-Based Exams: Perhaps the most attacked component of the present system is the EPPP. As we have seen before it has been argued that it unfairly discriminates against minorities, older applicants, and even those experienced applicants who have moved to a state which does not recognize their licenses. It is pointed out that there is no empirical evidence that this exam is in any way related to actual on-the-job competency. What is needed, instead, it is argued, are some measures of actual competency. The difficulty is that no such agreed upon measures exist. Consequently what is advocated is that such measures be developed through research. Two such critics, Bernstein and Lecomte (1981), advocate that a comprehensive research program be undertaken to establish links between professional entrance criteria and client outcomes. This program is to be based on a theoretical model of an ideal licensing system.

Increased Investigation by Boards: It is thought by some that it would be prohibitively expensive and thus impractical to utilize competency measures as the major criteria for credentialing, even if they could be developed.

> The identification of incompetence after the fact is more feasible. Accordingly, more adequate resources for the investigation of complaints and enforcement of statutory provisions should be made available to state regulatory boards. (Stigall in "Comment on Licensing," 1979, p. 37)

Even defenders of the present licensing system admit that the standards of practice that are established are seldom enforced. One corrective measure that is suggested is for the state boards to more thoroughly investigate the training programs of the applicants (Wiens & Menne, 1981).

> The main function of licensing boards should be an insistence upon competent, ethically proper, and nonnegligent practice on the part of all licensees, yet this does not seem to have been their main priority. Licensing boards must devote more of their effort and time to checking on the psychology training program. (pp. 394, 395)

They also concur that post-licensure investigation and enforcement is necessary (p. 391).

Expanded Public Membership on State Boards: Another reform addresses itself to the fact that the public has little direct control over regulation of licensed psychologists or over the licensing process. Only 10 of the 50 state boards have any lay members, and of those 10 that do have lay members, none have more than two lay representatives (Danish & Smyer, 1981). Thus, in effect, the profession decides both what is best for the public and what is best for itself. It is argued, more lay representation on the boards would increase the likelihood that the public's benefit would truly be uppermost. Shimberg ("Comment on Licensing," 1979) points out, however, that mere addition of lay members is insufficient: "To have any meaningful impact, public members must be carefully selected, thoroughly oriented and given adequate support" (p. 15).

Increased Disclosure to Public: One of the main features of Hogan's proposed system, but also something that has been advocated quite independently by many sources, is the mandatory disclosure of psychologist practitioners of more than just their "name, rank and serial number." In order for the consumer public to be in a position to intelligently choose among practitioners it needs to know more than just whether or not the practitioner is licensed, albeit as Wiens and Menne argue that is a significant disclosure in itself (1981, p. 394). Exactly what should be disclosed varies from list to list but among the suggestions are fee, the psychologist's academic and professional background, licenses held, approaches used, types of problems treated, and client improvement rate (Bernstein & Lecomte, 1981). Usually it is recommended that this disclosure be made in a statement that is sent to a central state registry and updated anually. Presumably the state would make it readily available to the public. It could also be mandated that it be available and provided to prospective clients upon their first contact with the practitioner.

Hogan's Proposal

Dan Hogan is both a law school graduate and a recent Ph.D. in psychology. His proposal for the regulation of psychotherapists is much more radical than a mere compilation of the reforms that have been mentioned. It is also far more extensive and is spelled out in four volumes, the first of which, A Study in the Philosophy and Practice of Professional Regulation (1979), is most germane to this section. I will briefly review the highlights of this proposal and comment as seems appropriate.

Hogan would do away with licensing of psychologists altogether, especially the licensing of certain professional groups and not of others. He argues that psychotherapy is what psychotherapists do, and this "do-ing" is not distinguishable from one professional group to another, nor is one group manifestly better or worse at it in terms of the crude criteria that exist for measuring successful therapy. Hence it makes no sense to separate out one group from another, or even one portion of a group from another, and certify its especial competency in any way.

Hogan advocates replacement of licensure with a registration system that would have to be utilized by all those who wish to claim that they practice psychotherapy. One essential feature of the registration system would be mandatory disclosure to a central registry maintained by each state of the therapist's "credentials," whatever they are. There would be no entry requirements, however, to get on the registry, such as minimal academic or training requirements.

In addition there would be a concerted effort at consumer education and utilization of client feedback. Each professional organization would be free to inform the public of the special "qualifications" of its members, but none would have the right to impose these qualifications as criteria for state-endorsement.

Consumers would be actively involved in several ways. Regulatory boards would be separated from disciplinary agencies, and consumers, as well as representatives of psychotherapy and non-mental health professionals, would serve on both boards. The disciplinary agencies would investigate and judge information provided both by clients and practitioners.

Finally, Hogan envisages a multitude of research efforts devoted to developing performance criteria and determining their relationships to various types of practitioner training. He believes insurance companies will find it in their interest to fund and direct such research, as well as professional groups, practitioner organizations, and governmental and educational institutions. Hogan is currently involved in establishing a center to conduct research on psychotherapy, including development of competency-based measures of practitioner performance.

Author's Comments: I concur in the main part with Hogan's analysis and proposals. His registration system is especially appealing; however, I do not believe it has "a snowball's chance in hell" of being adopted within the foreseeable future. Neither organized psychiatry nor psychology is apt to give up certification or licensure without a tremendous struggle. Psychiatry would probably be supported by the powerful medical lobby, since psychiatrists are first of all licensed physicians, and only later certified in the specialty of psychiatry. Psychology, having fought so long and so hard for parity with psychiatry, would never back down unless psychiatry did. Still other organizations are presently geared to getting licensure, and hopeful of doing so, and would not relinquish this orientation unless psychology and psychiatry did.

This does not mean that the political situation can't and won't change, especially if a sustained effort is made to bring about such change. It just means that only some of Hogan's proposals have much hope of implementation at present, and they are the same ones advocated by the reformers, the fixer uppers, rather than the revolutionaries. I refer here to the expansion of public membership on boards, increased efforts at disclosure and consumer education, and most especially, development of performance-based criteria. If such criteria are developed and are found to be related or not related to certain education or training experience, then these studies may be used to establish a more equitable system, one truly of benefit to the public.

I do not wish to imply that Hogan is blind to these

political realities. He admits that psychiatry would have to give up its privileged status among those practicing psychotherapy, and would not want psychology to do so first. It is also apparent that he recognizes the potential power of research to bring about changes, albeit, as Fairweather (1967) has pointed out, such changes only occur when there is a corresponding multifaceted effort to change the political infrastructure that ultimately implements or blocks the implementation of social change.

Comments on "Illustrative Cases"

As is apparent by the foregoing sections there are no generally accepted ethical stances, much less answers to the ethical issues evoked or alluded to in any of the "Illustrative Cases." There are some political realities, however, that apply. In *We too should be Licensed--help Us!* (p. 127) it seems clear that the American Psychological Association is not especially interested in helping other professional groups obtain licensure as psychotherapists. Whether it "should" or not, the facts of the matter are that it is still waging its own war to gain parity with psychiatry, and unless or until that goal has been secured, there will be few or no resources devoted to helping other organizations achieve similar goals.

The status of unlicensed psychologists, those with master's and doctor's degrees and even those licensed in other states (as in *Is he or is he not a "Psychologist"?* on page 127) is also a political football. The profession cannot put itself in the position of advocating the necessity of licensure in terms of protecting the public and yet resist stringent application of the resultant laws to its own kind. There may be some further accommodation that can be made to enlarge reciprocity of licensure among states and/or to lower the EPPP cutting score, but essentially the title of "psychologist" and other titles which include the prefix "psycho" (psychotherapist, psychological consultant, etc.) will continue to be restricted to those individuals who meet the qualifications established by the state in which they practice. Exactly what those qualifications are and other information about each state's statutes and their implementation can be obtained by writing the secretary of the state or provincial board for the relevant statutes. The addresses are published annually in the June issues of the *American Psychologist*.

Disqualified because of Training (p. 128) is less clear from both a political and an ethical point of view. An important factor would be the level of trust that individual faculty members have that the graduate students will not try to capitalize on their association with the university in attracting clients. Another factor would be the amount of knowledge that faculty have of actual questionable or unethical practices of those students in private practice. A few, isolated, but widely know incidents could adversely affect the position of all such practitioner-students.

CHAPTER VIII

MALPRACTICE

A major concern of almost any professional in our litigation-happy society is the possibility of being sued for malpractice by a client. It seems an almost daily occurrence to read a headline banner announcing the filing of a million dollar suit by someone who claims his life has been severely damaged as a result of professional mistreatment. Surgeons and other physicians who treat physical disorders are favorite targets of such suits, but occasionally psychiatrists and other psychotherapists are involved. The damages sought are so large and the publicity so great that it is little wonder that "how to prevent malpractice suits" has become a popular theme in recent publications and professional workshops.

Despite this furor, the actual incidence of successful malpractice suits against psychotherapists is quite low for reasons which will become clear in this chapter. If the therapist prescribes medication or makes an administrative decision, such as discharging a potentially dangerous patient, then the probability that the therapist may be sued, and sued successfully, may indeed be rising. However, as we shall see later, if the therapist sticks to doing psychotherapy, the likelihood of losing a malpractice suit is quite small.

In order to understand why this is true, and probably will remain true, it is necessary to understand tort law, and in particular that portion of tort law that pertains to professional malpractice claims. This chapter is devoted to a presentation of tort law and to a review of the data on malpractice suits against psychotherapists.

First the general body of tort law will be described, then how the definition of the legal duty of care is changed when the tort ("wrong") is committed by a professional rather than an ordinary citizen. The four legal elements of malpractice claim are depicted, and the role of expert witnesses is illustrated by a review of all the malpractice suits brought by clients against their therapists that reached the appellate court of this country and England during the period of 1959 to 1979. There are only six such cases in total. Daniel Hogan's review of 300 cases of psychotherapy malpractice from 1850 to 1977 is also referred to. The proper "defense" of the profession against the threat of malpractice is discussed in the concluding section.

The General Concept of Tort Law

The law of torts is the body of law that provides for monetary awards to clients of professionals who are injured as a result of malpractice. Tort law developed over centuries of Anglo-American jurisprudence as a system of private compensation for personal losses and harms resulting from the acts of omissions of others. Professional malpractice is a relatively recent addition to this time-honored compensation system.

Tort law is a private legal system which permits persons or enterprises to initiate suits for injuries and to collect awards of money damages. Some public systems of law provide for a representative of the government to initiate lawsuits. For example, if an intoxicated motorist who hits a pedestrian is arrested for drunk driving, a prosecutor initiates a lawsuit to obtain criminal remedies on behalf of the government. However, if the pedestrian wants to obtain the tort remedy of money damages, he will have to sue the motorist for compensation as a private party, probably with the assistance of an attorney retained at his expense.

Since tort law provides compensation for injuries caused by a variety of important social activities, from the delivery of professional services to the manufacture of retail goods, this body of law raises important public policy issues that may transcend the interests of the private parties to lawsuits. This is certainly true in the case of psychotherapeutic malpractice. To understand how the law works, however, it might be best to examine some fundamental principles of tort law first.

A "tort" is a legal course of action that an individual may pursue when someone else's conduct violates a duty established by law. This definition does not take us very far. We are left with some obvious questions. When is a duty established by law? If a duty is established, what is that duty?

For centuries, Anglo-American judges have been providing answers to these questions through the processes of the common law. Under a common law system, judges actually make law by deriving legal rules from prior reported cases involving similar circumstances and applying these rules to the cases before them. By studying the reported cases that contain the decisions and reasoning of judges, one can see laws created, revised and abandoned over time. Until quite recently, common law judges have used this decision-making process to establish, define and expand the duties of tort law without the help of legislatures.

The answers to the questions of when a duty is imposed by tort law and, if there is a duty, what that duty is depend first upon the circumstances in particular lawsuits. Who is the defendant from whom compensation is sought? What is the relationship between the plaintiff and the defendant? For example, a parent may have a duty in tort law to save her drowning child. A passing stranger, on the other hand, may have a moral, but not a legal, duty to save the child.

Although legal duties established by tort law emerge from private lawsuits, they also reflect choices of public policy. Through duties in tort law the legal system imposes an obligation to exercise reasonable care when the circumstances justify it. Whether a specific set of circumstances justifies the imposition of a duty depends upon a mix of value judgments including what is "fair," which persons or class of persons in society should bear the risk of loss, the relative importance of the social or economic activities of the parties to a lawsuit, and the magnitude of the future injuries that may be deterred by establishing a duty.

Through this common law process of resolving individual lawsuits, tort law has created a variety of legal duties in pursuit of important public policies, particularly in the modern era of complex social and economic relationships. For example, tort law imposes a duty on sellers of retail products not to distribute products that are unreasonably dangerous to consumers. It requires property owners to exercise reasonable care to seek out, discover and remedy hazards on their property for the benefit of invited guests. Tort law also establishes a duty for members of a recognized profession to exercise professional care and skill in providing services to their clients.

Tort Law as Applied to Professionals

The legal duty of professionals has been established under the most common tort known as negligence. In general, the tort of negligence imposes a legal duty on everyone to conduct themselves in a manner that does not create an unreasonable risk of harm to others. Therefore, when a person's conduct creates an unreasonable risk of harm, he is negligent. The standard for judging when conduct is negligent is often stated another way: "ordinary" or "reasonable care" measured against the hypothetical conduct of a "reasonable person." The question in a negligence case then becomes, what would the "reasonable person" have done under the same circumstances as those in which the defendant found himself?

When the defendant is a member of an established profession and his professional conduct is the subject of a negligence action, his duty, and the negligence standard used to evaluate his conduct, are different. Tort law imposes a legal duty on the professional to exercise a reasonable degree of professional skill and care. Instead of asking what a "reasonable person" would have done under the relevant set of circumstances, the law asks whether or not the conduct of the defendant represents "good professional practice" or "customary and usual practice" in the defendant's professional community. Originally applied in lawsuits against physicians, "good professional practice" or "customary and usual practice" is now the basic standard used to judge the professional conduct of a member of any recognized profession. This standard not only determines when a plaintiff can recover damages from a professional, it also insures a minimum level of competency through the deterrent effect of the risk of successful lawsuits.

In theory, a standard of professional skill and care should provide a remedy for injured clients in situations where the ordinary standard of care would not. Let's take Marcia's case as an example. Marcia has suffered from depression for years, and it has now become acute. She regularly considers the advantages of suicide. Marcia approaches a college classmate with her complaint and seeks advice. If Marcia is told by her classmate to "shake it off and forget about it," follows that advice, continues to be depressed and attempts suicide, she will not have much of a chance of recovering for her injuries in a tort action against her classmate. Although the classmate's advice is hardly thoughtful or sensitive, it probably does not violate the duty to exercise ordinary care. In other words, it is the kind of advice a "reasonable person," without special knowledge or skill, could be expected to give. As a matter of policy, tort law has not established a greater duty on the average person.

Suppose Marcia also approached a professional counselor at her college counseling center for help. Once again, she was advised "to shake it off and forget about it." Now Marcia's chances of successfully asserting a tort claim are much greater. The question becomes: Would such advice, under the circumstances, by a reasonably skilled, competent and experienced counselor who owes a special legal duty to this clients, represent "good professional practice" or what is "customary or usual practice" in the community? The answer would, no doubt, be no.

The Legal Elements of a Malpractice Claim

Marcia's claim of negligence against a professional counselor still may not result in monetary compensation. Every plaintiff suing a defendant for negligence must overcome other obstacles created by tort law. When a plaintiff is claiming negligent counseling or psychotherapy, these obstacles are so substantial that the chances of compensation for negligent counseling and psychotherapy, and therefore the threat of malpractice suits for counselors and psychotherapists, may be insignificant.

To obtain monetary compensation under any claim of negligence, a plaintiff must allege and prove four legal elements:

1. The defendant owed a legal duty to the plaintiff;

2. The defendant's conduct violated that duty by failing to conform to a legal standard established to prevent unreasonable risk or harm;

3. There is a sufficient causal connection between the conduct of the defendant and the harm suffered by the plaintiff; and

4. The harm to the plaintiff is an actual personal injury which can be measured in economic terms.

Marcia, as a former client of a professional psychotherapist seeking compensation for negligent professional practice, will have little trouble establishing the first element. However, the remaining elements will present problems for Marcia, or any other person who wants to recover damages from her therapist.

Expert Witnesses

With respect to the second element of a negligence action, we have already seen that the negligence standard for a professional's conduct is different from the standard for an ordinary person's conduct. Except in the most blatant cases of malpractice, where a physician amputates the wrong leg of her patient, for example, a plaintiff claiming professional negligence must retain an expert witness to establish this element of his cause of action.

An expert witness must be a qualified member of the profession who is willing to testify that the defendant's conduct fell below the standard of good professional practice or customary and usual practice in the defendant's professional community. Granting professions the privilege of setting their own legal standard of conduct in this manner has been criticized, but it is probably justifiable for the practical reason that judges or juries will be unable to establish the standard on their own.

In Marcia's suit against her therapist at the college counseling center, she and her attorney might conclude that professional advice to an acutely depressed person to "shake it off and forget about it" is analogous to amputating the wrong leg. Nevertheless, Marcia's case before a judge or jury would be strenghthened significantly by the testimony of a qualified psychotherapist who concludes that the defendant's conduct clearly violates a standard recognized in the profession. The need or desirability of an expert witness presents two obstacles that Marcia and her attorney must overcome. First, they must find the money to pay for an expert witness. Second, they must find an expert witness who will testify that the standard of good professional practice was violated.

The first obstacle is often overcome by an arrangement between plaintiffs and their attorneys known as a "contingency fee." Even if Marcia is a college student, on a shoe-string budget, her attorney may be willing to advance the money to hire an expert witness, based upon the prospects of recovering the cost and sharing in Marcia's recovery. Personal injury attorneys balance the prospects of recovering costs and the fee through successful verdict against the required expenditures of their time and money in deciding to represent a plaintiff. Let's assume that Marcia has found an attorney who is willing to take the risk.

The second obstacle involving expert witnesses, finding a favorable one, presents a special challenge in a suit for professional malpractice. Lawyers have complained for decades about the reluctance of physicians to testify against one another. This phenomenon is probably present in any profession. In the case of psychotherapy, the problem of finding a cooperative expert witness is complicated by the difficulty of determining what is good professional practice in the first place.

To illustrate this problem, let's consider another case. John also suffered from acute depression. In response to John's complaints and requests for help, his psychotherapist first administered "primal" therapy. When screaming proved unsuccessful, the psychotherapist administered "regressive hypnosis" to get at the "roots" of the problem. John attempted suicide soon after one of the sessions with the psychotherapist. He now seeks to recover for the injuries resulting from his suicide attempt by providing that the defendant psychotherapist was professionally negligent in his choice of "primal" therapy and in the manner in which he administered the "regressive hypnosis." John's attorney will argue that "primal" therapy itself does not amount to "good professional practice" or "customary and usual practice" and that the number and pacing of regressive hypnosis treatments were insufficient to affect acute depression under this standard.

Both of these arguments will reduce the field of potential experts. First, in a relatively young profession that encourages innovation and includes such diverse methods as Gestalt therapy, behavioral modification, and psychoanalysis, there will be a natural reluctance on the part of psychotherapists to condemn practices that fall short of physical assault or psychological exploitation. Second, to obtain an opinion that the manner in which a particular therapy has been administered is negligent, an expert witness must be found who uses or is knowledgeable about that therapy.

The rather unusual circumstances in John's case pose a problem in finding an expert witness to establish the violation of the duty to exercise professional skill and care. When the claim is that the psychotherapist negligently exercised his judgment in admimistering a more recognized form of therapy, the plaintiff's problem of finding an expert witness willing to condemn the defendant's conduct may be even more difficult. [For example, would a psychotherapist be negligent in ending a session at a particular point in the course of otherwise acceptable therapy, or would it be customary and usual to continue the session.] Now an expert will have to make a subtler distinction in concluding that the therapist exercised bad judgment amounting to negligence, instead of judgment that is customary and usual. The number of potential experts willing to make such a judgment with confidence may be quite small.

A Question of Professional Responsibility? I suggest that all professionals have some natural reluctance to criticize their colleagues or testify against them in court and that the problem of finding expert witnesses is a serious obstacle to recovering for injuries caused by negligent psychotherapists.

In his classic treatise on the tort law, Professor William Prosser (1971, p. 164) reports that several medical and bar associations have addressed this problem in their respective professions by establishing panels of qualified and disinterested experts. Professionals who serve on these panels receive professional fees for their services. Perhaps this procedure could also be adopted by the various mental health professions.

If plaintiffs can't find expert witnesses who are willing to testify that certain therapies do not constitute "good professional practice," another possibility would be for psychotherapists to collectively establish what is and is not "good professional practice." A court might be willing to admit these professional standards for the jury to consider in deciding whether or not a psychotherapist has violated his duty of care to a client. Such standards may even be accepted in place of an expert witness.

Consider the case of a psychotherapist who does nothing more than immerse his clients in warm water at regular intervals. Other than the testimonials of several clients, there is no empirical evidence that this practice has any positive effect on his clients' psychological conditions. Shouldn't a client whose condition would have improved through more conventional methods be able to recover for injuries resulting from the steady decline in his untreated condition? The client may be able to find an expert who rejected the defendant's methods as contrary to "good professional practice," but recovery would be more likely if the profession officially disapproves of "immersion therapy."

One problem with excluding therapies from "good professional practice" on the ground that they have no effect on psychological conditions is that many "customary and usual practices" would probably be eliminated as well. Still another problem with a profession officially certifying what is "good professional practice" is that in a profession that is as young and eclectic as psychotherapy, a collective determination by the profession of what is good practice may stifle innovation and further entrench more traditional forms of therapy. For example, nonmedical psychotherapists have often criticized the dominance of the "medical model" of psychiatry as an obstacle to the acceptance of more reliable clinical methods and as a means to keep psychiatrists at the top of the organization structure of mental health systems (Mischel, 1968).

Legal Causation

The third legal element of a negligence action, legal causation, presents another problem for plaintiffs claiming psychotherapeutic malpractice. To illustrate this problem, let's return to Marcia's case against a professional counselor at her college counseling center. Suppose Marcia has no difficulty establishing the counselor's legal duty to exercise professional skill and care, proving that all the counselor did was tell her to "shake off" her depression and "forget about it," and finding an expert who will testify that the advice given did not constitute good professional practice. She must still establish a causal connection between the negligent advice of the counselor and the injuries associated with her suicide attempt. This may be the greatest obstacle for plaintiff's claiming psychotherapeutic malpractice.

Marcia can expect the following argument on behalf of the defendant, probably based upon the testimony of an expert witness retained by the defendant:

> It has often been said that medicine is not an exact science. It is for this reason that physicians do not promise patients, or enter into contracts with them, to cure or improve their condition. This is true to an even greater degree of psychotherapy. Psychotherapists can identify and evaluate psychological problems, but they cannot predict the course of an illness based upon the present knowledge of the profession. It is common for a patient's condition

to worsen radically during psychotherapy. This is certainly true of the acutely depressed. There is no way to say that the defendant's advice had any effect on Marcia--or that it is probable that any other form of psychotherapy would have prevented her suicide attempt. If it is common for psychotherapy to have no effect, how can Marcia say that the defendant's failure to use a recognized therapy probably caused her injuries?

Actual Injury

The final legal element of a negligence action, the need to prove actual injury, can also present a problem for plaintiff claiming psychotherapeutic malpractice. However, recent developments in tort law may effectively eliminate this problem in the near future.

Tort law requires that a plaintiff's injury be real and measurable in money terms. As a consequence, plaintiffs have been denied recovery in cases where the defendant's conduct, although negligent, caused fright, shock, mental suffering or other mental disturbances, without any accompanying physical consequences. The requirement of proving some physical injury or consequences reflects the law's traditional concern over fictitious claims.

In addition to proof of physical consequences of emotional disturbance, the law once required proof of actual "impact" upon the plaintiff's body when the physical consequences were not immediate. Under this "impact" rule, a woman who suffered emotional trauma and a miscarriage could not recover from a negligent driver whose car just missed her. Although this rule has been rejected by most courts, proof of physical consequences is still a condition of recovery for negligently caused mental disturbances.

The requirement of proving actual injury can be satisfied in Marcia's case if her suicide attempt resulted in physical consequences that can be verified by witnesses who observed Marcia's injuries, medical reports, photographs or Marcia's own testimony. Most courts would also permit a jury to consider a plaintiff's claim when there is less substantial physical verification of mental disturbance, such as evidence of a rash, dizziness, headaches or nausea.

However, there is probably a substantial number of cases of negligent psychotherapy where the client suffers emotionally without any physical manifestations. In these cases, a plaintiff's prospects for recovery are still uncertain. The Supreme Courts of Hawaii and California have recently abolished the traditional requirement that there can be no recovery for the negligent infliction of emotional disturbance alone.

Other states may follow the lead of Hawaii and California, but a plaintiff must still overcome the natural skepticism of juries over claims for money damages that are based solely upon emotional injury. As the California Supreme Court put it in abolishing the traditional legal requirement of proving physical consequences for emotional injury before recovery is possible: " The jurors are best situated to determine whether and to what extent the defendant's conduct caused emotional distress" (Molien v. Kaiser Foundation Hospitals, 167 Cal. Rptr. 831, 616 P.2d 813, 1980).

How Real is the Threat of Malpractice?

To appreciate the kind of cases in which a plaintiff actually recovers for psychotherapeutic malpractice, I have summarized the facts in the reported decisions from the records of English and American appellate courts, as reviewed by Feldman and Ward (1980).

Nicholson v. Han

The Nicholsons were seen by Dr. Han for two years of marital counseling, which, however, ended in the couple's getting a divorce. During the last half of the counseling Mrs. Nicholson and Dr. Han had an affair. When Mr. Nicholson discovered this several years later, he sued Dr. Han for damages based on breach of contract, malpractice, assault and battery, trespass on the case, and fraud. The trial judge dismissed the suit, and the appellate court upheld the dismissal on the basis that the gist of the complaint, no matter how pleaded, was the tort of alienation of affections and this claim had been abolished by the state's legislature. The appellate court also reasoned that the facts presented did not constitute a claim of malpractice because the alleged wrongs were beyond the realm of professional practice.

In effect, the court recognized a defense to malpractice based on the argument that the conduct was so outrageous that the defendant was no longer practicing his profession. It is a matter for debate how generalizable to other jurisdictions such an argument would be.

Zipkin v. Freeman

After three years of treatment for extreme nervousness Mrs. Zipkin felt prepared to terminate. However, her psychiatrist, Dr. Freeman, persuaded her to continue, during the course of which they became sexually involved. Mrs. Zipkin divorced her husband at the therapist's suggestion, loaned him $14,000 to buy a farm, gave him the child support money from her former husband, stole Mr. Zipkin's suits and sewed Dr. Freeman's labels in them, perjured herself in frivolous lawsuits against relatives at his suggestion, and participated in nude swimming parties.

When therapy and the relationship finally terminated, Mrs. Zipkin brought a malpractice suit against Dr. Freeman and received $17,000 in damages. The insurance company disclaimed coverage and refused to pay.

The appellate court was only called upon to decide whether or not the insurance company should pay the $17,000 and concluded it should.

Roy v. Hartogs

Ms. Roy sought therapy for her lesbian tendencies. As part of the therapy Dr. Hartogs became sexually intimate with her. Upon termination, some 13 months later, Ms. Roy brought a malpractice suit and was awarded $150,000 in damages. The defendant appealed, and the appellate court agreed with the verdict, but ordered a new trial to reconsider the amount of damages unless Ms. Roy agreed to accept the sum of $25,000 instead.

Anclote Manor Foundation v. Wilkinson

Mrs. Wilkinson was placed in a hospital for psychiatric and medical care following commitment procedures instigated by her husband. During the course of psychotherapy the treating psychiatrist told Mrs. Wilkinson he wanted to marry her and was going to divorce his own wife.

Shortly after Mrs. Wilkinson was discharged from the hospital, her husband divorced her, and within a year she comitted suicide. Mr. Wilkinson subsequently sued the hospital and the staff psychiatrist for breach of contract and malpractice. The trial judge ruled in favor of the plaintiff, and damages equal to the amount the husband had paid for psychiatric care were awarded. The findings were affirmed upon appeal.

Landau v. Werner

Ms. Landau fell in love with her therapist, Dr. Werner. He reassured her that these feelings represented normal transference and would soon pass. When they didn't, they decided to terminate therapy, but to ease the seperation they were to do so in a gradual fashion. They met together socially on a number of occasions, discussed vacations together, and met once in Ms. Landau's domicile. Her condition deteriorated, and she attempted suicide. Therapy was resumed, but was unsuccessful in alleviating her mental distress. She sued, alleging malpractice, and prevailed. The appellate court affirmed.

Hammer v. Rosen

The defendant psychiatrist in this case had developed a method called "direct analysis" for treating schizophrenia. This method involved regressing patients to the period of their infancy and bringing them up again, including beatings. The patient, Ms. Hammer, endured this treatment over a period of seven years. The beatings were the basis for a malpractice suit which was dismissed by the trial court because the plaintiff, failing to produce an expert witness, had not established that the standard of good professional practice had been violated. The appellate court reversed the decision, stating that the beatings attested to by three lay witnesses, in conjunction with lack of credible explanation for them, was sufficient to show malpractice even with out supporting expert testimony.

The cases that have just been summarized represent all of the reported decisions involving psychotherapeutic malpractice in the appellate courts of this country and England over the twenty year period from 1959 to 1979. Books and articles written for psychologists or psychiatrists often warn of the increasing threat of malpractice suits by former clients (Knapp, 1980; Sherrer & Sherrer, 1980; Schwitzgebel & Schwitzgebel, 1980).

However, after considering the legal obstacles to recovery in tort law and the number and kind of reported cases, it would appear that these warnings are exaggerated.

Daniel Hogan's review of 300 cases of psychotherapeutic malpractice suits from 1850 to 1977 substantiates this conclusion. Although there has been an exponential increase in such suits, with a third of all decisions occurring in the ten year period from 1960 to 1969, "the therapists who restrict their practice to talk, interpretations, and advice . . . will remain nearly immune from suit" (1979, vol. III, p. 27). The reasons presented are:

> The problems of proof involved are little short of monumental, except in instances of negligent custodial care, physical assault, and several other categories of negligence. Where the particular act consists of words spoken by a therapist in private session with a client, it may be impossible to prove deeds actually took place. . . . Where the particular acts are not in question, proof that those acts were the proximate cause of the plaintiff's distress [is] enormous. . . . (p. 26)

Beyond the Scope of Tort Law

If legal recovery for psychotherapeutic malpractice is a remote possibility, should this be a cause of relief or alarm to us?

Aside from the legal obstacles, psychological dynamics may exist which discourage former clients from suing their psychotherapists. Two law professors (Feldman and Ward, 1980) hypothesize:

> a natural reluctance on the part of the patient to parade his illness before lawyers, judges and jurors, and the emotional difficulties that might attend a suit against a therapist who once held a deep, meaningful, and trusted position in the plaintiff's eye. (p. 69)

If the threat of malpractice claims is a serious one, Feldman and Ward's hypothesis suggests a strategy that protects the therapist from lawsuits but which may or may not be good for clients. Samuel Knapp, in

"A Primer on Malpractice for Psychologists," advises:

> Good relationships with clients substantially reduce the likelihood of a malpractice claim. Psychologists should use their skill in engendering positive feelings between themselves and their clients. People are less apt to sue someone they like or someone who claims to have their best interests in mind. (1980, p. 611)

This advice could lead to an ethical problem in some cases. The skills of psychologists should be put to other uses than "engendering positive feelings." Competent use of professional skills may actually cause negative feelings between psychologists and their clients. A preoccupation with threats of malpractice litigation could actually interfere with the delivery of competent professional services. This is one cost associated with a serious threat of malpractice suits and a cause for relief if the threat has been exaggerated.

On the other hand, if the system of tort law is presently not compensating many victims of malpractice and not deterring many forms of incompetent practice, then there may be a cause for concern and a need for more effective regulation. After studying all of the reported cases of psychiatric malpractice, the only advice about the likelihood of success that an attorney can confidently give a client seeking recovery from a psychotherapist is:

> Unless the court decides that your psychotherapist's conduct was so outrageous that he could no longer be considered to be practicing, or malpracticing, you can recover for your injuries if the therapist seduced you or assaulted you.

Responsible professionals would condemn these practices in the absence of tort law anyway and psychotherapist have. Principle 6 of the <u>Ethical Principles</u> requires that "Psychologists respect the integrity and protect the welfare of the people . . . with whom they work." Principle 6a specifically states that "Sexual intimacies with clients are unethical."

However, the profession may want to reach beyond the scope of tort law, to regulate conduct that falls short of seduction or assault but that is still incompetent, unethical or potentially harmful. The profession can condemn, deter or educate the psychologist who fails to use the most effective form of therapy because she is too lazy to keep informed of developments in her field since graduate school; the school counselor who advises students about emotional problems without adequate professional training or skill; or the psychotherapist who uses and promotes practices that he knows have at best only a placebo effect.

The last chapter of this book is devoted to consideration of alternative means of regulating professional practice in psychotherapy.

CHAPTER IX

IMPLICATIONS OF THE TARASOFF CASE

When Prorosenjit Poddar stabbed and killed Tatiana Tarasoff on October 27, 1969, he started a legal process whose repercussions are still being felt, and the eventual implications of which are still far from clear. This chapter is concerned with these implications. But before we examine the effects which have been documented, let us first briefly review the basic facts of the case and of the debate over the wisdom of the eventual decision by the Supreme Court of California. The reader may want to refer to Chapter V (pp. 73-74, 83-85) for previous details and discussion of the case as it pertains to breaching confidentiality. The following synopsis is derived from an article by Alan Stone (1976).

The Events Leading to the Murder

Prorosenjit Poddar had courted Tatiana Tarasoff for some time, but with little success. It may be presumed that her rebuff of him was a contributing factor to his seeking psychological help from the student health facility at the University of California at Berkley. There he was evaluated by a psychiatrist and referred to a psychologist for therapy as an out-patient. The psychologist subsequently decided that Poddar was dangerous, based on Poddar's pathological attachment to Tarasoff and evidence that he intended to purchase a gun. The psychologist consulted with the psychiatrist, and as a result notified the campus police, both orally and in writing, that Poddar was dangerous and should be taken to the facility for civil commitments.

The police questioned Poddar at length, decided he was not dangerous, especially in view of the fact that Tarasoff was in Brazil at the time, and released him. The psychiatrist, who had been away during the police investigation, returned, decided his staff had overreacted, requested the police to return the correspondence from the psychologist, and ordered it and all other records pertaining to this client destroyed. He also directed that no further action be taken to detain or commit Poddar.

Two months later Poddar went to Tarasoff's home and killed her.

The Subsequent Legal Process

Miss Tarasoff's parents attempted to sue the Regents of the University of California, the therapists involved, and the police. The trial court dismissed the complaint, the parents appealed, and the court of appeals affirmed the dismissal. The parents then appealed to the Supreme Court of California, arguing that the defendants had a duty to warn their daughter or themselves of the danger, and that they also had a duty to bring about Poddar's confinement through civil commitment.

The supreme court reversed, finding that the special relationship of the therapists to the patients had given them the duty to warn Miss Tarasoff. In addition, the court held that the police might be liable for failure to warn.

In a very rare action, the supreme court agreed to a rehearing upon being petitioned by the defendants, joined by several amici curiae, including the American Psychiatric Association. The court abandoned its position on the liability of the police, but formulated the duty of the therapists more broadly. According to Stone (1976, p. 361) the court held:

> that the relationship between a therapist and patient imposes on the therapist a duty to use reasonable care to protect third parties against danger posed by the patient. Whether this duty takes the form of a duty to warn, a duty to call the police, or some other form, will depend, in a way the court did not clarify, on the circumstances.

Rationale for the Duty and Rebuttal

The supreme court's decision was strongly influenced by an article by two law professors (Flemming and Maximov, 1974), published while the case was on appeal to the court. They argued that since civil commitment effectively deprives psychiatric patients of liberty, stigmatizes them, and destroys their will to resist, it should only be invoked as a last resort. Other, less dramatic means should be employed whenever feasible. Among such means is the warning of intended victims of threats to their health and safety.

Critics, such as Alan Stone (1976) and Toni Wise (1978), have argued that such an action may do little to actually protect possible victims, but would be likely to destroy the therapist-patient relationship, and, in particular, place the therapist on the "hit list" of the patient. Initiation of commitment proceedings, on the other hand, would be less disruptive of the therapeutic relationship in that commitment is generally accepted by everyone as an action which protects the patient as well as potential victims. Also, the patient is not apt to perceive the therapist as having aligned herself against him with his "enemy" or "prosecutor."

There are also those who worry about the erosion of confidentiality that would occur, and the effects of such erosion, if therapists are obliged to not only breach confidentiality when commitment is appropriate, but also when the less restrictive option of warning the intended victim might be considered appropriate.

Effects of Tarasoff

Survey results: One year following the second and final Tarasoff decision a survey of California psychotherapists was conducted to determine the effects of Tarasoff on their practice (Wise, 1978). A random sample of 530 of the list of 3,341 licensed psychologists and the total membership of the California Psychiatric Association, 3,155 psychiatrists, were sent questionnaires. A little more than a third of each group responded.

Given that these two groups had fought hard against the Tarasoff decisions[1], and that there were no "hard facts" or "benchmarks" against which to measure the accuracy of their response, it is little wonder that the results of the questionnaire reflected continued dissatisfaction with the decision. Nevertheless, the results contain interesting and perhaps useful information.

Predictably, many of the therapists reported having more anxiety about making judgments regarding the dangerousness of their clients and discussing limits of confidentiality more often with their clients than before Tarasoff. Also, they reported being more deliberate and careful in making predictions of dangerous

[1] Tarasoff v. Regents of University of California et al., 13 Cal.3d 177, 529 P.2d 553(1974), vacated, 17 Cal.3d 425, 551 P.2d 334(1976).

behavior, including more frequent consultation with other professionals. About one fourth of the therapists reported some reluctance by clients to discuss violent tendencies when the clients learned that their therapists might breach confidentiality.

Interestingly, some therapists claimed that, on occasion, they had voluntarily warned third parties prior to Tarasoff. Since Tarasoff, if anyone was warned, the intended victim was more apt to be among those included.

It would appear from this survey that the effects of Tarasoff may not be all bad, especially if they lead to more consultation and more careful deliberation in making predictions of dangerous behavior. However, whether such increased deliberation results in better predictions, or just in more expenditure of time and energy, remains to be seen.

It may also be argued that Tarasoff suggests a middle course of action for psychotherapists in those states where voluntary commitment is restricted to individuals who have already committed an overt action or have a severe degree of mental distress. Even if the therapist chooses not to warn the intended victim, some other sort of protective action, such as informing the police, may be in order. Apparently, some therapists have elected to do just that even before Tarasoff.

Legal Developments: Another way in which to assess the effects of Tarasoff is to analyze the results of similar legal suits since then, both in California and elsewhere. Samuel Knapp and Leon Vandecreek (1982) have done just that. It is interesting to note that only seven such cases have been reported during the five year period under review, three of which were in California. These cases have both limited the scope of Tarasoff and supported its basic premise.

In Bellah v. Greenson[2] the California court refused to find the therapist, Dr. Greenson, liable for not warning the parents of Tammy Bellah of the likelihood of her committing suicide, which she did in April, 1973. The court reasoned that self-inflicted harm or damage to property is not a strong enough public interest to violate the need for confidentiality.

---

[2] Bellah v. Greenson, Cal. App.3d, 141 Cal. Rptr. 92(1977).

In another California case[3] the victim's identity was unknown, and the question was how much effort should the psychotherapists at a hospital exert in trying to identify the victims, if any, of a potentially violent patient. The patient was a boy, who, when released to the custody of his parents, assaulted them with a hammer. The parents requested access to their son's psychiatric records to determine if the hospital could have anticipated such an assault. The court took the middle ground, as originally outlined in a footnote in the Tarasoff decision, that even if the patient did not specifically name an intended victim, it could be determined through a "moment's reflection" who it was. On the other hand, it recognized that therapists should not be required to interrogate patients or conduct special investigations to learn the identity of intended victims.

In still another California case[4] a juvenile made vague threats to kill someone if he were released. He was released to the custody of his mother and did, in fact, sexually assault and murder a neighborhood child. The court ruled that the juvenile justice authorities were not obliged to warn the community, since to require such warning in every case of threats against unspecified persons would be unwieldy, of little practical value, and would undermine the rehabilitation of parolees. A dissenting judge argued that the assailant's mother should have been notified of the vague threats.

A similar case was argued in Pennsylvania[5]. The assailant, Hartnett, had been in and out of veterans' hospitals for 20 years. After one discharge he stayed with a friend, Leedy, became drunk, and subsequently assaulted Leedy and Leedy's wife. Leedy charged that the hospital had a duty to warn him of Hartnett's violent tendencies. The defendants claimed Leedy was not an identifiable victim. The court found in favor of the defendants.

Thus, it would seem that the duty to warn does not apply to suicide and property damage, and in the case

---

[3] Mavroudis v. Superior Court for County of San Mateo, 162 Cal. Rptr. 724(Ct. App. 1980).

[4] Thompson v. County of Alameda, 614 P.2d 728 (Cal.1980).

[5] Leedy v. Hartnett, 510 F. Supp. 1125(M.D. Pa. 1981).

of third-party victims it only applies if the victim is identifiable without any special interrogation or investigation by the therapist.

The next issue is, will other states adopt Tarasoff? The preliminary answer is yes. Tarasoff has been found to apply in three out of four states in which related rulings have been made--Nebraska[6], Pennsylvania[5], and New Jersey[7]. The New Jersey case was quite similar. The patient, Lee Morganstein, had previously evinced his hostile feelings towards his ex-girlfriend by shooting at her car and house with a BB gun. One day after a therapy session, he obtained a pistol and killed her. The therapist was found negligent for not exercising the duty established by the special relationship he had with the patient of warning the intended victim, her parents, and the police.

A Maryland court, however, used the difference between its privileged communication laws and those of California in arriving at a different conclusion than the one reached in Tarasoff. Unlike California, the Maryland statutes do not allow for breach of confidentiality when the lives of others are threatened, except when involuntary commitment is sought. Shaw v. Glickman[8] concerns a group therapy situation in which a man, his wife, and her lover were participants. The man shot and seriously wounded his wife's lover upon learning of their relationship. The lover subsequently sued the group therapy team for not warning him of this possibility. The court exonerated the therapists since such warning would have been an impermissible breach of confidentiality under the state statutes.

This points out the value of knowing the statutes of the particular state in which the suit is brought, especially the statutes concerning allowable breaches of confidentiality. It is not safe to assume that a ruling in one state will be considered a precedent in another state, since its laws regulating the practice of psychotherapy may be significantly different.

---

6 Lipari v. Sears, Roebuck & Company, 497 F. Supp. 185(D. Neb. 1980).

7 McIntosh v. Milano, 403 A.2d 500(1979).

8 Shaw v. Glickman, 415 A.2d 625(Md. Ct. Spec. App. 1980).

Knapp and Vandecreek (1982) also point out that Tarasoff does not impose any new unrealistic standards on psychotherapists with regard to the prediction of violence.

> Psychotherapists need only follow reasonable standards in predicting violence. Psychotherapists are not liable for the failure to warn when the propensity toward violence is unknown or would be unknown by other psychotherapists using ordinary skill.

In summary, the full effects of Tarasoff are yet to be felt, but Slovenko's assessment of the situation back in 1975 (p. 392) seems to have been quite accurate:

> It may be predicted that Tarasoff, modified or unmodified, will not bring in a parade of horribles . . . the decision will make little or no difference . . . since the court would have to be convinced that the therapist believed that danger was imminent and then did nothing.

The legal actions which have occured since Slovenko's pronouncement appear to have modified the Tarasoff decision in several respects: suicide and property damage are excluded as grounds for warning third parties; the intended victim must be readily identifiable; and the state statutes on confidentiality must permit breaches in instances where voluntary commitment is not feasible, but danger to others still exists.

CHAPTER X

RESEARCH AND THE PRACTITIONER

It is presumptuous to write a chapter on the ethics of research for psychotherapists. It is no secret that research is an incidental aspect of most therapists' lives--reserved for the rare moment when enough time and interest can be summoned to sit down and read a journal article or answer a questionnaire. In fact, in a recent survey of 500 clinical psychologists, practitioners whose academic training specially prepares them for the dual role of scientist and practitioner, less than one percent of the respondents reported using tests as outcome research measures in their practice (Wade & Barker, 1977). Yet, perhaps the easiest and most common way to conduct evaluation of treatment studies is pre- and posttesting with standard instruments.

Why, then, should we concern ourselves with such an insignificant aspect of psychotherapeutic practice? First, it should be noted that many practitioners work at least part-time in agency or academic settings where they are exposed to, and sometimes participate in, research of various kinds. In such settings they have the opportunity to critically evaluate proposed and ongoing research projects, whether or not they utilize such opportunities. Second, it is also no secret that there is ever more pressure upon all agencies to justify their existence; thus the probability that some sort of evaluation research will become mandatory is increasing. Psychology's code (<u>Specialty Guidelines</u>, 3.3) stipulates that clinical service units should conduct evaluation studies on their effectiveness. Such pressure is not limited to agencies. As we have seen in the chapter on licensing, there are those who would require that individual therapists publish their "success rate" along with other credentials in describing their services.

Finally, and most important, therapists are curious and concerned about their effectiveness quite independently from outside pressure for accountability. It may also be presumed that we are curious about human psychological functioning in general, otherwise we would have never gone into such work. When we pursue those intrinsic interests in systematic ways, it is well for us to be knowledgeable about how to do so in an ethical manner, a manner that protects the integrity and well-being of the persons we study.

In pursuit of such knowledge, issues such as informed consent--what is it? when is it required? how to obtain it? deception and concealment--when permissible? and coercion--what sorts of pressure, what incentives are "legitimate"? become relevant. This chapter presents a rather full review of these and related issues.

In The Naked Truth a professor plans to require his students to participate in a study which involves deceiving subjects into believing they are "latent homosexuals." In On the other hand . . . a group leader is worried that formal informed consent procedures will interfere with the group process but doesn't want to evaluate members' progress in an unethical manner. Dreaming for Counseling poses the problem of doing basic research in a service setting. In Smoking Rights the issue is whether the rights of institutionalized patients are violated by using treatment means that they would not be likely to endorse.

The first two commentary sections point out the important role that "degree of risk" to the client plays in determining if it is necessary to formally obtain informed consent, and what the components of informed consent are. The following section reviews the ethical guidelines concerning the use of deception and/or concealment of information in research. Subtle and overt coercion of client participation is the theme of the next section. The final sections discuss the ethical responsibilities of "stooges" and other research assistants and the role of pilot studies in determining client risk of harm.

Illustrative Cases

The Naked Truth: A psychology instructor is interested in assessing the effect upon heterosexual social activity of thinking of oneself as "a latent homosexual." To that end he has designed a study in which a psychogalvanometer is attached to subjects as they view slides of same-sex nudes. The subjects are told that, if the needle deflects when they are viewing these slides, it will indicate latent homosexuality. The experimental subjects are given false feedback and led to believe they are, in fact, latent homosexuals. The control subjects are informed that they are "normal." Subjects are run singly and then sent to a waiting room prior to discussing the results with the experimenter. In this waiting room is a "stooge"--an attractive person of the opposite sex who presumably is there for other reasons and whose task is to flirt with the subject. The interaction is observed and recorded through a hidden camera and scored in terms of positive and negative responses to the flirtation. After ten minutes the subject is brought in to see the experimenter, and the actual purpose of the experiment is revealed.

The psychologist teaches an introductory course in psychology in a university and plans to use his students as subjects. He seeks you out as a consultant on the ethical issues involved. In particular, he wants to know if it is all right to require all his students to participate, and if not, how he should get them to participate. Also he wonders about the ethics of deceiving them as to the real purpose of the experiment, yet knows of no other way to assess this particular labeling effect. Finally he worries about how to handle the problem of there being some actual homosexually oriented students in his class, latent or overt. What is your response to his questions?

<u>On the other hand . . .</u> : Jacqueline is planning to conduct an eating disorders group and wishes to evaluate the effects of the experience on group members. To that end she has devised her own pre- and post-questionnaire to be administered along with a standard instrument. She does not consider the questionnaires especially threatening and wonders if it is necessary to formally obtain consent from group members prior to administering them. On the one hand she does not want to unduly emphasize the assessment process to the point where group members might consider themselves as guinea pigs in a research project rather than as potential beneficiaries of a group program for controlling eating disorders. Also she is afraid too many structured experiences at the beginning of the group program will make it difficult for the members to be spontaneous and open in the group interaction. Finally she suspects some members will refuse a formal request to participate in pre- and postassessment who would go along with an informal request. On the other hand, she doesn't want to do anything unethical, anything that might not protect the welfare of the group members. What should she do?

1. Should she go ahead and design the informed consent form and administer it on the basis it is better to be on the "safe side"?

2. Should she rely on her own judgement about the innocuousness of the research aspect of the group experience and simply introduce it in as unobtrusive and non demanding manner as possible, foregoing obtaining any formal consent or volunteering any information beyond that which is requested?

Dreaming for Counseling: Pete is interested in research on the function of dreaming. As a member of the staff of a college counseling center he has an easily accessible subject pool--the clients that come in for counseling. He would like to use them to gather some preliminary data and expects that all that would be required is a half hour of their time. He proposes this to the staff and, altough they agree the procedures he describes are not stressful in any way and that a half hour is not much to ask, there is some concern expressed that the clients did not come to participate in such research and that he ought to look elsewhere for subjects. What do you think?

1. Should Pete be permitted to conduct the preliminary research using counseling center clients? It could be argued that the clients might readily welcome the opportunity to do something in exchange for the counseling they receive.

2. Should Pete be asked to solicit subjects elsewhere? It may be that clients, even if given the opportunity to decline, may feel obligated to participate or will think that if they don't participate the center will feel less committed to helping them.

3. Should Pete be allowed to solicit subjects from the clients, but only if it is made abundantly clear that such participation is truly voluntary?

Smoking Rights: Alice is the director of therapeutic programming for a psychiatric ward in a mental hospital. This ward has a number of chronic, quite regressed patients. When left to their own devices they have demonstrated on numerous occasions that they will sit around or lie down on their beds for practically the whole day--only getting up to go to the bathroom, and then not always, or to be escorted to the canteen where they buy cigarettes and other goodies. They passively resist any active therapy such as occupational or work therapy--only going when commanded to do so and then just sitting and minimally responding. Normal incentives, such as prodding, encouragement, and praise are ineffective. Alice has noticed that most of them are heavy smokers and decides to use cigarettes as a reward for becoming more active. Specifically she plans to remove all their cigarettes and only give them out in proportion to the amount of willing participation each of them shows in the various therapy programs, using feedback from the ward personnel and the supervisors of the various programs as the criterion of "voluntary participation." She plans to carefully monitor the project and its success and, if successful, present a paper on it in a professional conference.

However, she must first get the approval of her immediate supervisors and of the hospital's research review committee. Their concern is that it seems the patients are being coerced into participation--they cannot opt out of the project. Also the question is raised whether or not the patients have a "right" to smoke if they want to, and it would be a violation of that right if she limited their access to cigarettes, unless it could be demonstrated that the smoking was physically harmful in some direct way, in which case they should not have any cigarettes, regardless of how active they were in therapy programs. What do you think?

1. Should Alice be allowed to institute the project? Obviously she is not harming the patients in any way, and something must be done to get them out of their lethargic, regressed condition. Only good could result from such a project. In fact, it would be irresponsible not to try out such a promising approach.

2. Should Alice be prohibited from carrying out the project? The regime smacks of punishment. It is not a positive reward system in the usual sense in which something additional is given upon successful performance; rather something is being given back that rightfully belonged to the patients in the first place. Surely other measures can be found that would be as effective and not punishing.

3. Should Alice be allowed to go ahead, but only under the condition that she devise one or more

alternative treatment programs and allow the patients to choose among them?

Commentary

"Minimal Risk"

The major source of guidelines for research in psychology is the report by the Committee for the Protection of Human Subjects (CPHS) of the American Psychological Association (APA) entitled *Ethical Principles in the Conduct of Research with Human Participants* which was published in 1973 and has recently undergone revision. One of the major revisions has been incorporated in the *Ethical Principles* and is reflected in 9b:

> Considering whether a participant in a planned study will be a "subject at risk" or a "subject at minimal risk," according to recognized standards is of primary ethical concern to the investigator.

This distinction is also made by the Department of Health and Human Services (DHHS) in the January 26, 1981, edition of the *Federal Register*. This document provides the following definition of "minimal risk":

> "Minimal risk" means that the risks of harm anticipated in the proposed research are not greater, considering probability and magnitude, than those ordinarily encountered in daily life or during the performance of routine physical or psychological examinations or tests. (Section 46.102.g)

This definition is used to determine whether or not research which is funded in whole or in part by DHHS can be exempted from the review process used to determine if proper precautions have been used to protect the human subjects from undue risk. It serves a similar function in psychological research in general:

> Except in minimal-risk research, the investigator establishes a clear and fair agreement with research participants, prior to their participation. . . . The investigator informs the participant of all aspects of the research that might reasonably be expected to influence willingness to participate. . . . (*Ethical Principles*, 9d)

Thus, it would seem in the case, <u>On the other hand . . .</u> (p. 177), that Jacqueline may not have to formally obtain the informed consent of the members of her eating disorders group to do pre- and postassessment. It would depend on how threatening the items of her pre- and postinventory and self-designed questionnaire are. She would do well to consult with someone about this prior to making a final decision.

Informed Consent Components

In other than "minimal-risk" research, however, informed consent is a standard requirement. What exactly are the components of informed consent in a research context? There is no single set of components that would apply to all research proposals, but the following guideline, based on DHHS regulations and developed by the Committee for the Protection of Human Subjects of the University of Oregon (1982), does a good job of incorporating the major points.

(1) A statement that the study involves research, an explanation of the purposes of the research and the expected duration of the subject's participation, a description of the procedures to be followed, and identification of any procedures which are experimental;

(2) A description of any reasonably foreseeable risks or discomforts to the subject;

(3) A description of any benefits to the subject or to others which may reasonably be expected from the research;

(4) A disclosure of appropriate alternative procedures or courses of treatment, if any, that might be advantageous to the subject;

(5) A statement describing the extent, if any, to which confidentiality of records identifying the subject will be maintained;

(6) For research involving more than minimal risk, an explanation as to whether any compensation and an explanation as to whether any medical treatments are available if injury occurs and, if so, what they consist of, or where further information may be obtained;

(7) An explanation of whom to contact for answers to pertinent questions about the research and research subjects' rights, and whom to contact in the event of a research-related injury to the subject;

(8) A statement that participation is voluntary, refusal to participate will involve no penalty or loss of benefits to which the subject is otherwise entitled, and the subject may discontinue participation at any time without penalty or loss of benefits to which the subject is otherwise entitled.

(9) If physical injury is a likely risk you must include the following statement or an acceptable paraphrase.

Should you suffer physical injury as a direct result of participating in this project, you may file a claim against the State of Oregon. Questions regarding coverage and claims should be directed to . . . .

Some subjects may not be capable of providing informed consent by virtue of insufficient background or intellectual capacity to comprehend the essentials of what is being asked of them. In some such cases it is a legal requirement to get agreement from parties who can legitimately represent the subjects. Those doing research with children should obtain the "Ethical Standards for Research with Children" developed by the Society for Research in Child Development[1] or the proposed federal rules for research involving children[2]. Those working with cross-cultural subjects would do well to obtain the publication on this matter by the Subcommittee on Cross-Cultural Research of the American Psychological Association Committee on International Relations in Psychology.

Research involving Deception and Concealment

Some research can not be carried out if the subjects are fully informed of the nature of the research prior to their participation in it. This would be true

---

[1] c/o University of Chicago Press, 5801 Ellis Ave., Chicago, Il 60637

[2] Federal Register, July 21, 1978

of any research in which it is important that the subjects' responses be spontaneous, not distorted by anticipation, or in the case of field observation studies, not affected by awareness of being systematically observed.

Before engaging in such research it is incumbent upon the researcher to justify the necessity of conducting it. As stated in the report by the APA Committee for the Protection of Human Subjects (1973):

> When ethical questions arise, the situation is usually one of weighing the advantages and disadvantages of conducting the research as planned. On the one hand, there is the contribution that the research may ultimately make to human welfare; on the other, there is the cost to the individual research participant. (p. 10)

Later the committee adds the following guideline:

> In general, after research participation, the participants' feelings about the experience should be such that they would willingly take part in further research. The requirements of the research should be ones that research psychologists would find acceptable were members of their immediate family to participate. (p. 11)

Finally, it is also recommended that:

> The investigator should not trust his own objectivity in balancing the pros and cons of going ahead with research that raises an ethical question for him. His personal involvement tends to lead him to exaggerate the scientific merit of what he is about to do and to underestimate the costs to the research participant. (p. 12)

These guidelines apply to any research project. When deception or concealment is involved it is additionally recommended that the researcher "determine whether alternative procedures are available . . . and ensure that the participants are provided with sufficient explanation as soon as possible" [underlining added] (*Ethical Principles*, 9e). Thus, in the illustrative case, *The Naked Truth* (p. 176), the instructor should seek consultation both to get a more objective assessment of the potential hazards of the research and, in conjunction with research of the literature, to determine if some non deceptive or otherwise less objectionable way of researching the question can be developed. If he proceeds with the study it is then incumbent upon him to give a full explanation of its actual purpose as soon as reasonably possible after its completion. In this particular study it appears problematic whether, in fact, subjects would " willingly take part in future research" unless the debriefing was done extremely skillfully.

More typical than research involving deception is research involving concealment--i.e. less than full disclosure of the purpose or possible consequences of the research. Deception involves deliberate misinformation, concealment is lack of information. This would occur, for example, in follow-up research of clients in which those who can reasonably be expected to be in the position to observe any changes in the client's behavior are contacted, without the client's knowledge or explicit permission, and asked if they had noticed any change. Again this is unethical if more than "minimal risk" to the client is involved--such as inadvertently disclosing to an employer that the person had been in psychotherapy, or breaking confidentiality regarding the focal areas of the psychotherapy. In such a case it seems unlikely that later debriefing with the client would be sufficient.

Coercion of Subject Participation

Another issue that is exemplified in The Naked Truth (p. 176) and also in Dreaming for Counseling (p. 178) is that of how much latitude should potential subjects have to not participate in research. Should students in introductory psychology classes have to participate in a particular experiment or in some experiments in order to pass the course or get an "A"? Is it ethically permissible to require that counseling center clients participate in a research project of the center prior to, or during counseling? Does it make any difference whether or not the project is related to the counseling received? Or if someone is an inmate of a regressed psychiatric ward, or a prisoner in a prison, is it okay to withhold certain privileges unless she participates in a research project, if the project is designed to benefit her? These are difficult questions which can not always be answered definitively. However, some rather complete guidelines do exist.

Perhaps because there has been such a plethora of studies using introductory psychology students as subjects a detailed set of guidelines has been proposed in this area. Following is a summary of the eight points found in the report by the CPHS (American Psychological Association, 1973):

> 1. Students are informed about the research requirement prior to entering the course, usually by an announcement in an official listing of courses. Also a detailed description of the requirement is provided, in writing, during the first class period.
>
> 2. Prior approval of research proposals is required, often by a departmental committee.
>
> 3. Options are commonly provided both among research projects and between research projects and other activities that do not require service as a research participant.
>
> 4. Before actual participation in a project the student receives a description of the procedures to be employed and is reminded of the option to drop out without penalty.
>
> 5. "Steps are taken to insure that the student is treated with respect and courtesy."
>
> 6. Participants receive a reward of some kind for their participation--at minimum as full an explanation of the purposes of the research as is possible.
>
> 7. There is a procedure whereby students may report any mistreatment.
>
> 8. The recruiting procedure is constantly monitored and periodically evaluated, both by students and by the researchers. (pp. 44-46)

Specific guidelines also exist with regard to the nature of research and the amount of coercion that is appropriate for clients of service-oriented psychological units, such as counseling centers (American Psychological Association, 1973):

> First, in a relationship defined primarily in terms of human service research that is undertaken must be compatible with the underlying expectation of service. For example, research in a counseling center requiring the participation of counseling center clients should involve the potential for improving the service program of the center. . . .
>
> Second, the strong motives inherent in the service relationship must not be exploited to the research participant's detriment. For example, the psychologist in a service context must be careful not to exercise undue coercion on the client . . . to participate in research by allowing the potential participant to draw incorrectly the inference that the service is contingent upon participation in the research. In situations in which services are contigent upon research participation, that fact must be made explicit. (p. 15)

Thus is would seem that it would be improper for the counselor in Dreaming for Counseling (p. 178) to in any way require counseling center clients to participate in such research, or even to let them assume that such participation is in any way related to the amount or quality of service they may receive.

The most difficult ethical issues arise in employment or institutional settings where the employee or inmate, respectively, is cognizant that there are many ways in which his life can be affected by the administration, depending on how "cooperative" he appears to be. There, almost any request by an administrator has a coercive aspect to it, whether intended or not. For this reason the Federal government has developed special regulations guiding biomedical and behavioral research involving prisoners and proposed rules for those institutionalized as "mentally disabled" (mentally ill, mentally retarded, emotionally disturbed, psychotic or senile)[3].

---

[3] The regulations for research with prisoners may be found in the November 16, 1978, Federal Register; the proposed rules for the other institutionalized categories are found in the November 17, 1978, Federal Register.

The guidelines developed by the CPHS of the APA (1973) cut across the various categories of institutional and organizational settings and do not specifically select out certain types of treatment for special consideration, such as biomedical and behavioral research. Thus they are of more value as general guidelines, and a summary follows:

The general context is that of an organizational or institutional setting in which the proposed research is to be conducted without the full voluntary consent of the participants. The common justification for such research is the value of it to institutional objectives, which objectives may be irrelevant or even objectionable to the participants. Three broad types of research are distinguished.

In the first type some aspects of the program of the institution or organization is being evaluated in the hope of improving its effectiveness. The example given is that of evaluating the comparative effectiveness of different types of psychiatric ward management. This is seen as analogous to comparing alternative curricula in educational research and as not requiring explicit informed consent of the participants. However, it is important to safeguard the interests of the participants by seeking "ethical consultation." If one or more of these alternative programs are a major departure from standard programs, and the participant is in danger of being handled in a way that will interfere with improvement or rehabilitation, then "the researcher incurs a special responsibility to assure the later provision of such benefits as the research participant may have been deprived of in the course of the research" (p. 48).

The second type of research requires the participation of persons like those found in a given institutional or organizational setting--i.e., the subjects are being used to "represent" other such subjects, rather than seen as directly benefitting from any research that is done on them.

> From one point of view . . . the investigator must respect the potential participants' freedom to decline participation. . . . From another point of view, however, [this] does not imply that the investigator may not communicate to the potential participant his sense of the possible value of the proposed

research and the need, as he sees it, for cooperation from individuals of the type represented by the potential participant. . . . (p. 49)

The proposed resolution of this dilemma is for the investigator to "provide the potential participant with a meaningful argument that his participation may help solve a serious problem without at the same time implying disapproval or punishment for refusal to take part" (pp. 49-50).

In the third type of research there is no special relationship between the nature of the research to either the program in the special setting or to the characteristics of persons in that setting. In such cases, "the argument that the potential participant is under some obligation to take part can no longer be made. Accordingly, the focus shifts to the kind and strength of incentives the investigator is warranted in using" (p. 50). It is often easy, in certain institutions, to find powerful incentives, incentives that are related to the disadvantaged circumstances of the potential participants--such as freedom to participate in leisure activities or better living accommodations. Again the guidelines specify the securing of ethical advice from consultants prior to establishment of incentives.

Let us now briefly return to our illustrative cases --what light do these guidelines throw on them? The Naked Truth (p. 176) and Dreaming for Counseling (p. 178) would fit into the third type of research, except that the potential participants are students, not inmates or employees of institutions or organizations. On the other hand . . . (p. 177) also has to do with potential participants who have much more latitude to refuse participation without penalty. The only relevant case, then, is that of Smoking Rights (p. 178). Here, the proposed research is likely to be of direct benefit to the potential participants, the regressed mental patients, and thus would fit under the first type of research. "Ethical consultation" is recommended in such cases.

In addition to voluntarily solicited ethical consultation, review by the requisite Institutional Review Board (IRB) is also required--i.e. by the board appointed by the institution to review the adequacy of the provisions for protection of human subjects in research projects within the institution. The IRB may well look to guidance from the federal "Proposed Rules on Research involving those institutionalized as Mentally Disabled" (see footnote 3). The most pertinent section there would seem to be 46.505, subsection (3), which, among other things, would require the investigator to obtain the consent of the inmate's "legally authorized representative" and the authorization "by a court of competent jurisdiction."

Role of "Stooges" and other Research Assistants

It is the rare research project that does not involve the assistance of one or more others in the data collection stage. In The Naked Truth (p. 176) it would be necessary for one or more research assistants, perhaps fellow students, to play flirtatious roles. In Smoking Rights (p. 178) it would be necessary to enlist the support of the nursing staff, including the psychiatric aides. In Dreaming for Counseling (p. 178) the assistance of the receptionist, and perhaps other office staff, would be required. What is the ethical responsibility of these individuals? The answer, in part, is provided by the ethical code, if any, of the occupation to which they belong. Other than that, assuming no illegal activities are involved, there is only their respective moral value systems to guide them. But for psychologists, or would-be psychologists, the ethical codes adopted by the APA are obviously relevant, although in the case of would-be psychologists, such as psychology students, the codes are not binding. The preamble of the Ethical Principals states: "Acceptance of membership in the American Psychological Association commits the member to adherence to these principles."

The most relevant part of the Ethical Principles is Principle 9c:

> The investigator always retains the responsibility for ensuring ethical practice in research. The investigator is also responsible for the ethical treatment of research participants by collaborators, assistants, students and employees, all of whom, however, incur similar obligations. [underlining added]

In other words, "responsibility can only be multiplied, never divided, by such collaboration" (American Psychological Association, 1973, p. 26). And later, "It in no way excuses impositions on research participants to say that one was ordered to perform such actions by an employer or teacher" (p. 27). For example, in the case of The Naked Truth (p. 176) it is the individual responsibility of each of the persons assigned the flirtatious role to decide whether or not this is an ethical role to assume, and in order to arrive at an informed opinion about that, each of them would need to know the nature of and justification for the experiment as a whole.

The Role of Pilot Studies

Often it is difficult, if not impossible, to "armchair" whether or not a particular procedure or combination of procedures will cause undue stress on subjects and result in some sort of relatively permanent negative change, such as assumption of a negative label about some aspect of personality or negative attitudes towards psychological research. In such cases it is advisable either not to conduct the research at all, or to do so only on a very limited, provisional scale until the likely effects can be determined. Pilot studies serve this "testing the water" function, as well as clarifying the workability of various components of the study, and the feasibility of the study as a whole.

Even pilot studies do not provide the investigator with carte blanche authority to try anything out. It is important to be equally as concerned for the welfare of the participants of these studies. Thus such studies are normally not only on a smaller scale than regular studies, but also may employ measures or procedures which are modified in such a way as to pose less threat, and/or use participants who may be presumed to be more emotionally and psychologically stable than the target population. If such modifications are used and do not result in any significant negative repercussions, then another pilot study, or perhaps a series of pilot studies, should be conducted, with the final one reproducing, as accurately as possible, the conditions of the planned research.

It is important to obtain full informed consent, insofar as this is feasible, from pilot study participants as well as from participants in any other study. In fact, the central message of this chapter is that informed consent is of crucial importance in the fulfillment of the researcher's obligation to treat potential participants with respect and concern for their dignity and welfare. The decision to forego obtaining of such consent is one that should never be made without consultation and considerable justification in terms of potential benefit to the participants, themselves, or to others.

> Ethical behavior, unlike legal behavior, cannot be operationally defined in precisely those areas where the risk is greatest, nor can it be considered apart from the issue of competency. In the counseling profession generally, and in group work specifically, the companion issues of competency and ethics still loom before us, unresolved and excruciatingly elusive. (Dye, 1981, p. 227)

CHAPTER XI

GROUPS

It is with considerable trepidation that I approach the problems posed in this chapter. As with most aspects of group work, there is nothing simple about the analysis of its ethical components. Every dilemma, every issue raised by individual therapy emerges in group therapy also, albeit in altered and often exacerbated form. In addition, a number of new concerns result from the expanded network of relationships--therapist(s)-client, therapist(s)-clients, client-client, and client-clients. In order to be effective and ethical the leader must somehow orchestrate this network.

To simplify the task, and to avoid needless duplication with what has been said in previous chapters, this chapter focuses on the distinctive features of group work and the ethical conundrums that issue from these features. The labeling and the classification of special characteristics are mine--I hope they will prove fruitful in clarifying the complexities of the topic.

We begin, as usual, with a series of concrete representations of dilemmas with which therapists may be faced. In _The "Nonparticipant"_ the group norm for self-disclosure is applied with some force to a noncontributing group member. The leader must decide if and how to protect him. In _The Extramarital Group Affair_ a full-fledged romance between two members of a married couples' group appears to be developing. The leader overhears the planning of a secret rendezvous and must decide if and how to enforce the group's rule of no out-of-group socializing. _The "Unfinished" Client_ features a timid woman who is just beginning to learn how to express a full range of emotions when the group ends abruptly (for her). What responsibility does the leader have to assist her further development? Lastly, Let's explore our Unconscious describes an all-too-successful growth group that threatens to take over the reins of control from the leader.

The first five parts of the commentary section are devoted to the description of five features of group work which do not find a ready parallel in individual counseling or therapy, and which therefore pose new or substantially altered ethical dilemmas for therapists who are group leaders. These distinctive features are: the dual role of members; the differing levels of readiness and development of members; the pressure to conform to group norms; the impact of out-of-group socializing; and the unexpected, creative, open-ended dimension of growth groups. There are still other relatively distinctive features that could be mentioned, such as the problems posed by simultaneous group and individual counseling, but I have selected these five as being most important and deserving of analysis.

The final sections of the commentary will present the resolutions, such as they are, to the ethical issues that have been delineated. Various sets of official guidelines will be utilized in this effort.

> The "Nonparticipant": Steve was referred for group therapy by the intake counselor. He would have preferred individual therapy, but when informed he would be placed on a waiting list with no guarantee of being removed in the near future, he reluctantly opted to join a newly opened group instead. His reluctance seems to have transferred into the group situation; he participates minimally, if at all, and appears to be bored and disgruntled most of the time. This behavior has persisted now for four sessions, and several members of the group have decided to confront Steve with their annoyance and discomfort. They ask him what he is doing in the group, and when he gives a noncommittal "same as everybody else" reply, they accuse him of wanting only to spectate, of being afraid to participate, and of being insensitive to the needs of others in the group. Their allegations are soon supported by other group members, and the situation is deteriorating into a "let's jump on Steve" competition. Should you intervene, and if so, how?

1. Interrupt, restate and summarize the remarks of the group members, thus ending the "attack" phase, and then turn to Steve and ask him if there is anything he wishes to say in return. You believe this will force him to come out of his shell and facilitate his integration into the group.

2. Use this as an opportunity to point out the difference between observations of behavior and imputing of motives, i.e., between the description of actual actions and the inferences made from these actions. You hope this instruction will serve the dual purpose of teaching the group members a valuble communication skill and act as a buffer for Steve, so he will have time to recover and constructively process the meaning of the group members' reactions.

3. Defend Steve, pointing out that although it would be nice if everyone were to participate equally, this is seldom, if ever, the case, and that you are sure that he will join in when he is ready.

The Extramarital Group Affair: You are running a group for couples with marital problems. During the course of the group it becomes apparent that two of the members, Jan and Lew, are responding positively to each other at a rapidly accelerating rate. Unfortunately, they are not one of the original pairs; rather each has a spouse in the group. During a break you overhear Jan and Lew arranging to meet privately later that week. One of the rules which the group has agreed to beforehand is that extra-group socializing would be forbidden until termination of the group. What should you do?

1. Should you immediately approach Jan and Lew and remind them of the rule, hoping that this will be effective?

2. Should you bring the issue up in the group, itself, when it reconvenes, but not mention any names, leaving that to the group members to handle as they want?

3. Should you focus instead on Jan and Lew's behavior within the group, noting that they seem especially positive about each other and wondering what that might mean?

4. Should you just ignore this potentially explosive situation in the hope that it will resolve itself without your intervention or that it will arise "naturally" in the group at some point, at which time you can promote resolution?

The "Unfinished" Client: When Elizabeth joined your ten-session interpersonal anxiety group, she was both frightened by and enthusiastic about the prospect of working through her anxieties within what promised to be a supportive social atmosphere. With some encouragement she has learned how to relate relatively comfortably both within and without the group situation by expressing positive feelings. However, this has made her painfully aware of feelings of anger that she has, which she has never learned to express. She has just begun to express these feelings within the protected confines of the group when it comes to an end. She expresses her frustration to you. What obligation do you have to help her with this problem?

1. None. You never promised any of the group members at any time that all or any particular amount of their personal goals and concerns would be met by the group. You did what you considered a good job with the group within the agreed-upon time limits, and your duty is discharged. Presumably, she can proceed on her own or seek out help by herself elsewhere.

2. You are obligated to either personally provide follow-up assistance or to refer her to someone who can.

Let's explore our Unconscious: You are the leader of a "growth group." It has been enormously successful to date. The group has achieved cohesion beyond your wildest dreams. You have completed most of the planned exercises in the earlier sessions of the group, exercises designed to help group members explore their various interpersonal limitations and acquire new skills for relating with each other. You are now in the later, deliberately more unstructured sessions in which spontaneity is encouraged. One member admits to a curiosity as to the effects of LSD on releasing one's unconscious, and this precipitates a discussion in which it evolves that almost everyone wants to try it out, and not only that, but do it as a group. Two of the members claim to have had a number of experiences with the drug state and offer to act as "monitors" for the others, yourself included. You are unwilling to abrogate your role as the group leader and fearful of the consequences, should anyone have a "bad trip," or worse yet, suffer physical injury while in the drug state. You admit these qualms to the group, and they reassure you that certain precautions will be taken, such as monitors driving everyone home and staying with members as long as it seems advisable. It is obvious that you are the only "holdout." What should you do?

1. Should you agree to the experiment, but only under the condition that it not be counted as a regular group session, and be held elsewhere than your place of business?

2. Should you put your foot down, refuse to participate and point out that the group members may be in violation of local or state law by purchasing or taking an illegal drug?

3. Should you agree, plan to video tape the session, and utilize the results in later group sessions--perhaps even as a basis for an article on potential benefits/hazards of dropping acid?

Commentary

Dual Role of Members

In many groups the members are explicitly instructed that they are to consider themselves as assistants, junior therapists, if you will, to the leader. Their task is to be extra eyes and ears for the leader, additional sounding boards for the members, and generally supportive of each other's efforts to make progress. Even in groups where the leader is clearly in command, such as in Gestalt "hot seat" procedures, the leader assumes that the members who are currently observing will participate as directed in order to assist the "hot seat" member in role-playing which requires interaction with the audience. And, of course, the debriefing that typically follows structured group exercises is designed to be helpful to not only the member offering comments but to those receiving them. This dual role as participant and as assistant to the leader is considered unique to group work (Grazda, Duncan, & Sisson, 1971).

Problems arise when the members, in their role as assistants, rather than acting in a manner that is helpful to the other members and/or to the group process, act in a way deemed destructive by the group leader. <u>The "Nonparticipant"</u> (p. 194) illustrates such a situation. If the leader criticizes the members who are attacking the "nonparticipant," she risks losing their cooperation at a later point. A leader cannot both give responsibility, implicitly or explicitly, and then arbitrarily take it back without destroying the mutual trust that must exist for a group to function effectively.

Another aspect of dual roles is the loss of confidentiality. Only the leader, if she is a professional therapist or counselor, is required by the guidelines of her profession, and sometimes also by law, to maintain confidentiality. The members have no corresponding obligation to provide such protection, and, as we shall see later, there is no sure solution to the problem. Also, it may be more of a problem from a professional's point of view than it is from that of the members.

Differential Readiness, Development of Members

In individual therapy the pacing of the therapy can be tailored to the readiness of the client. If the client is "left behind," this soon becomes apparent to the sensitive therapist, and a retracing is effected. If the pacing is too slow, the client can make his impatience known and prompt the therapist to adjust accordingly. Latitude to "digress," to explore areas for their potential significance, may also exist in goodly measure. This is not to say that there aren't limitations to such individual accommodations--frequently time and money are in short supply and a less-than-leisurely approach is called for. But within whatever confines there are, the therapist and the client are free to proceed at an individually determined judicious pace.

In group therapy, the more members there are, the more "paces" need to be accommodated. No two group members start at exactly the same psychological point (if, indeed, one could define such "points"), and no two members can be expected to be in exactly the same stage of development throughout the course of the group. Moments of communality, of community, are highly treasured, but may be illusory. This lack of synchronization results in internal strain, and the leader has the responsibility to try to set a pace that all can benefit from, not unlike the teacher in a one-room school, or in most classrooms.

The end point of term-limited groups is no different from other points in this respect. Not infrequently a client is "halfway there," as in The "Unfinished" Client" (p. 196), and wants very much to continue, whereas other group members may feel they have accomplished as much as they want for now. Whether or not such clients personally approach the leader and ask him for continuing assistance is irrelevant in an ethical sense; a sensitive, experienced leader will be aware of such "untimely" termination for some of the members and will have anticipated it. As we shall see later, there are recommended ways of handling such situations.

Pressure to Conform to Group Norms

Perhaps the most salient and most discussed aspect of group work, as well as one of the most investigated, is that of the psychological pressure that members of a group acting in concert can exert upon individual members. Strictly speaking, as any "people pleaser" can tell you, pressure to conform is not peculiar to groups of three or more--all it takes is one other person, especially an authority figure, to exert pressure on a second person to align her opinion to his. Thus, such pressure also exists in individual therapy. However, new wrinkles emerge in larger groups--cults can be formed in which the leader's wish is regarded as law, and ostracism becomes a potential reality, one which is feared to the proportion that the individual is attracted to the group and its activities. This force, if not kept in constant check, has unpredictable consequences--even the leader may risk being excluded from some groups as we have seen in Let's explore the Unconscious (p. 196). Typically, however, it is some group member that risks punishment, and almost always under the guise of treatment. A member of a "resocialization ward," for example, did not attempt a new behavior assigned to him by his group. As a result he was excluded from a long-anticipated trip to town. The staff subsequently observed marked regression in his behavior (Galinsky & Schopler, 1977, p. 92). One can argue that the potential reward (in terms of patient improvement) was worth the risk in such cases, but the need for ethical guidelines to frame such decisions is apparent.

Impact of Out-of-Group Socialization

I argued in Chapter IV that the distinctiveness of the client-therapist relationship was threatened by the introduction of small talk into the therapy sessions and by indiscriminate therapist self-disclosure, but most of all by forming a friendship or sexual involvement during the course of therapy. The resulting shift in focus from client to therapist concerns was listed as one of the hazards of such socialization. A similar argument can be made with respect to out-of-group socialization of group members. If the group members are unknown to each other at the time of the group inception and subsequently only meet each other within scheduled group meetings, a certain "privacy," sense of togetherness, and distinctiveness is built. This atmosphere may be utilized to promote explorative interpersonal behavior that would not otherwise be attempted. This, in turn, creates an even greater bonding and a sense of group integrity, not unlike the experience of communality that groups of individuals sometimes achieve who have suffered through danger together, such as soldiers in the same unit, or those who may have shared a "peak experience." A group leader may want such a group unity to develop, knowing how it will facilitate certain kinds of change.

If, however, certain portions of the group meet together outside of the scheduled sessions, it is inevitable that they will discuss their group experience, and, in so doing, may even draw non group members into the conversation. This talking about the therapy experience to others can be expected to happen in individual therapy also, but the distinct aspect of group therapy is that subgroup bondings can be formed between and among group members that threaten to violate the integrity of the larger group. Cliques of members or intimate pairings may develop, as in <u>The Extramarital Group Affair</u> (p. 195). To the degree that the rest of the group is aware of these subgroups, a division between those who are "in" a subgroup and those who are "out" is formed. Fears are aroused, such as "they are laughing at me" and "they are leaving me out." The resulting mistrust may destroy the efficacy of the group.

Many groups, such as groups of inmates in an institution or groups of employees, comprise people who already know each other and who may be interacting with each other on a regular basis outside of the group. In such cases it is often infeasible, or plain silly, to try to impose a "gag rule" on such individuals. However, the group members usually are cognizant of the preexising relationships and, supposedly, are mentally prepared to accept their continuance during the course of the group. It is newly formed relationships that are most threatening.

In view of the potential destructiveness of out-of-group socializing to some groups, how best to protect the welfare of all of the group members becomes an ethical issue. Several methods have been proposed which will be presented later.

The Creative, Experimental, Unexpected Aspect of Groups

Individual therapy is not devoid of a creative dimension. The skilled psychotherapist is able to tap into the creativeness of the client and use his own spontaneous, intuitive notions in resolving client dilemmas through mutual exploration and problem-solving. Often, unexpected actions and insights result in further clarification and precipitate therapeutic change. The added element of group therapy is that such a process may occur among the group members and threaten to become autonomous, escaping guidance or control by the constituted leader. Such is the case with Let's explore our Unconscious (p. 196). Often such "unexpected" developments would have been easily anticipated by the experienced leader. In The "Nonparticipant" (p. 194) the group's sudden outpouring of accusation and demand for self-disclosure was the usual consequence to any member who plays the spectator role in an ungracious manner. But even the most experienced leader will be surprised at times by the outcome of a subtle change in group norms and the emergence of nonofficial leaders in the group.

The encounter/sensitivity group movement of the 1960s and early 1970s, the heyday of small groups in American history, forced those professional organizations whose ranks included many who claimed expertise in group work to careful scrutiny of the ethical issues involved in running groups of all kinds, but especially "growth groups." The distinguishing feature of growth groups was the assumption that the members were relatively psychologically intact individuals who were seeking, not remedial help, but "self-actualization." Given this assumption, a number of things followed, including the increased latitude of groups to decide their own agendas, and the decreased need for guidance from expert leaders. In the first encounter/sensitivity groups, leaders typically lead the group members through structured exercises which were designed to expose hidden feelings and attitudes. But as group members went from group to group, more and more of them became exercise-wise and began to suggest and lead such exercises themselves. Also, leaders and members became increasingly creative in designing new experiences "on the spot." Finally, professionally trained leaders became superfluous--in fact, it seemed anybody and everybody who had been in several groups was willing and able to lead one himself. The language of group participation became (and is) distorted--instead of saying, "I was in a group led by Jill and John X," it became fashionable to say, "I worked with Jill and John X," as if the group member was a co-leader.

More disturbing, perhaps, was the accumulating evidence that there was negative "fallout" from encounter groups, and not just from nonprofessionally led ones. Estimates of "casualties" ranged from less than one percent to a high of fifty percent (Galinsky & Schopler, 1977). Probably the most comprehensive study was conducted at Stanford University on 210 students who had enrolled in an encounter course (Lieberman, Yalom, & Miles, 1973). The students were divided into 17 groups using 10 different approaches, including a National Training Laboratory model, Gestalt therapy, and "Esalen Eclectic." Despite the fact that the leaders had been screened as being experienced and esteemed by their colleagues, that 50 percent of the students had already had encounter group experiences, that they were warned beforehand that the experience might be stressful, and that they were informed of sources of help should they become emotionally stressed, one student committed suicide, and a number of others had less severe negative reactions, including three psychotic decompensations. A "casualty" was defined as:

> an individual who, as a direct result of his experience in the encounter group, became more psychologically distressed/or employed more maladaptive mechanisms of defense. Furthermore, to be so defined this negative change must not be transient, but enduring, as judged eight months after the group experience. (p. 171)

Almost 10 percent of those who completed 50 percent of the group meetings met this definition. The suicide victim did not, since he was receiving psychotherapy from two sources and was in another encounter group within this same time period. Group leaders "whose style is characterized by high aggressive stimulation, high charisma, high individual focus, high support, and high confrontation" were most apt to have casualties in their groups (p. 174). Overall, the leaders only perceived three percent of the participants as having undergone negative change, and identified only two of the 16 casualties (pp. 96, 176). Group members, in response to the question, "Who was hurt by the group?" were able to identify all but four of the casualties.

This sort of documented evidence of the potential destructiveness of encounter/sensitivity groups corresponded all to well with growing public distrust of such groups, and the professional reaction was soon forthcoming. A spate of articles (e.g.: Gazda, Duncan, & Sisson, 1971; Patterson, 1972; Peters, 1973; Zimpfer, 1971; Crogan, 1974; and Duncan, 1976) resulted, and the APA responded with "Guidelines for Psychologists Conducting Growth Groups" in 1973.

This adoption of the term "Growth Group" to stand for encounter and sensitivity groups has persisted and indicates an increased domain. The emphasis is still on enhancement of understanding and skills, rather than remediation, but the interpersonal element, especially the head-on encounter aspect that was previously featured, has diminished in favor of a broader range of concerns and means. In fact, the guidelines for growth groups readily apply to any type of group.

Application and Development of Guidelines

So far I have attempted only to sketch the situation, delineating its major complexities and distinguishing characteristics. I have made no attempt to resolve the multitude of ethical issues which have arisen in the course of this description. It is now time to face up to this monumental task. As aids in this task, I shall utilize the ethical codes developed by the APA, the APGA, and the Association for Specialists in Group Work (ASGW), but, as will soon be evident, some extrapolation and some bold independent assertions are necessary in order to deal with all of the issues that are presented. We shall proceed roughly in the order with which the issues were raised.

How Prevent Undue Group Pressure?

The potency of group pressure is most vividly apparent in the cases of The "Nonparticipant" (p. 194) and Let's explore our Unconscious (p. 196). It is a natural consequence of the dual role of group members as both clients and assistant leaders. As such, it is most apt to occur in "growth groups" where the members are expected to be capable of assisting the leader, but, as we have seen with the patient in the "resocialization ward" (p. 199), it may also happen with peer groups in institutions when such groups are given authority to grant to or withhold from its members certain rewards. Group pressure, in the abstract, is neither a negative nor a positive influence upon members; but, in the particular, it can precipitate quite negative reactions by individual members, and thus must be carefully monitored by the leader.

Several ways of instituting control have been suggested. Two ways are really catchalls for almost any given ethical problem in group work--screening of members for the group and obtaining informed consent to the goals and procedures of the group. Obviously, the two can be related, at least in time, in that part of the screening interview (or other procedure) can be devoted to informing the prospective members about the group. Specifically, with respect to the dual role of group members, the ability of members to assume the "assistant leader" role can be ascertained in the screening procedure and invoked as a criterion for acceptance/rejection for group membership. If a prospective member does not seem able to focus on anyone's concerns but her own, it is questionable how appropriate any group is for such a person, especially a growth group. The potential for learning within the group to focus on others' concerns is, of course, also relevant in this decision.

Other criteria for acceptance are the judgments as to the potential ability of the applicant to withstand group pressure, to constructively use criticism, and to control any tendency to negatively distort neutral or mildly negative comments. Zimpfer (1971, p. 282) goes so far as to advocate that group leaders should help prospective members develop "decision-making skills and independence of judgment" even before entering a group.

Screening of growth group members is proposed as an ethical guideline by several of the codes: the 1981

APGA Ethical Standards, the 1973 APA "Guidelines for Psychologists Conducting Growth Groups," and the 1980 Association for Specialists in Group Work (ASGW) "Ethical Guidelines for Group Leaders." The latter states:

> The group leader shall conduct a pre-group interview with each prospective member for purposes of screening, orientation, and, insofar as possible, shall select group members whose needs and goals are compatible with the established goals of the group; who will not impede the group process; and whose well-being will not be jeopardized by the group experience. (Section A-2)

Once the group is started, it is up to the leader to prevent undue group pressure upon individual members:

> Group leaders shall protect member rights against physical threats, intimidation, coercion, and undue peer pressure insofar as is reasonably possible. (ASGW Guidelines for Group Leaders, Section B-1, as cited in Roberts, 1982)

One way this can be done is reported in the Yalom and Lieberman article on the encounter group study (1971):

> One type B leader who led a low-risk group, very explicitly asked each member repeatedly to make the choice of what he wanted to work on and how far he wished to proceed in a particular meeting. This is in marked contrast to type A leaders who made that choice for their members and developed a hot-seat, no-escape-hatch format. (p. 26)

Informed Consent: Inasmuch as the members are expected to actively cooperate in establishing a therapeutic milieu, they should be so informed prior to entering the group, or, at the latest, very early in the group sessions. Such information will be as specific as the applicants/members can be expected to understand at each stage of the group process, and may well involve modeling how to express their negative reactions to other group members in ways which are least apt to be threatening and yet specific enough to be helpful. In the case of The "Nonparticipant" (p. 194), such prior training may well have greatly attenuated the potentially negative effects of the confrontation.

Another aspect of informed consent that is relevant to group pressure concerns the provision for voluntary participation in the group. Obviously, pressure to conform is attenuated to the degree that it is clear that members are free not to participate, and may withdraw from group membership at any time. The APA Guidelines say simply:

> Entering into a growth group experience should be on a voluntary basis; any form of coercion to participate is to be avoided. (Section 1)

It also asserts members' rights to leave the group at any time (Section gii). Similar statements are found in the ASGW Guidelines (Section A-7).

Information regarding the permissible limits of the group experience may also be appropriate prior to the actual onset of the group. Some writers have suggested this information be conveyed in a group contract which all members have to sign. One such contract even has a provision regarding use of drugs in group sessions, which may have been of aid to our besieged leader in Let's explore our Unconscious (p. 196). It states: "I will not use alcohol or drugs during group sessions. Smoking will be determined by the group members" (Johnson & Johnson, 1980, p. 96).

Advertising the group is another aspect of informed consent inasmuch as accurate advertisements inform prospective members of what to expect, both in terms of group goals and procedures, and with respect to the leader's qualifications. However, they have little to do with group pressure, so the reader is referred to pages 24-25 for further discussion of this topic.

Confidentiality

The other issue directly concerned with the dual role of members is the matter of confidentiality. As was stated earlier, only the group leader, if he is a professional practitioner, is obligated to maintain the confidence divulged by group members during the group sessions. Group members have neither an ethical nor a legal duty to do so, although, individually, they may assume a moral duty to retain such confidences.

How important it is that there be some modicum of confidentiality will vary from group to group. If Slovenko's experience (1977) is typical, the importance attributed to confidentiality differs between group leaders and members. He found in his interviews of group members that they were far less concerned about confidentiality than were their group leaders. These factors make it problematic that one can establish with any surety a group norm of confidentiality. Also, even if there is apparent group agreement to strict confidentality, the legal validity of such contracts is questionable, as we shall soon see.

Some group sessions have been held on public television, others have been developed for distribution as training films for audiences whose only credential for viewing the film may be having heard about it and having an interest in seeing it. Obviously, confidentiality is a null issue in such instances. At the other end of the dimension are individuals who are in sensitive public or private positions and whose jobs or political influence may be jeopardized by disclosure of the simple fact that they are members of a therapy group. Even if the group were a "growth group," they would have legitimate fears that disclosure of any personal weaknesses within the group to people outside the group might be used against them. Thus, the degree of confidentiality that is important to maintain, and the degree of importance of maintaining it, vary tremendously from group to group as well as among the individuals within each group. It is neither possible nor desirable to set a single norm to fit all occasions.

That the group leader has a responsibility to openly introduce the matter is not an issue, however, at least according to established guidelines. The ASGW code says it most succintly:

> Group leaders shall protect group members by defining clearly what confidentiality means, why it is important, and the difficulties involved in enforcement. (Section A-3)

Notice that this statement falls short of demanding that group leaders press for a group norm of confidentiality. It recognizes that to do so may: (1) be unrealistic; (2) push underground any resistance to such a norm and hence encourage deception; and (3) may actually push the group towards an intimacy they may not be willing to achieve, at least at the point of the group's inception (Lakin, cited in Capuzzi & Muffet, 1980).

The 1981 APGA Ethical Standards, however, go further:

> In a group counseling setting, the counselor must set a norm of confidentiality regarding all group participants' disclosures. (Section B-2)

Davies (1982, p. 200), in a survey of 12 groups and group leaders, found that even when the group leader explicitly told the members that "anything said in the group was to remain in the group, 24 of the 57 members [of the seven groups in which this was done] thought they could inform a friend and/or family member. . . . 13 of these members actually told a friend what another group member said, and 12 told a family member." So much for leaders "setting" group norms, at least in an informal way.

One proposed solution to this problem of trying to establish a secure group norm of confidentiality has been to have group members sign a group contract. R.K. Schwitzgebel (1980, Appendix M) has actually copyrighted such a statement of agreement, which even provides for monetary reimbursement to the "wronged" member by those members who breach her confidences. The legal validity of this contract has not as yet been determined. The author, himself, admits that, "to date . . . there are few precedents supporting an action for violation of confidentiality based on contract theory" (pp. 209-210). The primary advantage of a signed agreement would be that members would have available to them in written form exactly what it is that they have agreed to in the way of maintaining confidentiality.

Given this lack of firm assurance, even under the best of conditions, that what is disclosed in group sessions is to be kept within the confines of the group, it is little wonder that the courts are loath to recognize such communications as privileged.

> Present-day privilege laws . . . offer no assurance whatever in personal injury litigation where a group member makes his health a matter of issue. Likewise, should one member assault another in the course of therapy, and a suit ensue, the occurrence would not be shielded. (Slovenko, 1977, p. 415)

In instances where a non group member requests disclosure of what transpired in the group, a somewhat more optimistic situation obtains:

> For the most part, privilege tends to be ill-defined for the situation in which two or more clients are seen simultaneously in therapy. Since privilege only covers communications that are uttered in confidence, the question . . . arises of whether privilege covers client-to-client communications. Since some states extend privilege to persons who aid in the delivery of personal services and are present during the uttering of confidential information (e.g., nurses, technicians), a liberal interpretation of privilege statutes might show that family members (or group members) are agents of the therapist. (Attributed to Bersoff & Jain, cited in Margolin, 1982)

Colorado has provided some protection in a statutory amendment which "prohibits the questioning of any persons who have participated in group therapy sessions 'concerning any knowledge gained during the course of such therapy without the consent of the person or persons to whom the testimony sought relates'" (Schwitzgebel et al., 1980, p. 209). The American Group Psychotherapy Association is reportedly seeking further such enactments of testimonial privilege (Slovenko, 1977, p. 410).

As of the time of Slovenko's 1977 article, there had been no litigation that he could find which involved breach of confidentiality in a group setting. He points out that since groups seldom keep records of their interactions; it would be difficult for such a case to reach the courts.

How Handle Differential Readiness of Group Members?

The fact that the group members do not start a group from the same "starting line" and run breast to breast only in passing, results in the likelihood that some members at any given point in the group process are apt to "be out of it," and not getting any benefit from the group experience. In a multi-client situation it is literally impossible for the therapist to observe the general ethical rubric of always keeping the welfare of each client uppermost, since, under this rubric, he would, at times, have to deal simultaneously and individually with two or more clients. One way of coping with this dilemma is to provide special between-sessions help to those clients who are out of step with the rest of the group, analogous to the tutoring and special lab sessions offered to students who have fallen behind in their classes. If, at the end of the group, a member is not yet ready for termination, as was the case with <u>The "Unfinished" Client</u> (p. 196), then a follow-up help of some type is called for. Again the ASGW Guidelines say it best:

> Group leaders shall provide between-session consultation to group members and follow-up after termination of the group as needed or requested. (Section B-10)

<u>Encourage/Prohibit Out-of-Group Socializing</u>?

Although it is possible to take a pro or con position regarding encouraging or discouraging socializing of group members outside of group sessions, it makes no sense to do so in an overall, absolute fashion. One survey of group psychotherapists reflected the split in opinion on this issue: 54 percent believed such socializing to be contrary to the best interests of the members, and 33 percent "ignored" the problem (Mykel, 1971). I hold with the "ignorers" in the sense that I think it depends on the nature of the group as to whether or not out-of-group socialization is appropriate. In the case of <u>The Extramarital Group Affair</u> (p. 195) it is clear that certain social contacts between group members of different couples can destroy the group, and must be discouraged. With in-house groups, such as inmates on a psychiatric ward, a rule against social contacts outside the group might work to enforce the very tendency to withdrawal that the group may have been formed to counteract. Similarly, with community interpersonal anxiety groups, out-of-group interaction among group members can be conceived of as a bridge to forming relationships with non group members. Interestingly, a study of the effects of encouraging/discouraging out-of-group socializing among group members who were out-patients of a community health center indicated, contrary to the researcher's expectation, superior functioning for the members of the groups which discouraged socializing (Freedman, 1976).

In any case, the effects of out-of-group socializing are far from predictable in any but a few situations and may not be controllable by the leader in most situations. Again, such control may be enhanced by having members sign a group contract containing a provision which prohibits/requires such socializing (e.g., Johnson & Johnson, 1980). Another complementary way in which control can be maintained is to set up in advance what procedures will be followed if the rule is violated, and then, of course, to follow through if a violation occurs. Thus, in the case of The Extramarital Group Affair (p. 195), the leader should have recognized in advance the possibility of such an affair developing and should have discussed this with the group. Presumably, the group members would agree to prohibiting, for the length of the group, any contacts outside of the group between mates from different couples. The leader would then ask for guidance as to how she and the group can enforce this agreement if they note what appears to be a violation of it. These procedures would then be followed, if necessary. A similar process could be followed with any other anticipated conflict situation.

This is the ideal sequence of events, uncluttered with all the monkey wrenches that reality can throw in the way. Even the wisest and most ethical of group leaders will slip up in some way, miss giving some instructions, or be caught off guard in some situations. A retrieval technique is to bring such unanticipated occurrences to the group's attention, in an explicit as necessary but non confrontative manner, and ask for help in resolving the problem. Another retrieval technique would involve individual consultation with the immediately affected members. The one thing to be avoided is to take a "stick one's head in the sand" approach and hope everything will turn out all right. Sometimes, leaving things alone will work, but the leader has the responsibility to first gather enough data to reach a judicious decision on that, or some other course of action.

How to Avoid Losing Control of "Growth Groups"

At one time it was argued by several writers that it was not necessary, and even counterproductive, to establish limits on the activities of growth groups.

> The law sets limits on the behavior that one individual may show towards another, and these limits will surely apply within a group if its members call for aid. If they do not

> seek the protection of the law, then can we, as psychologists, set limits when the individual does not? Can we deny to any psychologist--or to anyone else--the right to lead a group based on his own responsibility, any group whatsoever, with whatever goals? Can we set ethical limits on whether a trainer should be able to choose to assault a group member, or to strip her, if in the situation, he thinks it appropriate, and she elected to accept it. . . .
>
> I think we cannot interfere, provided--and here we do encounter a principle that cannot and must not be violated--the individual in the group has freely chosen to join it, and to accept its styles. (Verplanck, cited in Patterson, 1972, p. 93)

A similar stance is assumed by Corsini:

> I think that the best thing right now is hands off. It is probably best not to try any policing. We just don't know enough. . . . We are in a mad wild period of uncontrolled growth, development and experimentation, and I think this is good. (Cited in Patterson, 1972, p. 93)

Well, we have survived this "mad wild period" and have rediscovered the effects of group and leader pressure upon the "free choice" of individual group members, with the result that a number of ethical guidelines have been adopted to prevent further casualties such as Yalom and Lieberman discovered in their study. Nevertheless, the basic issue of how to institute sufficient control to prevent casualties, and yet to allow creative experimentation by and within the group, might profit from some further examination and articulation of guidelines.

What is the responsibility of the leader in these instances where the group apparently has freely chosen to engage in an activity which, in the leader's opinion, is illegal or has other risks, the nature and probability of occurrence of which may not be immediately clear? In Let's explore our Unconscious (p. 196) one risk is that the group will be discovered taking an illegal drug. In other situations, such as disrobing in order to overcome fears of ridicule or shame with respect to one's body, engaging in marathon sessions in order to see what emerges when people are physically and/or psychologically worn down, or engaging in "group gropes" in order to experience one's feelings regarding personal space, the risk may be that one or more members will not handle the situation well, either at the time or later. Instead of "working things out," defensive, regressive reactions may set in. But without risk, there may be no progress.

One aspect of the leader's ethical responsibility is clear and has already been mentioned--and that is to carefully check with group members on an individual basis to be sure they are exercising their own independent judgments, and not merely succumbing to what they believe others want or have found to be true. Beyond that, it seems to me the leader has the responsibility to help the group identify the risks--physical, legal, and psychological--that are associated with the planned activities. He also has to encourage them to seriously consider these risks and not dismiss them in the heat of the moment. This may involve suggesting the group "think on it" for a week and then decide. Finally, the leader should decide for himself whether or not he wants to assume his special portion of risks, and not participate unless he is willing to accept the possible consequences. In the case of activities with legal implications, he may well seek legal consultation before deciding. Of course, any leader who works for an agency would jeopardize his job if he were to condone, implicitly or otherwise, any illegal activities in his group.

This ends our review of generic, clinical ethical issues. The next and final chapter is devoted to exploring ways of monitoring and handling violations that do occur.

CHAPTER XII

"POLICING" THE PROFESSION

Previously our concern has been on what the ethical issues are and how they are expressed in various codes of ethics. This chapter is a natural consequence of such a concern: Issues which are treated as only theoretical, result in codes which are only "on paper," whereas real sensitivity to issues may be expected to result in respect for, and adherence to those regulations and guidelines whose purpose it is to protect the public and insure the integrity of the profession. One test of the significance of the codes that professional groups have developed for their practitioners is the degree to which the practitioners conform to them; another is the vigor with which they are enforced. As we have already seen in Chapter VII on licensing, there are those who have found the implementation of licensing statutes wanting. Hogan (1979), for example, has said:

> A close analysis of licensing laws reveals that they have significant problems in performing their intended purpose of public protection. It is questionable whether the current credentials have much relationship with competent practice. It is indisputable that licensing boards have done a poor job of disciplining incompetent or unethical practitioners. (Vol. I, p. 4)

Hogan is equally pessimistic regarding the effectiveness of malpractice suits as a means of regulating the profession:

> In addition, a consensus is growing that judicial regulation of the professions through malpractice suits has proven ineffective, as have the attempts by professional associations to regulate themselves. (Vol. I, p. 4)

I accept Hogan's analysis of the situation as it existed at the time of his monumental research into the regulation of psychotherapy, but would temper it by pointing out that since then several changes have occurred which support a somewhat more optimistic view. I refer to the recent revisions of the Ethical Principles (1981), the Specialty Guidelines (1981), the

Ethical Standards (1981) of the American Personnel and Guidance Association (APGA), and The Principles of Medical Ethics: with Annotations especially applicable to Psychiatry (1981), as well as corresponding changes in casebooks. None of these new codes is considered a finished work, and the respective organizations have established committees devoted to further refinement of the codes as well as development of proposals for special situations and clientele, such as APA's Task Force on Minority Education and Training which was established in 1981. It is apparent, at least at the national organizational level, that there is a great deal of effort being extended to educate, guide, and regulate the profession regarding ethical and legal issues. How much of this does or will sift down to the general membership remains to be seen.

My purpose in this chapter is to inform practitioners of the various resources and procedures available to them for implementation of ethical courses of action. I have also taken the liberty to suggest some general procedures myself which I believe conform to the spirit of the existing regulations and guidelines. As is my custom, I first illustrate some representative dilemmas in concrete form. In the first case, "My therapist took advantage of me," you are asked to assume the role of a therapist whose client complains about a former therapist, who apparently has treated her unethically--what is your responsibility as her current therapist? In the second case, "We thought you knew what you were doing," the client is complaining about your incompetence, and the question is what obligation do you have to acknowledge and further the complaint. In the third case, How to build a Private Practice, a fellow instructor appears to be sollіciting clients among the students--what is your responsibility in the matter? In the final case, The "Unforgettable Learning Experience," you see an ad by another psychologist which appears to offer more than might be delivered. What obligation do you have to support "truth in advertising" in the profession, and how do you discharge it?

The first commentary section describes the four basic ethical codes of the American Psychological Association and the corresponding codes of other professional organizations. The "casebooks" which show how the APA codes are applied in actual situations are then listed. Another section informs the reader where to obtain the names and addresses of APA boards and committees that may be involved in ethical complaints.

The following section reviews various types of ethical complaints and the procedures for processing them. A flow chart is provided that handles a variety of complaints within a single framework. Finally, the outcomes of complaints--the kind of sanctions available to various regulatory entities, and who is informed of what actions--are articulated.

Illustrative Cases

"My therapist took advantage of me": Fay is a conventionally attractive but obviously insecure young woman whom you are seeing in therapy. In the course of the therapy she claims that her former therapist "took advantage" of her, that under the guise of providing her personal support he met her outside of office hours and eventually entered a sexual liaison with her. Soon thereafter he discontinued the therapy sessions as "superfluous" and continued to see her once or twice a week, but only in her home. She found this increasingly demeaning and unsatisfactory and finally refused to see him anymore.

From what you know of the client, you have no reason to doubt the veracity of her allegations and can well imagine how she might allow herself to be exploited by a male authority figure. Her former therapist is a colleague of yours, a licensed psychologist in the state. What is you responsibility in the matter?

1. Should you treat this as any other situation in which this client would complain of being "taken advantage of"?--that is, would you simply incorporate this complaint into the therapy and help her work through it? If she has no special wish to rectify the injustice, there is no reason to convince her to do so. Your task is solely to help her avoid being placed in such a position again.

2. Should you suggest to Fay that she could pursue this matter by formally complaining to the state licensing board, that this clearly was unethical behavior on the part of her former therapist and that he should have to face up to the consequences? If she decided to complain to the board, should you provide emotional support and advice during the course of the proceedings?

3. Do you perceive an obligation to confront your colleague yourself with this complaint, assuming

Fay does not object? Suppose your colleague admits the behavior, but sees nothing wrong with it since he did terminate therapy as soon as he saw that the sexual involvement was going to be more than "incidental." What then do you do?

"We thought you knew what you were doing": You have been seeing a young married couple for counseling. Their original complaints centered aroung the inequity of the division of household chores (his standards are higher than hers, and so he ends up having to clean up after her), financial disagreements (she considers him too "tight-fisted"; he says she "throws money away"), and sexual incompatibility (they haven't enjoyed having sex together for two months). You have tried a number of approaches with them, but to no avail. Their initial optimism regarding counseling has changed to disappointment and now anger. They have been talking with other couples who have seen other counselors and "everyone else is doing great." They ask if you have ever done marriage counseling before, and you have to admit that you haven't. This makes them even angrier, and they claim you should have so informed them at the outset. They are thinking of pursuing a formal complaint process. Which of the following options seem most ethical to you?

1. Point out to them that you are but a "tool," and how they use you is up to them--that no one can solve their problems but themselves and making you the scapegoat isn't going to help. That, as a matter of fact, this characterizes their basic problem--unwillingness to accept responsibility for each of their own actions. If they do that, they will find your counseling helpful.

2. Admit you should have warned them about your lack of experience in this area. Offer to refund them their money and to find a suitable referral. Inform them of the procedures for complaining to the ethics committee of the state professional organization, of which you are a member.

3. Some combination of the two approaches--such as admitting you may have let them assume more competency and experience on your part than you possess, and yet pointing out that, even so, they had a role in the matter.

How to build a Private Practice: Ann, a fellow instructor in clinical psychology, has a part-time private practice. Most of it seems to consist of present or former students of hers, especially those she has seen in supervision. Several of these students have talked with you and with other members of the department and have openly stated that they are seeing Ann for therapy. When asked how that came about, their response is that Ann either asked to see them after class or saw them in a supervisory session, at which time she offered her observations of some behavior indicative of personality problems that were likely to affect their performance as future therapists. She stated that, in her opinion, they needed personal therapy and she would be willing to provide it. None of them report any direct threat that their grades would be affected or that they would get a bad recommendation if they didn't follow through with Ann's suggestions.

Do you, as a recipient of this information, have any responsibility in this matter? and, if so, what might you do about it?

The "Unforgettable Learning Experience": You are perusing the newspaper and run across a prominent ad describing a training program as being an "unforgettable learning experience" and one that would teach a form of psychotherapy "that works." You notice the ad mentions a local psychologist--a "Ph.D. and member of the American Psychological Association" --as being the trainer. You do not know the individual. What should you do?

1. Nothing. The ad in no way directly affects you, and as far as you know it could be relatively accurate.

2. Write the APA, include a copy of the ad, and ask them to look into the matter. If so, why?--what is unethical about such an ad? Where do you find out whom to contact in APA and what the address is?

Commentary

In order to determine if, in fact, an ethical violation has occurred, it is necessary to be acquainted with the ethical principles involved. In order to understand the application of these principles it is helpful to have cases developed which illustrate their usage. In order to know to whom and where to refer violations and complaints, it is necessary to have a list of the various referral sources, their addresses and a description of their functions. This information is provided in the immediately following sections.

Ethical Codes

There are four basic ethical codes that have been developed by the American Psychological Association that are currently in force. Two of them replace previous codes, and a new, expanded version of another will soon be released. Each is designed for a different audience and subject matter, although they interface broadly. Below is a description of each code and its year of last revision.

Ethical Principles of Psychologists (1981) (Appendix A): This is the basic generic code to which all APA members are committed. It represents a substantial revision of the latest Ethical Standards (1979), which it replaces, and includes a new tenth principle entitled "Care and Use of Animals."

The corresponding codes for other organizations, some members of which practice psychotherapy, include: National Association of Social Workers, Inc.: Code of Ethics (1980); American Personnel and Guidance Association: Ethical Standards (1981); American Psychiatric Association: The Principles of Medical Ethics with Annotations especially applicable to Psychiatry (1981); and American Association for Marriage and Family Therapy: Code of Ethical Principles for Family Therapists (1982).

Standards for Providers of Psychological Services (1977): As the title indicates this set of guidelines is directed at those who are involved in the direct provision of psychological services to others--practitioners in clinical, counseling, industrial-organizational, and school psychology. However, no division between the responsibilities of the four types of practitioners is made; rather the standards refer to psychological functions which may be common to all practitioners. "Minimally acceptable" levels of quality assurance and performance are established. They apply not only to individual providers of such services as evaluation, program development, consultation, and supervision, but also to psychological service units. The units are responsible for provision of adequate staffing, of adequate information regarding the services to users, of a suitable environment to facilitate "optimal human functioning," and of a record-keeping system that protects the confidentiality of the users.

Specialty Guidelines for the Delivery of Services (1981): This is an elaboration of the Standards for Providers of Psychological Services for the specialties of clinical (Appendix B), counseling, industrial-organizational, and school psychology.

> [They] are intended to educate the public, the profession, and other interested parties regarding specialty professional practices. They are also intended to facilitate the continued systematic development of the profession.

A different set of guidelines is elaborated for each of the four specialties, albeit the major divisions in each set parallel those of the Standards, and many subunits thereof use similar or even identical wording, especially for clinical and counseling psychology. Each set is preceeded by a definition of the class of psychologists it covers.

Ethical Principles in the Conduct of Research with Human Participants (1973): This document was developed by the Committee for Protection of Human Subjects (CPHS) of APA, and an updated version will soon be forthcoming. The document provides full discussion of the ethical issues that "arise in the actual course of planning and conducting psychological research with human beings" in an attempt "to foster responsible decisions" (p. 6). Many issues are left unresolved since there are no clear right or wrong courses of action, given the complexities of the practical situations. A special section is planned consisting solely of incidents linked with specific ethical principles.

Casebooks

"Complaints against psychologists adjudicated informally by APA's Committee on Scientific and Professional Ethics and Conduct" (CSPEC) (Sanders, 1979), "Formal and informal adjudication of ethics complaints against psychologists" (Sanders & Keith-Spiegel, 1980) and "Procedures for responding to ethics complaints against psychologists" (Hare-Mustin & Hall, 1981) are articles that consist of selected, disguised summaries of cases involving alleged violations that came before CSPEC during the immediately previous year. They have appeared in the December issue of the *American Psychologist* for the past three years, and presumably this practice will be continued. These articles replace the *Casebook on Ethical Standards of Psychologists* (American Psychological Association, 1974), that became outdated with successive revision of the *Ethical Standards* (1974, 1977, 1979), and thus represent "the state of the art" with regard to what is considered unethical by the profession and how such violations are handled.

"Casebook for providers of psychological services" (Committee on Professional Standards, 1982) appeared for the first time in the June edition of the *American Psychologist* and consists of summaries of three cases--one each for counseling, industrial-organizational, and school psychology--that were developed to illustrate the application of the guidelines found in the *Specialty Guidelines*. The Committee on Professional Standards (COPS) of the Board of Professional Affairs (BPA) plans to develop three to four such cases each year and present them in the June edition of the *American Psychologist*.

Names and Addresses

The annual June issue of the *American Psychologist* contains the current names of each of the members of the various APA boards, committees and task forces. It also provides the names of the officers of APA-affiliated state, provincial and territorial psychological associations, the names and addresses of the secretaries of these associations, and the names and addresses of the secretaries of the state and provincial boards and agencies for the statutory licensure or certification of psychologists. Should you want to correspond with an APA board, committee or task force, or with the state, provincial and territorial psychological associations you can either write in care of APA, or locate the address of one of the officers in a recent APA membership directory. APA's address is:

American Psychological Association, Inc.
1200 Seventeenth Street, NW
Washington, D.C. 20036

Procedures for Handling Complaints

This section reviews mandatory and recommended procedures for handling complaints. I will first describe procedures that are germane to particular types of complaints, and then note the general features that apply to all complaints.

Direct Complaints--Clients to their Therapist: Hare-Mustin et al. (1979), in their signal article regarding the responsibility of psychotherapists for recognizing and promoting the rights of clients, made several suggestions for therapists whose clients complain to them about the therapy they are receiving. Most important is the advice not to assume that any complaint is solely or simply another instance of distorted perception by the client; that, in fact, a complaint may have a "reality component" that should be "respected and validated" (p. 10). Such would seem to be true in the illustrative case, "We thought you knew what you were doing" (p. 218) since the counselor had, as a matter of fact, not had any prior experience in marriage counseling and had not informed the couple beforehand.

Once a valid or partially valid complaint has been made, what responsibility does the therapist have to implement it, to "cut her own throat" by forwarding it to a regulatory board? Hare-Mustin et al. admit that "it may be difficult for therapists to suggest means of protest when the client is complaining about the therapist's own practices." Also, "paradoxically, at this point, when the information is most needed, it may be least useful because the client no longer trusts the therapist" (p. 15). Given these difficulties, they recommend that clients be informed at an early opportunity of grievance procedures, i.e., before any complaint is apt to occur.

Provision of such information would not, of course, preclude trying to work out with the client(s) any legitimate complaint in an open, non defensive manner, thus obviating any need on the client's part to proceed further.

Indirect Complaints--Clients about their Therapists: A more common situation is for clients to complain about former therapists to their current therapists, such as illustrated in the case, "My therapist took advantage of me," (p. 217). What is the responsibility of the current therapist in such situations? As any practitioner knows all such allegations must be taken with a grain of salt, that is, they are not likely to represent a complete, "unvarnished" account of what actually occurred. Some allegations, even if true, would not constitute ethical violations, but simply dissatisfaction by the client with the therapist's failure to live up to the client's expectations. Assuming, however, an ethical violation may have occurred, what should be done? [1]

First of all, it is appropriate to discuss the matter with the client and determine what he is willing to do to try to pursue the complaint. The client may decide not to confront his former therapist directly but does want to pursue another option. One that may be applicable is for the client to give permission to his current therapist to take the matter up with his former therapist. This would be especially appropriate if the matter were fairly minor and would seem to accord with a recommendation found in the Hare-Mustin & Hall "casebook" article (1981):

> It is clear that not all ethical violations should be brought to CSPEC. In accord with Principle 7g of the Ethical Principles of Psychologists, psychologists are expected to attempt informally to resolve issues of ethical violations by other psychologists. Such informal solutions are usually appropriate for misconduct of a minor matter and/or when such misconduct appears to be due to a member's lack of sensitivity, knowledge or experience. (p. 1495)

Obviously, therapists do not routinely volunteer to intercede in this way since it promotes client dependence rather than encouraging independent action. However, in some instances it may be appropriate, especially if the therapist has heard of several such ethical violations from different clients, none of whom has been willing to pursue the complaint himself. In this case it may be the therapist can even guarantee her client a measure of anonymity in breaching the matter with the offending therapist. Furthermore, violations

---

[1] One technical point that should be kept in mind is that complaints by non APA members about violations that occurred over five years "from the time the complainant discovered or reasonably should have discovered the alleged unethical behavior" may not be admissible according to CSPEC rules (Sanders & Keith-Spiegel, 1980, p. 1096).

involving sexual intimacy between therapists and clients during the course of therapy are not apt to be of a minor type requiring only education of the offending therapist. However, allegations of such intimacy may be exaggerated and could be clarified through discussion with the therapist.

Should the matter not prove to be a minor ethical violation, then the client should be fully informed of the more formal complaint channels--the therapist's supervisor, if any, or employer and the ethics committees of any professional organizations to which the therapist belongs, both state or provincial and national. The most potent options, in terms of possible negative effects on the offending therapist, are the state licensing board and the court. Once a formal complaint has been lodged at any level, the possibility exists that it will be forwarded or made accessible to an affiliated organization and the court. A motion was introduced at the January, 1981, APA Council of Representatives meeting, "requesting that CSPEC, BSERP [Board of Social and Ethical Responsibility for Psychology] , and BPA [Board of Professional Affairs] recommend to the Council a plan for integrating national and state ethics committees and ethics activities so as to avoid duplication and systematize ethics activities" (Abeles, 1982, p. 644). Currently, CSPEC "may disclose information to members, committees, and divisions of the Association; affiliated State and Regional Associations; the ABPP; state licensing and certification boards, as the Committee shall deem necessary to maintain ethical practice by psychologists at the highest professional level" (Article X, Section 5, Paragraph 2 of APA Bylaws). Also, "all records and proceedings of peer review and ethics committees can be subject to subpoena" (Sinnet & Linford, 1982, p. 332).

Violation but no Complaint: Sometimes a fellow therapist may be engaged in what appears to you to be unethical practice, but there are no complainants in the usual sense--that is, those most directly affected inform you of the practice but do not really complain about it. This was the situation with the students who became clients in their instructor's private practice in the How to build a Private Practice illustrative case (p. 219). Although the students did not complain about being unduly pressured to become clients, it is difficult to see how it would be possible for some pressure not to exist in view of the faculty member's power to influence their future careers, either by actions taken while they were still in school, or by subsequent willingness to give positive letters of recommendation. Thus her behavior seems clearly to violate Principle 6a of the Ethical Principles:

> Psychologists are continually cognizant of their own needs and of their potentially influential position vis-a-vis persons such as clients, students, and subordinates . . . Psychologists make every effort to avoid dual relationships. . . Examples of such dual relationships include research with and treatment of employees, students, supervisees, close friends, or relatives.

Principle 7g requires psychologists to report known ethical violations by fellow psychologists. Psychiatrists admonish themselves simularly: Their code directs them to "strive to expose those physicians deficient in character or competence or who engage in fraud or deception" (American Psychiatric Association, 1981, section 2). On the one hand it is difficult to see how such admonishments are enforceable, but on the other unless psychotherapists are willing to incur the displeasure of their colleagues by pointing out professional lapses, it is hard to believe that the welfare of the public is truly being served by these codes. The codes become "window-dressing"--something to show others but basically irrelevant to actual practice. In a case where the violation is blatant and no one steps forward to report it, then the lack of action speaks loudly to all who are in a position to observe, and the reputation of the profession is bound to suffer. The meaningfulness of the codes varies in direct proportion to the willingness of its members to police themselves.

Admittedly it is a difficult and often thankless task to call a colleague to account, but sometimes it can be made easier by concerted action. Consultation with other colleagues, if available, and enlistment of their aid is an appropriate first step. The subsequent step of informally discussing the matter with the alleged offender can be devoted to ascertaining the full picture and determining her sensitivity to the ethical issues involoved. CSPEC'S policy is:

> The objective with regard to the individual shall in all cases be constructive and educative rather than punitive in character, the intent being to exert a salutary influence

> on members found to have violated ethical principles. (cited in Sanders & Keith-Spiegel, 1980, p. 1096)

If, however, the informal discussion with the offender is not productive in that it does not immediately produce or seem to promise to produce a positive change, then it becomes appropriate to proceed further. Again, CSPEC provides guidance:

> However, when the interests of the public or of the profession are in conflict with personal interests, the former must be of overriding concern. (cited in Sanders & Keith-Spiegel, 1980, p. 1096)

This does not necessarily mean a formal complaint must be filed. It may be that an administrative superior can be informed of the ethical situation. In the case of <u>How to build a Private Practice</u> (p. 219) the chairperson of the psychology department should be informed, and a few words from this person may rectify the situation.

Should such informal channels prove insufficient, or for some reason inappropriate, then the only remaining recourse is to file a formal complaint with the appropriate committee of the professional organization to which the offender belongs, such as the state psychological association ethics committee or an ethics committee of the national organization, which, for practitioner-psychologists, would in most instances be APA's Committee of Scientific and Professional Ethics and Conduct (CSPEC). If the therapist is licensed or certified by a state licensing or certification board, a formal complaint could be lodged with it. Since such boards have the authority to revoke or suspend licenses or certificates, whereas the "ultimate" penalty a professional organization can mete out is expulsion from membership, filing a complaint with state boards should probably be reserved for serious matters or when no other recourse exists.

<u>Improper Advertisement of Psychotherapeutic Services</u>: Another situation in which there may be no client complainant because clients or potential clients would lack the knowledge to recognize the breach of professional ethics occurs when a therapist's public description of his services does not accord with professional guidelines, such as Principle 4 of <u>Ethical Prin-</u>

ciples on public statements. An example was provided in the commentary section of Chapter II (p. 24) as well as in this chapter in the case, The "Unforgettable Learning Experience" (p. 219). It is undoubtedly difficult for licensed professionals to refrain from describing their services in highly positive terms, given the fact that much of the literature of the competition is loaded with superlatives. One can only hope that modest, dignified, and presumably accurate descriptions will attract the discerning seeker, and that a sufficient number of them exists to provide a reasonable income. The alternative is to engage in a war of words which threatens to degenerate into a battle of grandiose claims which reflect adversely upon all professionals involved.

Practical aspects aside, the central ethical precept underlying Principle 4 is that it is wrong to lie, to deceive by intimidating or promising that one can deliver more than can be reasonably expected, given one's own actual knowledge of the effects of any particular treatment, or, lacking that, the general repertoire of experience of the profession with such treatments. Accordingly, to describe a training program as "an unforgettable learning experience" is to intimate that it is extraordinary in some way, and not simply one of many possible programs of equal, or near-equal potential for help. To couple this with claiming to teach a form of therapy "that works" is to intimate that other potential programs by other practitioners will not work, a claim that seems irresponsible in view of the multitude of positive results claimed and to some extent documented by every school of psychotherapy.

The ad may also violate Principle 4 in the manner in which membership in the American Psychological Association is introduced. APA membership status may be included, along with other information, in announcements of professional services (Principle 4a). However, ". . . psychologists do not state APA membership or fellow status in a way to suggest that such status implies special professional competence or qualifications" (Principle 4b). Given the rather grandiose aspects of the other statements in the ad, and the fact that APA membership is highlighted rather than simply listed along with other objective qualifications, the inference could be drawn by the ad's readers that this is the mark of special competency.

Such an ad then seems a clear violation of Principle 4--what is the responsibility of a fellow psychologist who notices the ad? She is not ethically required to act, and if the ad-placer is not known to her it is easy for her to shrug her shoulders and say to herself that someone else, someone who knows this psychologist personally and who has seen the ad, should pursue the matter. Such other persons may, if they exist, say to themselves that it would be awkward for them to risk whatever personal relationship they have with the ad-placer and hope some disinterested "third-party" psychologist will act in their stead.

Suppose our ad-reader did choose to act, what are the options? Again, she could first speak to the offender informally, bringing to his attention her ethical concern and determining by his response whether or not he has knowingly violated the ethical principle, is insensitive to the violation, or ignorant and willing to be educated, or ignorant and not willing to be educated. If it appears he is recalcitrant in the matter, and especially if future actions should prove him so, then it would be appropriate to take the issue to his administrative superior, if he has any. If not, then formal complaint to a relevant professional organization or to the state licensing or certification board would be the logical next step.

Anonymous Complaints--what happens to them? The situation of the improper ad might seem, at first appearance, resolvable by turning in an anonymous complaint. After all, such an ad "speaks for itself"--i.e., there is no necessity to provide any additional evidence of a violation, so why should it be necessary to personally identify oneself as the sender of the ad, assuming it was sent to the appropriate organization? Whether or not it should be necessary, it may be so for the complaint to be acted upon. CSPEC, for example, "does not act on the basis of anonymous complaints" (Hare-Mustin & Hall, 1981, p. 1496). State professional organizations and licensing and certification boards may have similar policies, and for the large part they make sense in that it is the rare case in which the information is so patently complete that there is no need to acquire more, or to see if more is available, in order to be sure that a violation has actually occurred or to be able to judge the seriousness of it. An ad from a local paper with a circulation of a few hundred, for example, might be considered less of a violation than one appearing in a newspaper with a large circulation, or an ad which is placed in several media. Only the local sender may be able to readily provide such additional information.

CSPEC does, however, reserve the authority to act on its own initiative ("sua sponte"), and has done so on several occasions. One example was when it received, anonymously, a copy of a journal article and a copy of a dissertation whose discussion sections appeared identical, yet were allegedly by different authors (Hare-Mustin & Hall, 1981, 1501-1502).

It is also possible to keep the identity of the complainant confidential under certain circumstances. One case is reported in which this was done since release of this information might have jeopardized the informant's employment, and CSPEC was able to proceed using only available public records (Hare-Mustin & Hall, 1981, p. 1499).

Counter-Complaints--are they a Hazard? One of the disturbing aspects of the legal system is the possibility of counter-suits. In fact, one of the most common "triggers" for malpractice suits is the attempt by a psychotherapist to collect an outstanding debt by turning over the account to a collection agency or initiating civil suit (Wrights, 1981, p. 1491). CSPEC has found that "countercharges are often initiated to harass or intimidate a complainant" (Hare-Mustin & Hall, 1981, p. 1496), hence does not accept counter-complaints during the course of an investigation of a complaint. However, they may be considered after the initial complaint is settled.

Overview of Complaint Procedures and Flow Chart: A review of the preceeding sections would show that a general procedure could be derived that, with minor modifications, would apply to each of the various situations. Such a procedure is outlined in the Flow Chart that follows. According to this chart the first step is to determine whether or not there is sufficient basis to initiate a complaint. This involves validating hearsay information, insofar as this is pragmatically feasible, and consulting the ethical codes and/or those familiar enough with the codes to be able to provide an informed opinion on the matter. Client complainants would normally have to consult other psychotherapists. If the possibility exists that the alleged behavior is also illegal, an attorney could also be consulted.

The next step is to confront the apparently errant therapist and determine her side of the issue, the degree of her sensitivity to the ethical violation and her willingness to make amends, if this is a possibility. If her immediate response is not satisfactory, inform her of any contemplated further actions and provide time for the effects of this communication "to sink in." It may be that a reasonably satisfactory solution can be achieved at this initial level without going further, if the offender has a chance to reflect on the matter and has an oppportunity to rectify it herself.

If not, the next step is to take the matter to the therapist's supervisor and/or administrator, if any. Therapeutic supervisors are inevitably drawn into such complaints in any case, and indeed, their own license and/or membership in professional organizations are vulnerable if one of their supervisees acts unethically. Often the power of a supervisor or an administrator, especially if the therapist's employment is involved, is greater than that of a professional organization in which the errant therapist holds voluntary membership. For this reason, alone, it is probable an informal solution could be reached at this level. Also, for this reason, there will be instances in which it might be best to skip this step, even if it were a possibility.

The next step is to inform the ethics committee of a professional organization in which the therapist holds membership. This, then, initiates the formal complaint process which requires, except in rare instances, disclosure of the identification of the complainant to the therapist, exact specification and documentation of the complaint, and, if the complainant is a client, release of confidentiality regarding any client-therapist interactions that may be relevant to the complaint. Every attempt will be made to keep all such information confidential to the investigators, but this does preclude clients having to undergo what may prove to be emotionally stressful questioning during the course of the investigation. At the state level it is not uncommon for representatives of the state psychological organization's ethics committee to personally interview the complainant. At the national CSPEC level the investigation is more apt to be a "paper" one, without any necessity for personal appearances before hearing committees, but even such investigations can involve a number of requests for further information over a long period of time. Critics have noted that "it is not uncommon to take as long as 2 years before a case is adjudicated" (Sinnett & Linford, 1982, p. 332).

Should the therapist not be a member of a state or national professional organization, or if the violation

Flow Chart for Making Complaints regarding Unethical Behavior

A therapist ("T") has committed what appears to be an ethical violation. How might the complainant or his advocate proceed?

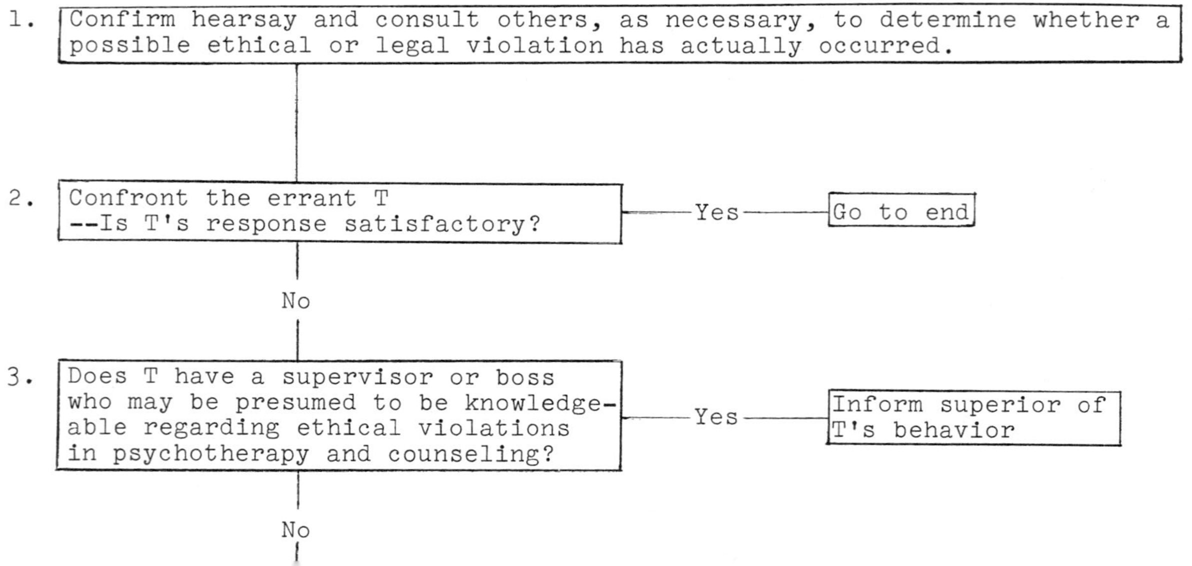

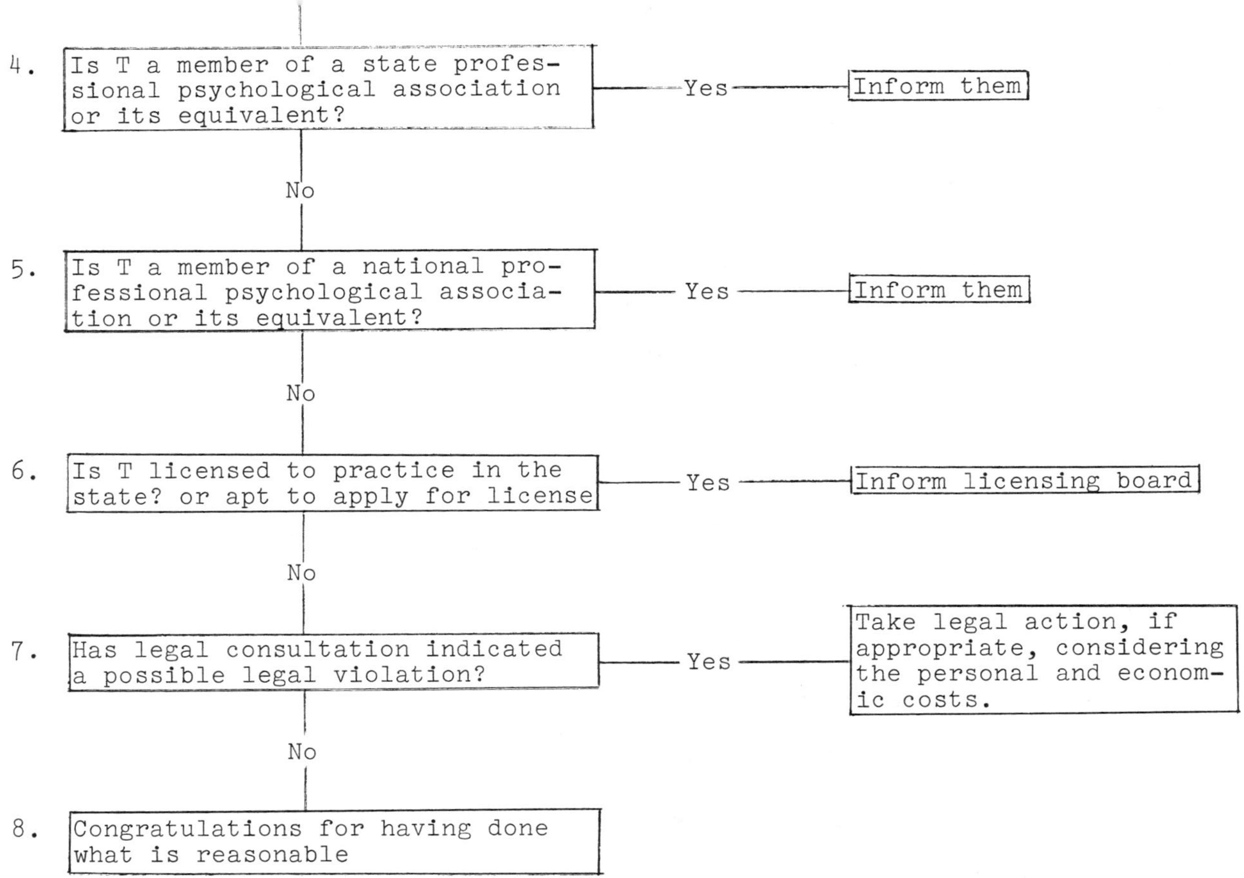
4. Is T a member of a state professional psychological association or its equivalent?
Yes
Inform them
No
5. Is T a member of a national professional psychological association or its equivalent?
Yes
Inform them
No
6. Is T licensed to practice in the state? or apt to apply for license
Yes
Inform licensing board
No
7. Has legal consultation indicated a possible legal violation?
Yes
Take legal action, if appropriate, considering the personal and economic costs.
No
8. Congratulations for having done what is reasonable

is one that clearly pertains to licensing or certification, as would be the case of someone who is using the title of "psychologist" without being licensed or certified to do so, then the complaint should be forwarded to the state licensure or certification board. Again this is a formal procedure requiring identification of the complainant, etc. as specified above.

What if nothing satisfactory to the complainant issues from any or all of the above procedures--what further steps could be considered? If the violation appears to be illegal, then it may be that a legal action could be initiated. It is possible that the therapist acted illegally and not unethically, as well as vice versa. "A member of APA may be found guilty of a misdemeanor that would have no corresponding ethical violation" (Hare-Mustin & Hall, 1981, p. 1495). It is much more likely, however, that a complaint would have both ethical and legal aspects, or only ethical aspects. But if the grounds for the ethical complaint are insufficient, it is highly dubious that they would suffice for successful legal action since the burden of proof of legal violation is apt to be more stringent and ranges from substantial evidence, to preponderance of evidence, to proof beyond a reasonable doubt, depending on the alleged violation. As we have seen in Chapter VIII on malpractice suits it is very difficult to meet the legal criteria for malpractice, especially if only verbal therapy is involved.

Another recourse the complainant could consider is to contact the original referral source and voice his dissatisfaction with the treatment or to do so with potential clients of the therapist. At some point, however, it would make sense for the individual to congratulate himself for having made a good effort to rectify what he believed to be an injustice and to go on with his life.

Possible Actions taken on Complaints

The type of action that can result from complaints that are deemed valid will depend upon the agency which executes them. Any agency, however, will dismiss complaints which seem misdirected, trivial, or lack sufficient substantiation. Even those which pass the initial screening may later be dismissed because of lack of timely follow-through by the complainant or because an informal resolution had been worked out between the complainant and the complainee during the formal proceedings. Also an agency may refer the complaint to one better equipped to handle it. In one instance a complaint was referred because a hearing officer for a licensing board had made what appeared to be a procedural error (Hare-Mustin & Hall, 1981, p. 1495).

Voluntary membership organizations are limited to imposing corrective actions on those who wish to remain members, or, in the extreme, to expelling members. This latter action, however, may have implications for obtaining or keeping employment, licensure, and malpractice insurance--so it is not entirely "toothless." The gambit of potential actions includes reprimand, requiring a cease and desist of unethical behavior, censure, stipulated resignation, requiring the offender to obtain supervision and/or personal therapy and/or further training of some specified kind and amount, placing on probation, suspending membership for specified periods of time and expulsion--in short, anything that promises to be both effective and educative. National organizations may refer members to state or regional associations for monitoring compliance.

State psychology licensing and certification boards are limited in their formal actions to those which affect the license or certificate, or which may, in the case of candidates, affect their eligibility for such status. These boards may act to deny, restrict, suspend, or revoke the offender's license or certificate. They may refer complaints about cases which do not involve currently licensed or certified individuals or applicants for licensure or certification to the appropriate legal authorities. This might occur, for instance, when a "non-psychologist" (as defined by the state statutes) holds himself out to be one in violation of state law. The boards may also refer complaints which would not affect the licensure or certification of psychologists to other appropriate individuals or groups with the consent of the complainant, or informally handle them themselves.

Who gets what Information regarding the Disposition of the Cases?

The issue of whom to inform of any actions taken in response to complaints is one which is currently still very much a matter of debate. Obviously, the complainee, the one who is the recipient of the action, is informed, but the complainant may receive only general information at best. Whether or not the complainee's colleagues or others are informed, and how, is often not spelled out and is left a matter of judgment by the agency taking the action.

There is legislation now pending before the APA membership which would make the situation somewhat clearer for CSPEC actions. Under the current bylaw (Article X, Section 5, Paragraph 2) CSPEC "may disclose information to members, committees, and divisions of the Association; affiliated State and Regional Associations, the ABPP; and state and regional licensing and certification boards, as the Committee shall deem necessary to maintain ethical practice by psychologists at the highest professional level."

The pending legislation, if adopted, would amend this legislation to extend the communication to the courts "when compelled by a validly issued subpoena or when otherwise required by law." Also, "in serious cases which have resulted in a member's probation, suspension, or stipulated resignation, the Committee may communicate these actions to legal counsel of the Association, staff of the Association's Center Office designated by the Executive Officer to assist the Committee with its work, AASPB Register and other individuals and organizations as the Committee shall deem necessary to protect the public."

Also to be added, if passed, is a directive for CPSEC to "inform the complainant and complainee of its action when the matter is resolved with the Committee, including the Principles violated, should there be any, and the rationale for its actions." Thus there would be a formal requirement to fully inform the complainant as well as the complainee of any final actions taken by CSPEC, itself.

There is already a policy to provide such information to the complainant and complainee when "formal" action has been taken, action requiring the APA Board of Directors' authority. CSPEC refers matters to this governing board "when a complainee rejects CSPEC's attempts to dispose of the matter informally, when the complainee rejects the recommendation of a stipulated resignation, or after reviewing all the information in an accepted complaint" (Hare-Mustin & Hall, 1981, p. 1504). "The Board of Directors also reports annually and in confidence to the membership the names of members who have been expelled and the respective ethical principles involved. [These names were enclosed with the dues statement in September, 1982.] The Board also notifies other entities when it deems it necessary to protect the public or to maintain the standards of APA" (Hare-Mustin & Hall, 1981, p. 1505).

State licensing and certification boards, insofar as they conduct formal investigations, whether utilizing an adversary model with both the complainant and the complainee having an attorney, or following state administrative procedures, have to make the findings available to both parties, and their attorneys, if any.

This then concludes the discussion on policing the profession. Again the readers are cautioned that each state association and state licensing or certification board will vary in terms of exact complaint procedures. Up-to-date descriptions of such procedures are usually available upon request; however, the foregoing material should be sufficient for general purposes.

Notes

1. Acker, M. Personal communication, March 24, 1982.

2. Swanson, L.M. J.D. Personal communication, January 21, 1983.

3. Spero, H. Health Services Director of SelectCare. Personal communication, February 9, 1982.

4. Swanson, J.L. Oregon counselor licensure: A status report. Printed circular distributed to Oregon psychologists and counselors, 1980.

5. Reaves, R.P. Survey of cut-off scores for EPPP. Printed reference material for the Legal Issues Workshop at 1982 APA National Conference.

References

Abeles, M. Proceedings of the American Psychological Association, Inc. for the year 1981: Minutes of the annual meeting of the council of representatives. _American Psychologist_, 1981, _37_, 632-666.

Allender, J.A. Absurdity. Letter to the editor in _APA Monitor_, March and June 1982.

American Association of Marriage and Family Therapy. _Code of Ethical Principles for Family Therapists_. Upland, CA: Author, 1982.

American Association of State Psychology Boards. _Guidelines for the employment and supervision of uncredentialed persons providing psychological services_. Montgomery, AL: Author, 1980.

American Board of Professional Psychology. _Policies and procedures for the creation of diplomates in professional psychology_. Washington, D.C.: Author, 1979.

American Personnel and Guidance Association. _Ethical Standards_. Washington, D.C.: Author, 1981.

American Psychiatric Association. _The principles of medical ethics with annotations especially applicable to psychiatry_. Washington, D.C.: Author, 1981.

American Psychological Association. *Ethical principles in the conduct of research with human participants*. Washington, D.C.: Author, 1973. (a)

American Psychological Association. Guidelines for psychologists conducting growth groups. *American Psychologist*, 1973, *28*, 933. (b)

American Psychological Association. *Casebook on Ethical Standards of Psychologists*. Washington, D.C.: Author, 1974.

American Psychological Association. *Ethical Standards of psychologists* (Rev. ed.). Washington, D.C.: Author, 1977. (a)

American Psychological Association. *Standards for providers of psychological services* (Rev. ed.). Washington, D.C.: Author, 1977. (b)

American Psychological Association. Report on the task force on the role of psychology in the criminal justice system. *American Psychologist*, 1978, *32*, 1099-1113.

American Psychological Association. Who is the client? The ethics of psychological intervention in the criminal justice system. Monahan, J. (Ed.). Washington, D.C.: Author, 1980.

American Psychological Association. Specialty Guidelines for the delivery of services. *American Psychologist*, 1981, *36*, 639-686.

American Psychological Association, American Education Research Association, & National Council on Measurement in Education. *Standards for educational and psychological tests and manuals*. Washington, D.C.: American Psychological Association, 1974.

Anderten, P., Staulcup, U. & Grisso, T. On being ethical in legal places. *Professional Psychology*, 1980, *11*, 764-773.

APA committee on legislation. A model for state legislation affecting the practice of psychology. *American Psychologist*, 1967, *22*, 1095-1103.

APA sued in Florida. *APA Monitor*, March 1982 (as corrected in April 1982, p.2) p.2.

APA cleared in Florida suit. *APA Monitor*, December 1982, p.2.

Bazar, J. Warning: sex with your therapist may be dangerous to your mental health. *APA Monitor*, October 1981, p.4.

Bergin, A.E. Carl Rogers' contribution to a fully functioning psychology. In A.R. Mahrer & L. Pearson (Eds.), *Creative developments in psychotherapy*. (Vol. 1). Cleveland, Ohio: Case Western University Press, 1971.

Bergin, A.E. Psychotherapy and religious values. *Journal of Consulting and Clinical Psychology*, 1980, *48*, 95-105.

Bersoff, D.M. Testing and the law. *American Psychologist*, 1981, *36*, 1047-1956.

Bernstein, B.C. & Lecomte, C. Licensure in psychology: alternative directions. *Professional Psychology*, 1981, *12*, 200-208.

Beutler, L.E. Toward specific psychological therapies for specific conditions. *Journal of Consulting and Clinical Psychology*, 1979, *47*, 882-897.

Brill, N.Q., Koegler, R.R., Epstein, L.J., & Forgy, E.W. Controlled study of psychiatric outpatient treatment. *Archives of General Psychiatry*, 1964, *10*, 581-595.

Budd, K.S. & Baer, D.M. Behavior modification and the law. *Journal of Psychiatry and Law*, 1976, *4*, No. 2, 171-245.

Butcher, J.N. & Koss, M.P. Research on brief and crisis-oriented therapies. In S.L. Garfield & A.E. Bergin (Eds.), *Handbook of psychotherpay and behavior change*. New York: Wiley, 1978.

Capuzzi, D., & Muffett, L. An overview of ethical standards for group facilitators. *Journal for Specialists in Group Work*, 1980, *5*, 98-106.

Chodoff, P. The effect of third-party payment on the practice of psychotherapy. *American Journal of Psychiatry*, 1972, *129*, 540-545.

Claiborn, W.L. The problem of professional incompetence. Professional Psychology, 1982, 13, 153-158.

Cleary, E.W. (Ed.). McCormick on evidence. (2nd ed.). St. Paul, Minn.: West, 1972.

Comment on Licensing. APA Monitor, September/October 1979, pp. 15, 36.

Committee for the protection of human subjects/institutional review board, University of Oregon. Policy and procedures governing the protection of human subjects. University of Oregon Graduate School, Office of Research Administration, 1982.

Committee on Professional Standards. Casebook for providers of psychological services. American Psychologist, 1982, 37, 698-701.

Corey, G., Corey, M.S., & Callanan, P. Professional and ethical issues in counseling and psychotherapy. Monterey, CA: Brook-Cole Publishing Company, 1979.

Council for the National Register of Health Service Providers in Psychology. National Register of Health Service Providers in Psychology. Baltimore, Maryland: Port City Press, 1981.

Council for the National Register of Health Service Providers in Psychology. Register Report, May 1982, No. 16, 1-6.

Council pursues ethics reforms, other business. APA Monitor, March 1981, pp. 1, 4 & 5.

Coyne, J.C. & Widiger, T.A. Toward a participatory model of psychotherapy. Professional Psychology, 1978, 9, 700-709.

Craddick, R.A. Sharing oneself in the assessment procedure. Professional Psychology, 1975, 6, 279-282.

Croghan, L.M. Encounter groups and the necessity for ethical guidelines. Journal of Clinical Psychology, 1974, 30, 438-445.

Cummings, N.A. Anatomy of psychotherapy under national health insurance. American Psychologist, 1977, 13, 711-718.

Danish, S.J. & Symer, M.A. Unintended consequences of requiring a license to help. American Psychologist, 1981, 36, 13-21.

Davis, K.L. Is confidentiality in group counseling realistic? Personnel and Guidance Journal, 1982, 59, 197-201.

Dekarii, M.B. & Sales, B.C. Privileged communications of psychologists. Professional Psychology, 1982, 13, 372-388.

Department of Health and Human Services. Final regulations amending basic HHS policy for the protection of human research subjects. Federal Register, January 26, 1981, 46, 8366-8392.

Duncan, J.A. Ethical considerations in peer group work. Elementary School Guidance and Counseling, 1976, 11, 59-60.

Dye, A. Challenges to ethical behavior in group work. Counseling and Values, 1981, 25, 227-235.

Edmonston, W.E. Neutral hypnosis as relaxation. American Journal of Clinical Hypnosis, 1977, 20, 69-75.

Ellis, A. Psychotherapy and atheistic values: A response to A.E. Bergin's "Psychotherapy and religious values." Journal of Consulting and Clinical Psychology, 1980, 48, 635-639.

Epstein, G.N., Steingarten, J, Weinstein, H.C., & Nashel, H.M. Panel report: Impact of law on the practice of psychotherapy. Journal of Psychiatry and Law, 1977, 5, No. 1, 7-40.

Everstine, L, Everstine, D.S., Heymann, G.M., True, R.H., Frey, D.G., Johnson, H.G., & Seiden, R.H. Privacy and confidentiality in psychotherapy. American Psychologist, 1980, 35, 828-840.

Eysenck, H.J. The effects of psychotherapy: an evaluation. Journal of Consulting Psychology, 1952, 16, 319-324.

Eysenck, H.J. The effects of psychotherapy. International Journal of Psychiatry, 1965, 1, 97-168.

Fairweather, G.W. Methods for experimental social innovation. New York: John Wiley & Sons, Inc., 1967.

Farrely, F. & Brandsma, J. Provocative therapy. San Francisco: Shield Publishing Company, 1974.

Feigl, H. The "mental" and the "physical"; the essay and a postscript. Minneapolis: University of Minnesota Press, 1967.

Feldman, S.R. & Ward, T.M. Psychotherapeutic injury: reshaping the implied contract as an alternative to malpractice. North Carolina Law Review, 1980, 58, 63-96.

Fleming, J.G. & Maximor, B. The patient or his victim. California Law Review, 1974, 62, 1025-1068.

Flexner, A. Medical education in the United States and Canada. New York: Carnegie Foundation, 1910.

Foltz, D. CHAMPUS peer review set to begin shortly. APA Monitor, January 1979, pp. 1, 9.

Foltz, D. California charges bias in psychology licensing exam. APA Monitor, August-September, 1981, pp. 4, 50. (a)

Foltz, D. CHAMPUS peer review under fire from the field. APA Monitor, May 1981, pp. 1, 12, 37. (b)

Foltz, D. South Dakota lawmakers re-enact licensing for psychologists. APA Monitor, April 1981, p.1. (c)

Foster, H.H. An overview of confidentiality and privilege. Journal of Psychiatry and Law, 1976, 4, 393-401.

Frank, J.D. The role of hope in psychotherapy. International Journal of Psychotherapy, 1968, 5, 386.

Frank, J.D. Persuasion and healing: a comparative study of psychotherapy. (rev. ed.) Baltimore: John Hopkins University Press, 1973.

Frank, J.D. The present status of outcome studies. Journal of Consulting and Clinical Psychology, 1979, 47, 310-316.

Freedman, R.J. The effects of extra-group socializing and alternate sessions on group psychotherapy outcome (Doctoral dissertation, Temple University, 1976). Dissertation Abstracts International, 1976, 37(4-B), 1896-1897.

Freud, S. Recommendations on treatment. Collected Works, (Vol. 2). New York: Basic Books, 1959. (originally published in Zentralblatt, Bd. II, 1912; reprinted in Sammlung, Urentfolge.)

Galinsky, M.J. & Schopler, J.H. Warning: groups may be dangerous. Social Work, 1977, 22(2), 89-94.

Garfield, S.L. Introductory clinical psychology. New York: The MacMillan Company, 1957.

Gaza, G.M., Duncan, J.A., & Sisson, P.J. Professional issues in group work. Personnel and Guidance Journal, 1971, 49, 637-643.

Goldberg, C. Therapeutic partnership. New York: Springer Publishing Company, 1977.

Gordon, E.W. & Terrell, M.D. The changed social content of testing. American Psychologist, 1981, 36 1167-1171.

Gross, M.L. The psychological society. New York: Random House, 1978.

Gross, S.J. The myth of professional licensing. American Psychologist, 1978, 33, 1009-1016.

Hadley, S.W. & Strupp, H.H. Contemporary view of negative effects in psychotherapy. Archives of General Psychiatry, 1976, 33, 1291-1302.

Haley, J. Uncommon therapy. New York: W.W. Morton and Company, 1973.

Hare-Mustin, R.T. & Hall, J.E. Procedures for responding to ethics complaints against psychologists. American Psychologist, 1981, 36, 1494-1505.

Hare-Mustin, R.T., Marecek, J., Kaplan, A.G., & Liss-Levinson, N. Rights of clients, responsibilities of therapists. American Psychologist, 1979, 35, 3-16.

Hays, J.R. Privacy and confidentiality. In Comment section of the _American Psychologist_, 1981, _36_, 914.

Herbert, W. New York Medicaid inquiry tests psychologist-client privilege. _APA Monitor_, February 1979, p. 40.

Historic agreement on parity signals end of psychologist-psychiatrist war. _Behavior Today_, April 28, 1980, pp. 1-2.

Hogan, D.B. Series on _The regulation of psychotherapists:_
A study in the philosophy and practice of professional regulation. (Vol. I)
A handbook of state licensure laws. (Vol. II)
A review of malpractice suits in the United States. (Vol. III)
A resource bibliography. (Vol. IV)
Cambridge: Ballinger Publishing Company, 1979.

Holroyd, J.C. & Brodsky, A.M. Psychologists' attitudes and practices regarding erotic and nonerotic physical contacts with patients. _American Psychologist_, 1977, _32_, 843-849.

Holroyd, J.C. & Brodsky, A.M. Does touching patients lead to sexual intercourse? _Professional Psychology_, 1980, _11_, 807-811.

Huffman, J.C. _Ethical confrontations in counseling_. Chicago: University of Chicago, 1979.

Insurance Committee of Oklahoma Psychological Association. A code of ethics for insurance procedures. _APA Monitor_, April 1981, p. 16.

Jaffe, L. CHAMPUS protest. Letter to the editor in _APA Monitor_, November 1981, pp. 2, 3, 11.

Johnson, N. & Johnson, S.C. A group counseling contract. _Journal for Specialists in Group Work_, 1980, _5_, 93-97.

Jourard, S.M. _The transparent self_. (1st ed.). Princeton, N.J.: Van Nostrand, 1964.

Jourard, S.M. _The transparent self_. Princeton, N.J.: Van Nostrand, 1971.

Judicial notebook. APA Monitor, March 1982, p. 42.

Kardener, S.H., Fuller, M., & Mensh, I.N. A survey of physicians' attitudes and practices regarding erotic and nonerotic contact with patients. American Journal of Psychiatry, 1973, 130, 1077-1081.

Katz, J. Who's afraid of informed consent? Journal of Psychiatry and Law, 1976, 4, No. 2, 315-325.

Katz, N.W. Behavioral hypnotic inductions. Journal of Consulting and Clinical Psychology, 1979, 47, 119-127.

Kelly, G.A. The theory and technique of assessment. In P.R. Farnsworth & Q. McNemar (eds.) Annual Review of Psychology. Vol. 9. Palo Alto: Annual Review, 1958, pp. 323-352.

Kitchener, R.F. Ethical relativism and behavior therapy. Journal of Consulting and Clinical Psychology, 1980, 48, 1-6.

Knapp, S. A primer on malpractice for psychologists. Professional Psychology, 1980, 11, 606-612.

Knapp, S. & Vandecreek, L. Tarasoff: five years later. Professional Psychology, 1982, 13, 511-516.

Koocher, G. Credentialing in psychology: close encounters with competence? American Psychologist, 1979, 34, 696-702.

Lazarus, A.A. Behavior therapy and beyond. New York: McGraw-Hill Book Company, 1971.

Liebeman, M.A., Yalom, I.D., & Miles, M.B. Encounter groups: first facts. New York: Basic Books, 1973.

Lifespring suit cites D.C. law. APA Monitor, April 1982, p. 2.

London, P. The modes and morals of psychotherapy. New York: Holt, Rinehart and Wilson, Inc., 1964.

Lowental, U. The vicissitudes of discretion in psychotherapy. American Journal of Psychotherapy, 1974, 28, 235-242.

Mac Houec, F. In-competence. Letter to the editor in APA Monitor, March 1982, p. 6.

Mahoney, M.J. Cognition and behavior modification. Cambridge, Mass.: Ballinger Publishing Company, 1974.

Mahoney, M.J. Publication prejudices: an experimental study of confirmatory bias in the peer review system. Cognitive Therapy and Research, 1977, 1, 161-175.

Margolin, G. Ethical and legal considerations in marital and family therapy. American Psychologist, 1982, 37, 788-801.

Masters, W.H., Johnson, V.E., & Kolodny, R.C. (Eds.) Ethical issues in sex therapy and research. Boston: Little, Brown and Company, 1977.

Meehl, P.E. Clinical vs. statistical prediction. Minneapolis: University of Minnesota Press, 1954.

Messick, S. Test validity and the ethics of assessment. American Psychologist, 1980, 35, 1012-1027.

Mischel, W. Personality and assessment. New York: Wiley, 1968.

Morton, S.I. Peer review: a view from within. Professional Psychology, 1982, 13, 141-144.

Murray, E.J. A content-analysis method for studying psychotherapy. Psychological Monographs, 1956, 70, (13, Whole No. 420).

Mykel, N. The application of ethical standards to group psychotherapy in a community. International Journal of Group Psychotherapy, 1971, 21(2), 248-254.

National Association of Social Workers, Inc. Code of Ethics. Washington, D.C.: Author, 1980.

Noll, J.O. Material risks and informed consent to therapy. American Psychologist, 1981, 36, 915-916.

Oklahoma Psychological Association Insurance Committee. A code of ethics for insurance procedures. APA Monitor, April, 1981, p. 16.

Oregon Revised Statutes. Salem, Oregon: Legislative Counsel Committee of the Legislative Assembly of the State of Oregon, 1981.

Ozanne, P.A. Psychology and the law: Part II. OPA Newsletter, July 1977, p. 1.

Parish, S.J. & Smyer, M.A. Unintended consequences of requiring a license to help. American Psychologist, 1981, 36, 13-21.

Parloff, M.B. Can psychotherapy research guide the policymaker? American Psychologist, 1979, 34, 296-306.

Patterson, C.H. Ethical standards for groups. The Counseling Psychologist, 1972, 3, 93-101.

Peters, J.J. Do encounter groups hurt people? Psychotherapy: Theory and Practice, 1973, 10, 33-35.

Plotkin, R. Through the looking glass: clients' access to their own records. APA Monitor, December 1978.

Prosser, W.L. Law of Torts (4th Ed.). St. Paul, Minnesota: West Publishing Company, 1971.

Rappaport, R.G. Crisis in confidentiality, ethics and legality for a psychiatrist. Journal of Psychiatry and Law, 1977, 5, No. 3, 467-498.

Redd, W.H., Andresen, G.U., & Minagawa, R.Y. Hypnotic control of anticipatory emesis in patients receiving cancer chemotherapy. Journal of Consulting and Clinical Psychology, 1982, 30, 14-19.

Reimbursement: How to get along with Blue Shield. Psychotherapy Finances, April 1980, Section 1.

Rimland, B. Death Knell for psychotherapy? In comment section of American Psychologist, 1979, 34, 192.

Roberts, A.L. Ethical guidelines for group leaders. Journal for Specialists in Group Work, 1982, 7, 174-181.

Robitscher, J. Informed consent for psychoanalysis. Journal of Psychiatry and Law, 1978, 6, No. 3, 363-370.

Rogers, C.R. *Client-centered therapy*. Boston: Houghton Mifflin, 1951.

Rogers, C.R. *Carl Rogers on encounter groups*. New York: Harper & Row, 1970.

Roskam, P. First-person review: CHAMPUS hit on confidentiality. *APA Monitor*, March 1979, pp. 3, 18.

Sanders, J.R. Complaints against psychologists adjudicated informally by APA's Committee on Scientific and Professional Ethics and Conduct. *American Psychologist*, 1979, *34*, 1139-1144.

Sanders, J.R. & Keith-Spiegel, P. Formal and informal adjudication of ethics complaints against psychologists. *American Psychologist*, 1980, *35*, 1096-1105.

Schofield, W. *Psychotherapy: The purchase of friendship*. Englewood Cliffs, N.J.: Prentice-Hall, 1964.

Schwitzgebel, R.L. & Schwitzgebel, R.K. *Law and Psychological Practice*. New York: John Wiley & Sons, 1980.

Scriven, M. 'First, the roses...' A letter to the editor in *APA Monitor*, January 1975, pp. 2-3.

Sherrer, C.W. & Sherrer, S.S. *Ethical and professional standards for academic psychologists and counselors*. Springfield, Ill.: Charles C. Thomas, 1980.

Shimberg, B. Testing for licensure and certification. *American Psychologist*, 1981, *36*, 1138-1146.

Siegel, M. Privacy, ethics, and confidentiality. *Professional Psychology*, 1979, *10*, 249-258.

Sinnet, E.R. & Linford, O. Is there a crisis in professional self-regulation of the practice of psychology? In Forum section of *Professional Psychology*, 1982, *13*, 332-333.

Slovenko, R. Psychotherapy and confidentiality. *Cleveland State Law Review*, 1975, *24*, 375-396.

Slovenko, R. Group psychotherapy: privileged communication and confidentiality. *Journal of Psychiatry and Law*, 1977, *5*, No. 3, 405-466.

Slovenko, R. On the need for recordkeeping in the practice of psychiatry. Journal of Psychiatry and Law, 1979, 7, No. 4, 399-440. (a)

Slovenko, R. Series foreword. In D. Hogan, The regulation of psychotherapists, Cambridge: Ballinger Publishing Company, 1979. (b)

Smith, M.L. & Glass, G.U. Meta-analysis of psychotherapy outcome studies. American Psychologist, 1977, 32, 752-760.

Starr, R.H., Jr. Child abuse. American Psychologist, 1979, 34, 872-878.

Stolz, S. & Associates. Ethical issues in behavior modification. San Francisco: Jossey-Bass, 1978.

Stone, A.A. The Tarasoff decisions: suing psychotherapists to safeguard society. Harvard Law Review, 1976, 90, 358-378.

Sundberg, N.D. & Tyler, L.E. Clinical psychology. New York: Appelton-Century-Crofts, 1962.

Truax, C.B. Reinforcement and nonreinforcement in Rogerian psychotherapy. Journal of Abnormal Psychology, 1966, 71, 1-9.

Tyler, L. The work of the counselor. New York: Appleton-Century-Crofts, 1961.

Van Hoose, W.H. & Kottler, J.A. Ethical and legal issues in counseling and psychotherapy. San Francisco: Jossey-Bass, 1977.

Van Hoose, W.H. & Paradise, L.V. Ethics in counseling and psychotherapy. Cranston, R.I.: The Carroll Press, 1979.

Wade, T.C. & Baker, T.B. Opinions and use of psychological tests: A survey of clinical psychologists. American Psychologist, 1977, 32, 874-882.

Walls, G.B. Values and psychotherapy: a comment on "Psychotherapy and religious values." Journal of Consulting and Clinical Psychology, 1980, 48, 640-641.

Ward, L.C. Behavior therapy and ethics: a response to Kitchener. Journal of Consulting and Clinical Psychology, 1980, 48, 646-648.

Watzlawick, P., Beavin, J., & Jackson, D. Pragmatics of human communication. New York: W.W. Norton and Company, 1967.

Weinstock, M., & Haft, J.I. The effect of illness on employment opportunities. Archives of Environmental Health, 1974, 29, 79-83.

Wiens, A.N. & Menne, J.W. On disposing of "straw people." American Psychologist, 1981, 36, 390-395.

Wise, T.P. Where the public peril begins: a survey of psychotherapists to determine the effects of Tarasoff. Standford Law Review, 1978, 31, 165-190.

Wright, R.H. Psychologists and professional liability (malpractice) insurance. American Psychologist, 1981, 36, 1485-1493. (a)

Wright, R.H. What to do until the malpractice lawyer comes: a survivor's manual. American Psychologist, 1981, 36, 1535-1541. (b)

Yalom, I.D. & Lieberman, M.A. A study of encounter group casualties. Archives of General Psychiatry, 1971, 25, 16-30.

Young, H.H. A brief history of quality assurance and peer review. Professional Psychology, 1982, 13, 9-13.

Zimpfer, D.G. Needed: professional ethics for working with groups. Personnel and Guidance Journal, 1971, 50, 280-287.

Ethical Principles of Psychologists

PREAMBLE

Psychologists respect the dignity and worth of the individual and strive for the preservation and protection of fundamental human rights. They are committed to increasing knowledge of human behavior and of people's understanding of themselves and others and to the utilization of such knowledge for the promotion of human welfare. While pursuing these objectives, they make every effort to protect the welfare of those who seek their services and of the research participants that may be the object of study. They use their skills only for purposes consistent with these values and do not knowingly permit their misuse by others. While demanding for themselves freedom of inquiry and communication, psychologists accept the responsibility this freedom requires: competence, objectivity in the application of skills, and concern for the best interests of clients, colleagues, students, research participants, and society. In the pursuit of these ideals, psychologists subscribe to principles in the following areas: 1. Responsibility, 2. Competence, 3. Moral and Legal Standards, 4. Public Statements, 5. Confidentiality, 6. Welfare of the Consumer, 7. Professional Relationships, 8. Assessment Techniques, 9. Research With Human Participants, and 10. Care and Use of Animals.

Acceptance of membership in the American Psychological Association commits the member to adherence to these principles.

Psychologists cooperate with duly constituted committees of the American Psychological Association, in particular, the Committee on Scientific and Professional Ethics and Conduct, by responding to inquiries promptly and completely. Members also respond promptly and completely to inquiries from duly constituted state association ethics committees and professional standards review committees.

Principle 1
RESPONSIBILITY

In providing services, psychologists maintain the highest standards of their profession. They accept responsibility for the consequences of their acts and make every effort to ensure that their services are used appropriately.

a. As scientists, psychologists accept responsibility for the selection of their research topics and the methods used in investigation, analysis, and reporting. They plan their research in ways to minimize the possibility that their findings will be misleading. They provide thorough discussion of the limitations of their data, especially where their work touches on social policy or might be construed to the detriment of persons in specific age, sex, ethnic, socioeconomic, or other social groups. In publishing reports of their work, they never suppress disconfirming data, and they acknowledge the existence of alternative hypotheses and explanations of their findings. Psychologists take credit only for work they have actually done.

b. Psychologists clarify in advance with all appropriate persons and agencies the expectations for sharing and utilizing research data. They avoid relationships that may limit their objectivity or create a conflict of interest. Interference with the milieu in which data are collected is kept to a minimum.

c. Psychologists have the responsibility to attempt to prevent distortion, misuse, or suppression of psychological findings by the institution or agency of which they are employees.

d. As members of governmental or other organizational bodies, psychologists remain accountable as individuals to the highest standards of their profession.

e. As teachers, psychologists recognize their primary obligation to help others acquire knowledge and skill. They maintain high standards of scholarship by presenting psychological information objectively, fully, and accurately.

f. As practitioners, psychologists know that they bear a heavy social responsibility because their recommendations and professional actions may alter the lives of others. They are alert to personal, social, organizational, financial, or political situations and pressures that might lead to misuse of their influence.

This version of the Ethical Principles of Psychologists (formerly entitled Ethical Standards of Psychologists) was adopted by the American Psychological Association's Council of Representatives on January 24, 1981. The revised Ethical Principles contain both substantive and grammatical changes in each of the nine ethical principles constituting the Ethical Standards of Psychologists previously adopted by the Council of Representatives in 1979, plus a new tenth principle entitled Care and Use of Animals. Inquiries concerning the Ethical Principles of Psychologists should be addressed to the Administrative Officer for Ethics, American Psychological Association, 1200 Seventeenth Street, N.W., Washington, D.C. 20036.

These revised Ethical Principles apply to psychologists, to students of psychology, and to others who do work of a psychological nature under the supervision of a psychologist. They are also intended for the guidance of nonmembers of the Association who are engaged in psychological research or practice.

Any complaints of unethical conduct filed after January 24, 1981, shall be governed by this 1981 revision. However, conduct (a) complained about after January 24, 1981, but which occurred prior to that date, and (b) not considered unethical under prior versions of the principles but considered unethical under the 1981 revision, shall not be deemed a violation of ethical principles. Any complaints pending as of January 24, 1981, shall be governed either by the 1979 or by the 1981 version of the Ethical Principles, at the sound discretion of the Committee on Scientific and Professional Ethics and Conduct.

Principle 2
COMPETENCE

The maintenance of high standards of competence is a responsibility shared by all psychologists in the interest of the public and the profession as a whole. Psychologists recognize the boundaries of their competence and the limitations of their techniques. They only provide services and only use techniques for which they are qualified by training and experience. In those areas in which recognized standards do not yet exist, psychologists take whatever precautions are necessary to protect the welfare of their clients. They maintain knowledge of current scientific and professional information related to the services they render.

a. Psychologists accurately represent their competence, education, training, and experience. They claim as evidence of educational qualifications only those degrees obtained from institutions acceptable under the Bylaws and Rules of Council of the American Psychological Association.

b. As teachers, psychologists perform their duties on the basis of careful preparation so that their instruction is accurate, current, and scholarly.

c. Psychologists recognize the need for continuing education and are open to new procedures and changes in expectations and values over time.

d. Psychologists recognize differences among people, such as those that may be associated with age, sex, socioeconomic, and ethnic backgrounds. When necessary, they obtain training, experience, or counsel to assure competent service or research relating to such persons.

e. Psychologists responsible for decisions involving individuals or policies based on test results have an understanding of psychological or educational measurement, validation problems, and test research.

f. Psychologists recognize that personal problems and conflicts may interfere with professional effectiveness. Accordingly, they refrain from undertaking any activity in which their personal problems are likely to lead to inadequate performance or harm to a client, colleague, student, or research participant. If engaged in such activity when they become aware of their personal problems, they seek competent professional assistance to determine whether they should suspend, terminate, or limit the scope of their professional and/or scientific activities.

Principle 3
MORAL AND LEGAL STANDARDS

Psychologists' moral and ethical standards of behavior are a personal matter to the same degree as they are for any other citizen, except as these may compromise the fulfillment of their professional responsibilities or reduce the public trust in psychology and psychologists. Regarding their own behavior, psychologists are sensitive to prevailing community standards and to the possible impact that conformity to or deviation from these standards may have upon the quality of their performance as psychologists. Psychologists are also aware of the possible impact of their public behavior upon the ability of colleagues to perform their professional duties.

a. As teachers, psychologists are aware of the fact that their personal values may affect the selection and presentation of instructional materials. When dealing with topics that may give offense, they recognize and respect the diverse attitudes that students may have toward such materials.

b. As employees or employers, psychologists do not engage in or condone practices that are inhumane or that result in illegal or unjustifiable actions. Such practices include, but are not limited to, those based on considerations of race, handicap, age, gender, sexual preference, religion, or national origin in hiring, promotion, or training.

c. In their professional roles, psychologists avoid any action that will violate or diminish the legal and civil rights of clients or of others who may be affected by their actions.

d. As practitioners and researchers, psychologists act in accord with Association standards and guidelines related to practice and to the conduct of research with human beings and animals. In the ordinary course of events, psychologists adhere to relevant governmental laws and institutional regulations. When federal, state, provincial, organizational, or institutional laws, regulations, or practices are in conflict with Association standards and guidelines, psychologists make known their commitment to Association standards and guidelines and, wherever possible, work toward a resolution of the conflict. Both practitioners and researchers are concerned with the development of such legal and quasi-legal regulations as best serve the public interest, and they work toward changing existing regulations that are not beneficial to the public interest.

Principle 4
PUBLIC STATEMENTS

Public statements, announcements of services, advertising, and promotional activities of psychologists serve the purpose of helping the public make informed judgments and choices. Psychologists represent accurately and objectively their professional qualifications, affiliations, and functions, as well as those of the institutions or organizations with which they or the statements may be associated. In public statements providing psychological information or professional opinions or providing information about the availability of psychological products, publications, and services, psychologists base their statements on scientifically acceptable psycholog-

ical findings and techniques with full recognition of the limits and uncertainties of such evidence.

a. When announcing or advertising professional services, psychologists may list the following information to describe the provider and services provided: name, highest relevant academic degree earned from a regionally accredited institution, date, type, and level of certification or licensure, diplomate status, APA membership status, address, telephone number, office hours, a brief listing of the type of psychological services offered, an appropriate presentation of fee information, foreign languages spoken, and policy with regard to third-party payments. Additional relevant or important consumer information may be included if not prohibited by other sections of these Ethical Principles.

b. In announcing or advertising the availability of psychological products, publications, or services, psychologists do not present their affiliation with any organization in a manner that falsely implies sponsorship or certification by that organization. In particular and for example, psychologists do not state APA membership or fellow status in a way to suggest that such status implies specialized professional competence or qualifications. Public statements include, but are not limited to, communication by means of periodical, book, list, directory, television, radio, or motion picture. They do not contain (i) a false, fraudulent, misleading, deceptive, or unfair statement; (ii) a misinterpretation of fact or a statement likely to mislead or deceive because in context it makes only a partial disclosure of relevant facts; (iii) a testimonial from a patient regarding the quality of a psychologists' services or products; (iv) a statement intended or likely to create false or unjustified expectations of favorable results; (v) a statement implying unusual, unique, or one-of-a-kind abilities; (vi) a statement intended or likely to appeal to a client's fears, anxieties, or emotions concerning the possible results of failure to obtain the offered services; (vii) a statement concerning the comparative desirability of offered services; (viii) a statement of direct solicitation of individual clients.

c. Psychologists do not compensate or give anything of value to a representative of the press, radio, television, or other communication medium in anticipation of or in return for professional publicity in a news item. A paid advertisement must be identified as such, unless it is apparent from the context that it is a paid advertisement. If communicated to the public by use of radio or television, an advertisement is prerecorded and approved for broadcast by the psychologist, and a recording of the actual transmission is retained by the psychologist.

d. Announcements or advertisements of "personal growth groups," clinics, and agencies give a clear statement of purpose and a clear description of the experiences to be provided. The education, training, and experience of the staff members are appropriately specified.

e. Psychologists associated with the development or promotion of psychological devices, books, or other products offered for commercial sale make reasonable efforts to ensure that announcements and advertisements are presented in a professional, scientifically acceptable, and factually informative manner.

f. Psychologists do not participate for personal gain in commercial announcements or advertisements recommending to the public the purchase or use of proprietary or single-source products or services when that participation is based solely upon their identification as psychologists.

g. Psychologists present the science of psychology and offer their services, products, and publications fairly and accurately, avoiding misrepresentation through sensationalism, exaggeration, or superficiality. Psychologists are guided by the primary obligation to aid the public in developing informed judgments, opinions, and choices.

h. As teachers, psychologists ensure that statements in catalogs and course outlines are accurate and not misleading, particularly in terms of subject matter to be covered, bases for evaluating progress, and the nature of course experiences. Announcements, brochures, or advertisements describing workshops, seminars, or other educational programs accurately describe the audience for which the program is intended as well as eligibility requirements, educational objectives, and nature of the materials to be covered. These announcements also accurately represent the education, training, and experience of the psychologists presenting the programs and any fees involved.

i. Public announcements or advertisements soliciting research participants in which clinical services or other professional services are offered as an inducement make clear the nature of the services as well as the costs and other obligations to be accepted by participants in the research.

j. A psychologist accepts the obligation to correct others who represent the psychologist's professional qualifications, or associations with products or services, in a manner incompatible with these guidelines.

k. Individual diagnostic and therapeutic services are provided only in the context of a professional psychological relationship. When personal advice is given by means of public lectures or demonstrations, newspaper or magazine articles, radio or television programs, mail, or similar media, the psychologist utilizes the most current relevant data and exercises the highest level of professional judgment.

l. Products that are described or presented by means of public lectures or demonstrations, newspaper or magazine articles, radio or television programs, or similar media meet the same recognized standards as exist for products used in the context of a professional relationship.

Principle 5
CONFIDENTIALITY

Psychologists have a primary obligation to respect the confidentiality of information obtained from persons in the course of their work as psychologists. They reveal such information to others only with the consent of the person or the person's legal representative, except in those unusual circumstances in which not to do so would result in clear danger to the person or to others. Where appropriate, psychologists inform their clients of the legal limits of confidentiality.

a. Information obtained in clinical or consulting relationships, or evaluative data concerning children, students, employees, and others, is discussed only for professional purposes and only with persons clearly concerned with the case. Written and oral reports present only data germane to the purposes of the evaluation, and every effort is made to avoid undue invasion of privacy.

b. Psychologists who present personal information obtained during the course of professional work in writings, lectures, or other public forums either obtain adequate prior consent to do so or adequately disguise all identifying information.

c. Psychologists make provisions for maintaining confidentiality in the storage and disposal of records.

d. When working with minors or other persons who are unable to give voluntary, informed consent, psychologists take special care to protect these persons' best interests.

Principle 6
WELFARE OF THE CONSUMER

Psychologists respect the integrity and protect the welfare of the people and groups with whom they work. When conflicts of interest arise between clients and psychologists' employing institutions, psychologists clarify the nature and direction of their loyalties and responsibilities and keep all parties informed of their commitments. Psychologists fully inform consumers as to the purpose and nature of an evaluative, treatment, educational, or training procedure, and they freely acknowledge that clients, students, or participants in research have freedom of choice with regard to participation.

a. Psychologists are continually cognizant of their own needs and of their potentially influential position vis-à-vis persons such as clients, students, and subordinates. They avoid exploiting the trust and dependency of such persons. Psychologists make every effort to avoid dual relationships that could impair their professional judgment or increase the risk of exploitation. Examples of such dual relationships include, but are not limited to, research with and treatment of employees, students, supervisees, close friends, or relatives. Sexual intimacies with clients are unethical.

b. When a psychologist agrees to provide services to a client at the request of a third party, the psychologist assumes the responsibility of clarifying the nature of the relationships to all parties concerned.

c. Where the demands of an organization require psychologists to violate these Ethical Principles, psychologists clarify the nature of the conflict between the demands and these principles. They inform all parties of psychologists' ethical responsibilities and take appropriate action.

d. Psychologists make advance financial arrangements that safeguard the best interests of and are clearly understood by their clients. They neither give nor receive any remuneration for referring clients for professional services. They contribute a portion of their services to work for which they receive little or no financial return.

e. Psychologists terminate a clinical or consulting relationship when it is reasonably clear that the consumer is not benefiting from it. They offer to help the consumer locate alternative sources of assistance.

Principle 7
PROFESSIONAL RELATIONSHIPS

Psychologists act with due regard for the needs, special competencies, and obligations of their colleagues in psychology and other professions. They respect the prerogatives and obligations of the institutions or organizations with which these other colleagues are associated.

a. Psychologists understand the areas of competence of related professions. They make full use of all the professional, technical, and administrative resources that serve the best interests of consumers. The absence of formal relationships with other professional workers does not relieve psychologists of the responsibility of securing for their clients the best possible professional service, nor does it relieve them of the obligation to exercise foresight, diligence, and tact in obtaining the complementary or alternative assistance needed by clients.

b. Psychologists know and take into account the traditions and practices of other professional groups with whom they work and cooperate fully with such groups. If a person is receiving similar services from another professional, psychologists do not offer their own services directly to such a person. If a psychologist is contacted by a person who is already receiving similar services from another professional, the psychologist carefully considers that professional relationship and proceeds with caution and sensitivity to the therapeutic issues as well as the client's welfare. The psychologist discusses these issues with the client so as to minimize the risk of confusion and conflict.

c. Psychologists who employ or supervise other professionals or professionals in training accept the obligation to facilitate the further professional development of these individuals. They provide appropriate working conditions, timely evaluations, constructive consultation, and experience opportunities.

d. Psychologists do not exploit their professional relationships with clients, supervisees, students, employees, or research participants sexually or otherwise. Psychologists do not condone or engage in sexual harassment. Sexual harassment is defined as deliberate or repeated comments, gestures, or physical contacts of a sexual nature that are unwanted by the recipient.

e. In conducting research in institutions or organizations, psychologists secure appropriate authorization to conduct such research. They are aware of their obligations to future research workers and ensure that host institutions receive adequate information about the research and proper acknowledgment of their contributions.

f. Publication credit is assigned to those who have contributed to a publication in proportion to their professional contributions. Major contributions of a professional character made by several persons to a common project are recognized by joint authorship, with the individual who made the principal contribution listed first. Minor contributions of a professional character and extensive clerical or similar nonprofessional assistance may be acknowledged in footnotes or in an introductory statement. Acknowledgment through specific citations is made for unpublished as well as published material that has directly influenced the research or writing. Psychologists who compile and edit material of others for publication publish the material in the name of the originating group, if appropriate, with their own name appearing as chairperson or editor. All contributors are to be acknowledged and named.

g. When psychologists know of an ethical violation by another psychologist, and it seems appropriate, they informally attempt to resolve the issue by bringing the behavior to the attention of the psychologist. If the misconduct is of a minor nature and/or appears to be due to lack of sensitivity, knowledge, or experience, such an informal solution is usually appropriate. Such informal corrective efforts are made with sensitivity to any rights to confidentiality involved. If the violation does not seem amenable to an informal solution, or is of a more serious nature, psychologists bring it to the attention of the appropriate local, state, and/or national committee on professional ethics and conduct.

Principle 8
ASSESSMENT TECHNIQUES

In the development, publication, and utilization of psychological assessment techniques, psychologists make every effort to promote the welfare and best interests of the client. They guard against the misuse of assessment results. They respect the client's right to know the results, the interpretations made, and the bases for their conclusions and recommendations. Psychologists make every effort to maintain the security of tests and other assessment techniques within limits of legal mandates. They strive to ensure the appropriate use of assessment techniques by others.

a. In using assessment techniques, psychologists respect the right of clients to have full explanations of the nature and purpose of the techniques in language the clients can understand, unless an explicit exception to this right has been agreed upon in advance. When the explanations are to be provided by others, psychologists establish procedures for ensuring the adequacy of these explanations.

b. Psychologists responsible for the development and standardization of psychological tests and other assessment techniques utilize established scientific procedures and observe the relevant APA standards.

c. In reporting assessment results, psychologists indicate any reservations that exist regarding validity or reliability because of the circumstances of the assessment or the inappropriateness of the norms for the person tested. Psychologists strive to ensure that the results of assessments and their interpretations are not misused by others.

d. Psychologists recognize that assessment results may become obsolete. They make every effort to avoid and prevent the misuse of obsolete measures.

e. Psychologists offering scoring and interpretation services are able to produce appropriate evidence for the validity of the programs and procedures used in arriving at interpretations. The public offering of an automated interpretation service is considered a professional-to-professional consultation. Psychologists make every effort to avoid misuse of assessment reports.

f. Psychologists do not encourage or promote the use of psychological assessment techniques by inappropriately trained or otherwise unqualified persons through teaching, sponsorship, or supervision.

Principle 9
RESEARCH WITH HUMAN PARTICIPANTS

The decision to undertake research rests upon a considered judgment by the individual psychologist about how best to contribute to psychological science and human welfare. Having made the decision to conduct research, the psychologist considers alternative directions in which research energies and resources might be invested. On the basis of this consideration, the psychologist carries out the investigation with respect and concern for the dignity and welfare of the people who participate and with cognizance of federal and state regulations and professional standards governing the conduct of research with human participants.

a. In planning a study, the investigator has the responsibility to make a careful evaluation of its ethical acceptability. To the extent that the weighing of scientific and human values suggests a compromise of any principle, the investigator incurs a correspondingly serious obligation to seek ethical advice and to observe stringent safeguards to protect the rights of human participants.

b. Considering whether a participant in a planned

study will be a "subject at risk" or a "subject at minimal risk," according to recognized standards, is of primary ethical concern to the investigator.

c. The investigator always retains the responsibility for ensuring ethical practice in research. The investigator is also responsible for the ethical treatment of research participants by collaborators, assistants, students, and employees, all of whom, however, incur similar obligations.

d. Except in minimal-risk research, the investigator establishes a clear and fair agreement with research participants, prior to their participation, that clarifies the obligations and responsibilities of each. The investigator has the obligation to honor all promises and commitments included in that agreement. The investigator informs the participants of all aspects of the research that might reasonably be expected to influence willingness to participate and explains all other aspects of the research about which the participants inquire. Failure to make full disclosure prior to obtaining informed consent requires additional safeguards to protect the welfare and dignity of the research participants. Research with children or with participants who have impairments that would limit understanding and/or communication requires special safeguarding procedures.

e. Methodological requirements of a study may make the use of concealment or deception necessary. Before conducting such a study, the investigator has a special responsibility to (i) determine whether the use of such techniques is justified by the study's prospective scientific, educational, or applied value; (ii) determine whether alternative procedures are available that do not use concealment or deception; and (iii) ensure that the participants are provided with sufficient explanation as soon as possible.

f. The investigator respects the individual's freedom to decline to participate in or to withdraw from the research at any time. The obligation to protect this freedom requires careful thought and consideration when the investigator is in a position of authority or influence over the participant. Such positions of authority include, but are not limited to, situations in which research participation is required as part of employment or in which the participant is a student, client, or employee of the investigator.

g. The investigator protects the participant from physical and mental discomfort, harm, and danger that may arise from research procedures. If risks of such consequences exist, the investigator informs the participant of that fact. Research procedures likely to cause serious or lasting harm to a participant are not used unless the failure to use these procedures might expose the participant to risk of greater harm, or unless the research has great potential benefit and fully informed and voluntary consent is obtained from each participant. The participant should be informed of procedures for contacting the investigator within a reasonable time period following participation should stress, potential harm, or related questions or concerns arise.

h. After the data are collected, the investigator provides the participant with information about the nature of the study and attempts to remove any misconceptions that may have arisen. Where scientific or humane values justify delaying or withholding this information, the investigator incurs a special responsibility to monitor the research and to ensure that there are no damaging consequences for the participant.

i. Where research procedures result in undesirable consequences for the individual participant, the investigator has the responsibility to detect and remove or correct these consequences, including long-term effects.

j. Information obtained about a research participant during the course of an investigation is confidential unless otherwise agreed upon in advance. When the possibility exists that others may obtain access to such information, this possibility, together with the plans for protecting confidentiality, is explained to the participant as part of the procedure for obtaining informed consent.

Principle 10
CARE AND USE OF ANIMALS

An investigator of animal behavior strives to advance understanding of basic behavioral principles and/or to contribute to the improvement of human health and welfare. In seeking these ends, the investigator ensures the welfare of animals and treats them humanely. Laws and regulations notwithstanding, an animal's immediate protection depends upon the scientist's own conscience.

a. The acquisition, care, use, and disposal of all animals are in compliance with current federal, state or provincial, and local laws and regulations.

b. A psychologist trained in research methods and experienced in the care of laboratory animals closely supervises all procedures involving animals and is responsible for ensuring appropriate consideration of their comfort, health, and humane treatment.

c. Psychologists ensure that all individuals using animals under their supervision have received explicit instruction in experimental methods and in the care, maintenance, and handling of the species being used. Responsibilities and activities of individuals participating in a research project are consistent with their respective competencies.

d. Psychologists make every effort to minimize discomfort, illness, and pain of animals. A procedure subjecting animals to pain, stress, or privation is used only when an alternative procedure is unavailable and the goal is justified by its prospective scientific, educational, or applied value. Surgical procedures are performed under appropriate anesthesia; techniques to avoid infection and minimize pain are followed during and after surgery.

e. When it is appropriate that the animal's life be terminated, it is done rapidly and painlessly.

Specialty Guidelines for the Delivery of Services by Clinical Psychologists

The Specialty Guidelines that follow are based on the generic *Standards for Providers of Psychological Services* originally adopted by the American Psychological Association (APA) in September 1974 and revised in January 1977 (APA, 1974b, 1977b). Together with the generic *Standards*, these Specialty Guidelines state the official policy of the Association regarding delivery of services by clinical psychologists. Admission to the practice of psychology is regulated by state statute. It is the position of the Association that licensing be based on generic, and not on specialty, qualifications. Specialty guidelines serve the additional purpose of providing potential users and other interested groups with essential information about particular services available from the several specialties in professional psychology.

Professional psychology specialties have evolved from generic practice in psychology and are supported by university training programs. There are now at least four recognized professional specialties—clinical, counseling, school, and industrial/organizational psychology.

The knowledge base in each of these specialty areas has increased, refining the state of the art to the point that a set of uniform specialty guidelines is now possible and desirable. The present Guidelines are intended to educate the public, the profession, and other interested parties regarding specialty professional practices. They are also intended to facilitate the continued systematic development of the profession.

The content of each Specialty Guideline reflects a consensus of university faculty and public and private practitioners regarding the knowledge base, services provided, problems addressed, and clients served.

Traditionally, all learned disciplines have treated the designation of specialty practice as a reflection of preparation in greater depth in a particular subject matter, together with a voluntary limiting of focus to a more restricted area of practice by the professional. Lack of specialty designation does not preclude general providers of psychological services from using the methods or dealing with the populations of any specialty, except insofar as psychologists voluntarily refrain from providing services they are not trained to render. It is the intent of these Guidelines, however, that after the grandparenting period, psychologists not put themselves forward as *specialists* in a given area of practice unless they meet the qualifications noted in the Guidelines (see Definitions). Therefore, these Guidelines are meant to apply only to those psychologists who voluntarily wish to be designated as *clinical psychologists*. They do not apply to other psychologists.

These Guidelines represent the profession's best judgment of the conditions, credentials, and experience that contribute to competent professional practice. The APA strongly encourages, and plans to participate in, efforts to identify professional practitioner behaviors and job functions and to validate the relation between these and desired client outcomes. Thus, future revisions of these Guidelines will increasingly reflect the results of such efforts.

These Guidelines follow the format and, wherever applicable, the wording of the generic *Standards*.[1] (Note: Footnotes appear at the end of the Specialty Guidelines. See pp. 648–651.) The intent of these Guidelines is to improve the quality, effectiveness, and accessibility of psychological services. They are meant to provide guidance to providers, users, and sanctioners regarding the best judgment of the profession on these matters. Although the Specialty Guidelines have been derived from and are consistent with the generic *Standards*, they may be used as separate documents. However, *Standards for Providers of Psychological Services* (APA, 1977b) shall remain the basic policy statement and shall take precedence where there are questions of interpretation.

Professional psychology in general and clinical psychology as a specialty have labored long and diligently to codify a uniform set of guidelines for the delivery of services by clinical psychologists that would serve the respective needs of users, providers, third-party purchasers, and sanctioners of psychological services.

The Committee on Professional Standards, established by the APA in January 1980, is charged with keeping the generic *Standards* and the Specialty Guidelines responsive to the needs of the public and the profession. It is also charged with continually reviewing, modifying, and extending them progressively as the profession and the science of psychology develop new knowledge, improved methods, and additional modes of psychological services.

The Specialty Guidelines for the Delivery of Services by Clinical Psychologists that follow have been established by the APA as a means of self-regulation to protect the public interest. They guide the specialty practice of

These Specialty Guidelines were prepared through the cooperative efforts of the APA Committee on Standards for Providers of Psychological Services (COSPOPS) and many professional clinical psychologists from the divisions of APA, including those involved in education and training programs and in public and private practice. Jules Barron, succeeded by Morris Goodman, served as the clinical psychology representative on COSPOPS. The committee was chaired by Durand F. Jacobs; the Central Office liaisons were Arthur Centor and Richard Kilburg.

clinical psychology by specifying important areas of quality assurance and performance that contribute to the goal of facilitating more effective human functioning.

Principles and Implications of the Specialty Guidelines

These Specialty Guidelines have emerged from and reaffirm the same basic principles that guided the development of the generic *Standards for Providers of Psychological Services* (APA, 1977b):

1. These Guidelines recognize that admission to the practice of psychology is regulated by state statute.

2. It is the intention of the APA that the generic *Standards* provide appropriate guidelines for statutory licensing of psychologists. In addition, although it is the position of the APA that licensing be generic and not in specialty areas, these Specialty Guidelines in clinical psychology provide an authoritative reference for use in credentialing specialty providers of clinical psychological services by such groups as divisions of the APA and state associations and by boards and agencies that find such criteria useful for quality assurance.

3. A uniform set of Specialty Guidelines governs the quality of services to all users of clinical psychological services in both the private and the public sectors. Those receiving clinical psychological services are protected by the same kinds of safeguards, irrespective of sector; these include constitutional guarantees, statutory regulation, peer review, consultation, record review, and supervision.

4. A uniform set of Specialty Guidelines governs clinical psychological service functions offered by clinical psychologists, regardless of setting or form of remuneration. All clinical psychologists in professional practice recognize and are responsive to a uniform set of Specialty Guidelines, just as they are guided by a common code of ethics.

5. Clinical psychology Guidelines establish clearly articulated levels of quality for covered clinical psychological service functions, regardless of the nature of the users, purchasers, or sanctioners of such covered services.

6. All persons providing clinical psychological services meet specified levels of training and experience that are consistent with, and appropriate to, the functions they perform. Clinical psychological services provided by persons who do not meet the APA qualifications for a professional clinical psychologist (see Definitions) are supervised by a professional clinical psychologist. Final responsibility and accountability for services provided rest with professional clinical psychologists.

7. When providing any of the covered clinical psychological service functions at any time and in any setting, whether public or private, profit or nonprofit, clinical psychologists observe these Guidelines in order to promote the best interests and welfare of the users of such services. The extent to which clinical psychologists observe these Guidelines is judged by peers.

8. These Guidelines, while assuring the user of the clinical psychologist's accountability for the nature and quality of services specified in this document, do not preclude the clinical psychologist from using new methods or developing innovative procedures in the delivery of clinical services.

These Specialty Guidelines have broad implications both for users of clinical psychological services and for providers of such services:

1. Guidelines for clinical psychological services provide a foundation for mutual understanding between provider and user and facilitate more effective evaluation of services provided and outcomes achieved.

2. Guidelines for clinical psychologists are essential for uniformity in specialty credentialing of clinical psychologists.

3. Guidelines give specific content to the profession's concept of ethical practice as it applies to the functions of clinical psychologists.

4. Guidelines for clinical psychological services may have significant impact on tomorrow's education and training models for both professional and support personnel in clinical psychology.

5. Guidelines for the provision of clinical psychological services in human service facilities influence the determination of acceptable structure, budgeting, and staffing patterns in these facilities.

6. Guidelines for clinical psychological services require continual review and revision.

The Specialty Guidelines here presented are intended to improve the quality and delivery of clinical psychological services by specifying criteria for key aspects of the practice setting. Some settings may require additional and/or more stringent criteria for specific areas of service delivery.

Systematically applied, these Guidelines serve to establish a more effective and consistent basis for evaluating the performance of individual service providers as well as to guide the organization of clinical psychological service units in human service settings.

Definitions

Providers of clinical psychological services refers to two categories of persons who provide clinical psychological services:

A. Professional clinical psychologists.[2] Professional clinical psychologists have a doctoral degree from a regionally accredited university or professional school providing an organized, sequential clinical psychology program in a department of psychology in a university or college, or in an appropriate department or unit of a professional school. Clinical psychology programs that are accredited by the American Psychological Association are recognized as meeting the definition of a clinical psychology program. Clinical psychology programs that are not accredited by the American Psychological Association meet the definition of a clinical psychology program if they satisfy the following criteria:

1. The program is primarily psychological in nature and stands as a recognizable, coherent organizational entity within the institution.

2. The program provides an integrated, organized sequence of study.

3. The program has an identifiable body of students who are matriculated in that program for a degree.

4. There is a clear authority with primary responsibility for the core and specialty areas, whether or not the program cuts across administrative lines.

5. There is an identifiable psychology faculty, and a psychologist is responsible for the program.

In addition to a doctoral education, clinical psychologists acquire doctoral and postdoctoral training. Patterns of education and training in clinical psychology[3] are consistent with the functions to be performed and the services to be provided, in accordance with the ages, populations, and problems encountered in various settings.

B. All other persons who are not professional clinical psychologists and who participate in the delivery of clinical psychological services under the supervision of a professional clinical psychologist. Although there may be variations in the titles of such persons, they are not referred to as clinical psychologists. Their functions may be indicated by use of the adjective *psychological* preceding the noun, for example, *psychological associate, psychological assistant, psychological technician*, or *psychological aide*. Their services are rendered under the supervision of a professional clinical psychologist, who is responsible for the designation given them and for quality control. To be assigned such a designation, a person has the background, training, or experience that is appropriate to the functions performed.

Clinical psychological services refers to the application of principles, methods, and procedures for understanding, predicting, and alleviating intellectual, emotional, psychological, and behavioral disability and discomfort. Direct services are provided in a variety of health settings, and direct and supportive services are provided in the entire range of social, organizational, and academic institutions and agencies.[4] Clinical psychological services include the following:[5]

A. Assessment directed toward diagnosing the nature and causes, and predicting the effects, of subjective distress; of personal, social, and work dysfunction; and of the psychological and emotional factors involved in, and consequent to, physical disease and disability. Procedures may include, but are not limited to, interviewing, and administering and interpreting tests of intellectual abilities, attitudes, emotions, motivations, personality characteristics, psychoneurological status, and other aspects of human experience and behavior relevant to the disturbance.

B. Interventions directed at identifying and correcting the emotional conflicts, personality disturbances, and skill deficits underlying a person's distress and/or dysfunction. Interventions may reflect a variety of theoretical orientations, techniques, and modalities. These may include, but are not limited to, psychotherapy, psychoanalysis, behavior therapy, marital and family therapy, group psychotherapy, hypnotherapy, social-learning approaches, biofeedback techniques, and environmental consultation and design.

C. Professional consultation in relation to A and B above.

D. Program development services in the areas of A, B, and C above.

E. Supervision of clinical psychological services.

F. Evaluation of all services noted in A through E above.

A *clinical psychological service unit* is the functional unit through which clinical psychological services are provided; such a unit may be part of a larger psychological service organization comprising psychologists of more than one specialty and headed by a professional psychologist:

A. A clinical psychological service unit provides predominantly clinical psychological services and is composed of one or more professional clinical psychologists and supporting staff.

B. A clinical psychological service unit may operate as a professional service or as a functional or geographic component of a larger multipsychological service unit or of a governmental, educational, correctional, health, training, industrial, or commercial organizational unit.[6]

C. One or more clinical psychologists providing professional services in a multidisciplinary setting constitute a clinical psychological service unit.

D. A clinical psychological service unit may also be one or more clinical psychologists in a private practice or a psychological consulting firm.

Users of clinical psychological services include:

A. Direct users or recipients of clinical psychological services.

B. Public and private institutions, facilities, or organizations receiving clinical psychological services.

C. Third-party purchasers—those who pay for the delivery of services but who are not the recipients of services.

D. Sanctioners—those who have a legitimate concern with the accessibility, timeliness, efficacy, and standards of quality attending the provision of clinical psychological services. Sanctioners may include members of the user's family, the court, the probation officer, the school administrator, the employer, the union representative, the facility director, and so on. Sanctioners may also include various governmental, peer review, and accreditation bodies concerned with the assurance of quality.

Guideline 1
PROVIDERS

1.1 *Each clinical psychological service unit offering psychological services has available at least one professional clinical psychologist and as many more professional clinical psychologists as are necessary to assure the adequacy and quality of services offered.*

INTERPRETATION: The intent of this Guideline is that one or more providers of psychological services in any clinical psychological service unit meet the levels of training and experience of the professional clinical psychologist as specified in the preceding definitions.[7]

When a facility offering clinical psychological services does not have a full-time professional clinical psychologist available, the facility retains the services of one or more professional clinical psychologists on a regular part-time basis. The clinical psychologist so retained directs and supervises the psychological services provided, participates sufficiently to be able to assess the need for services, reviews the content of services provided, and has the authority to assume professional responsibility and accountability for them.

The psychologist directing the service unit is responsible for determining and justifying appropriate ratios of psychologists to users and psychologists to support staff, in order to ensure proper scope, accessibility, and quality of services provided in that setting.

1.2 *Providers of clinical psychological services who do not meet the requirements for the professional clinical psychologist are supervised directly by a professional clinical psychologist who assumes professional responsibility and accountability for the services provided. The level and extent of supervision may vary from task to task so long as the supervising psychologist retains a sufficiently close supervisory relationship to meet this Guideline. Special proficiency training or supervision may be provided by a professional psychologist of another specialty or by a professional from another discipline whose competence in the given area has been demonstrated by previous training and experience.*

INTERPRETATION: In each clinical psychological service unit there may be varying levels of responsibility with respect to the nature and quality of services provided. Support personnel are considered to be responsible for their functions and behavior when assisting in the provision of clinical psychological services and are accountable to the professional clinical psychologist. Ultimate professional responsibility and accountability for the services provided require that the supervisor review and approve reports and test protocols, review and approve intervention plans and strategies, and review outcomes. Therefore, the supervision of all clinical psychological services is provided directly by a professional clinical psychologist in individual and/or group face-to-face meetings.

In order to meet this Guideline, an appropriate number of hours per week are devoted to direct face-to-face supervision of each clinical psychological service unit staff member. In no event is such supervision less than 1 hour per week. The more comprehensive the psychological services are, the more supervision is needed. A plan or formula for relating increasing amounts of supervisory time to the complexity of professional responsibilities is to be developed. The amount and nature of supervision is made known to all parties concerned.

Such communications are in writing and describe and delineate the duties of the employee with respect to range and type of services to be provided. The limits of independent action and decision making are defined. The description of responsibility also specifies the means by which the employee will contact the professional clinical psychologist in the event of emergency or crisis situations.

1.3 *Wherever a clinical psychological service unit exists, a professional clinical psychologist is responsible for planning, directing, and reviewing the provision of clinical psychological services. Whenever the clinical psychological service unit is part of a larger professional psychological service encompassing various psychological specialties, a professional psychologist is the administrative head of the service.*

INTERPRETATION: The clinical psychologist coordinates the activities of the clinical psychological service unit with other professional, administrative, and technical groups, both within and outside the facility. This clinical psychologist, who may be the director, chief, or coordinator of the clinical psychological service unit, has related responsibilities including, but not limited to, recruiting qualified staff, directing training and research activities of the service, maintaining a high level of professional and ethical practice, and ensuring that staff members function only within the areas of their competency.

To facilitate the effectiveness of clinical services by raising the level of staff sensitivity and professional skills, the clinical psychologist designated as director is responsible for participating in the selection of staff and support personnel whose qualifications and skills (e.g., language, cultural and experiential background, race, sex, and age) are directly relevant to the needs and characteristics of the users served.

1.4 *When functioning as part of an organizational setting, professional clinical psychologists bring their backgrounds and skills to bear on the goals of the organization, whenever appropriate, by participation in the planning and development of overall services.*[8]

INTERPRETATION: Professional clinical psychologists participate in the maintenance of high professional standards by representation on committees concerned with service delivery.

As appropriate to the setting, their activities may include active participation, as voting and as office-holding members, on the professional staffs of hospitals and other facilities and on other executive, planning, and evaluation boards and committees.

1.5 *Clinical psychologists maintain current knowledge of scientific and professional developments to preserve and enhance their professional competence.*[9]

INTERPRETATION: Methods through which knowledge of scientific and professional developments may be gained include, but are not limited to, reading scientific and professional publications, attendance at workshops, participation in staff development programs, and other forms of continuing education. The clinical psychologist has ready access to reference material related to the provision of psychological services. Clinical psychologists are prepared to show evidence periodically that they are staying abreast of current knowledge and practices in the field of clinical psychology through continuing education.

1.6 *Clinical psychologists limit their practice to their demonstrated areas of professional competence.*

INTERPRETATION: Clinical psychological services are offered in accordance with the providers' areas of competence as defined by verifiable training and experience. When extending services beyond the range of their usual practice, psychologists obtain pertinent training or appropriate professional supervision. Such training or supervision is consistent with the extension of functions performed and services provided. An extension of services may involve a change in the theoretical orientation of the clinical psychologist, a change in modality or technique, or a change in the type of client and/or the kinds of problems or disorders for which services are to be provided (e.g., children, elderly persons, mental retardation, neurological impairment).

1.7 *Professional psychologists who wish to qualify as clinical psychologists meet the same requirements with respect to subject matter and professional skills that apply to doctoral and postdoctoral education and training in clinical psychology.*[10]

INTERPRETATION: Education of doctoral-level psychologists to qualify them for specialty practice in clinical psychology is under the auspices of a department in a regionally accredited university or of a professional school that offers the doctoral degree in clinical psychology. Such education is individualized, with due credit being given for relevant course work and other requirements that have previously been satisfied. In addition, doctoral-level training plus 1 year of postdoctoral experience supervised by a clinical psychologist is required. Merely taking an internship in clinical psychology or acquiring experience in a practicum setting is not adequate preparation for becoming a clinical psychologist when prior education has not been in that area. Fulfillment of such an individualized educational program is attested to by the awarding of a certificate by the supervising department or professional school that indicates the successful completion of preparation in clinical psychology.

1.8 *Professional clinical psychologists are encouraged to develop innovative theories and procedures and to provide appropriate theoretical and/or empirical support for their innovations.*

INTERPRETATION: A specialty of a profession rooted in a science intends continually to explore and experiment with a view to developing and verifying new and improved methods of serving the public in ways that can be documented.

Guideline 2
PROGRAMS

2.1 *Composition and organization of a clinical psychological service unit:*

2.1.1 *The composition and programs of a clinical psychological service unit are responsive to the needs of the persons or settings served.*

INTERPRETATION: A clinical psychological service unit is structured so as to facilitate effective and economical delivery of services. For example, a clinical psychological service unit serving predominantly a low-income, ethnic, or racial minority group has a staffing pattern and service programs that are adapted to the linguistic, experiential, and attitudinal characteristics of the users.

2.1.2 *A description of the organization of the clinical psychological service unit and its lines of responsibility and accountability for the delivery of psychological services is available in written form to staff of the unit and to users and sanctioners upon request.*

INTERPRETATION: The description includes lines of responsibility, supervisory relationships, and the level and extent of accountability for each person who provides psychological services.

2.1.3 *A clinical psychological service unit includes sufficient numbers of professional and support personnel to achieve its goals, objectives, and purposes.*

INTERPRETATION: The work load and diversity of psychological services required and the specific goals and objectives of the setting determine the numbers and qualifications of professional and support personnel in the clinical psychological service unit. Where shortages in personnel exist, so that psychological services cannot be rendered in a professional manner, the director of the clinical psychological service unit initiates action to remedy such shortages. When this fails, the director appropriately modifies the scope or work load of the unit to maintain the quality of the services rendered.

2.2 *Policies:*

2.2.1 *When the clinical psychological service unit is composed of more than one person or is a component of a larger organization, a written statement of its objectives and scope of services is developed, maintained, and reviewed.*

INTERPRETATION: The clinical psychological service unit reviews its objectives and scope of services annually and revises them as necessary to ensure that the psychological services offered are consistent with staff competencies and current psychological knowledge and practice. This statement is discussed with staff, reviewed with the appropriate administrator, and distributed to users and sanctioners upon request, whenever appropriate.

2.2.2 *All providers within a clinical psychological service unit support the legal and civil rights of the users.*[11]

INTERPRETATION: Providers of clinical psychological services safeguard the interests of the users with regard to personal, legal, and civil rights. They are continually sensitive to the issue of confidentiality of information, the short-term and long-term impacts of their decisions and recommendations, and other matters pertaining to individual, legal, and civil rights. Concerns regarding the safeguarding of individual rights of users include, but are not limited to, problems of self-incrimination in judicial proceedings, involuntary commitment to hospitals, protection of minors or legal incompetents, discriminatory practices in employment selection procedures, recommendation for special education provisions, information relative to adverse personnel actions in the armed services, and adjudication of domestic relations disputes in divorce and custodial proceedings. Providers of clinical psychological services take affirmative action by making themselves available to local committees, review boards, and similar advisory groups established to safeguard the human, civil, and legal rights of service users.

2.2.3 *All providers within a clinical psychological service unit are familiar with and adhere to the American Psychological Association's* Standards for Providers of Psychological Services, Ethical Principles of Psychologists, Standards for Educational and Psychological Tests, Ethical Principles in the Conduct of Research With Human Participants, *and other official policy statements relevant to standards for professional services issued by the Association.*

INTERPRETATION: Providers of clinical psychological services maintain up-to-date knowledge of the relevant standards of the American Psychological Association.

2.2.4 *All providers within a clinical psychological service unit conform to relevant statutes established by federal, state, and local governments.*

INTERPRETATION: All providers of clinical psychological services are familiar with appropriate statutes regulating the practice of psychology. They observe agency regulations that have the force of law and that relate to the delivery of psychological services (e.g., evaluation for disability retirement and special education placements). In addition, all providers are cognizant that federal agencies such as the Veterans Administration, the Department of Education, and the Department of Health and Human Services have policy statements regarding psychological services, and where relevant, providers conform to them. Providers of clinical psychological services are also familiar with other statutes and regulations, including those addressed to the civil and legal rights of users (e.g., those promulgated by the federal Equal Employment Opportunity Commission), that are pertinent to their scope of practice.

It is the responsibility of the American Psychological Association to maintain current files of those federal policies, statutes, and regulations relating to this section and to assist its members in obtaining them. The state psychological associations and the state licensing boards periodically publish and distribute appropriate state statutes and regulations.

2.2.5 *All providers within a clinical psychological service unit inform themselves about and use the network of human services in their communities in order to link users with relevant services and resources.*

INTERPRETATION: Clinical psychologists and support staff are sensitive to the broader context of human needs. In recognizing the matrix of personal and societal problems, providers make available to users information regarding human services such as legal aid societies, social services, employment agencies, health resources, and educational and recreational facilities. Providers of clinical psychological services refer to such community resources and, when indicated, actively intervene on behalf of the users.

Community resources include the private as well as the public sectors. Private resources include private agencies and centers and psychologists in independent private practice. Consultation is sought or referral made within the public or private network of services whenever required in the best interest of the users. Clinical psychologists, in either the private or the public setting, utilize other resources in the community whenever indicated because of limitations within the psychological service unit providing the services. Professional clinical psychologists in private practice are familiar with the types of services offered through local community mental health clinics and centers, including alternatives to hospitalization, and know the costs and eligibility requirements for those services.

2.2.6 *In the delivery of clinical psychological services, the providers maintain a cooperative relationship with colleagues and co-workers in the best interest of the users.*[12]

INTERPRETATION: Clinical psychologists recognize the areas of special competence of other professional psychologists and of professionals in other fields for either consultation or referral purposes. Providers of clinical psychological services make appropriate use of other professional, research, technical, and administrative resources to serve the best interests of users and establish and maintain cooperative arrangements with such other resources as required to meet the needs of users.

2.3 *Procedures:*

2.3.1 *Each clinical psychological service unit follows a set of procedural guidelines for the delivery of psychological services.*

INTERPRETATION: Providers are prepared to provide a statement of procedural guidelines, in either oral or written form, in terms that can be understood by users, including sanctioners and local administrators. This statement describes the current methods, forms, procedures, and techniques being used to achieve the objectives and goals for psychological services.

2.3.2 *Providers of clinical psychological services develop plans appropriate to the providers' professional practices and to the problems presented by the users.*

INTERPRETATION: A clinical psychologist develops a plan that describes the psychological services, their objectives, and the manner in which they will be provided.[13,14] This plan is in written form; it serves as a basis for obtaining understanding and concurrence from the user and provides a mechanism for subsequent peer review. This plan is, of course, modified as new needs or information develops.

A clinical psychologist who provides services as one member of a collaborative effort participates in the development and implementation of the overall service plan and provides for its periodic review.

2.3.3 *Accurate, current, and pertinent documentation of essential clinical psychological services provided is maintained.*

INTERPRETATION: Records kept of clinical psychological services may include, but are not limited to, identifying data, dates of services, types of services, significant actions taken, and outcome at termination. Providers of clinical psychological services ensure that essential information concerning services rendered is recorded within a reasonable time following their completion.

2.3.4 *Each clinical psychological service unit follows an established record retention and disposition policy.*

INTERPRETATION: The policy on record retention and disposition conforms to federal or state statutes or administrative regulations where such are applicable. In the absence of such regulations, the policy is (a) that the full record be retained intact for 3 years after the completion of planned services or after the date of last contact with the user, whichever is later; (b) that a full record or summary of the record be maintained for an additional 12 years; and (c) that the record may be disposed of no sooner than 15 years after the completion of planned services or after the date of the last contact, whichever is later. These temporal guides are consistent with procedures currently in use by federal record centers.

In the event of the death or incapacity of a clinical psychologist in independent practice, special procedures are necessary to ensure the continuity of active services to users and the proper safeguarding of inactive records being retained to meet this Guideline. Following approval by the affected user, it is appropriate for another clinical psychologist, acting under the auspices of the local professional standards review committee (PSRC), to review the records with the user and recommend a course of action for continuing professional service, if needed. Depending on local circumstances, the reviewing psychologist may also recommend appropriate arrangements for the balance of the record retention and disposition period.

This Guideline has been designed to meet a variety of circumstances that may arise, often years after a set of psychological services has been completed. More and more records are being used in forensic matters, for peer review, and in response to requests from users, other professionals, or other legitimate parties requiring accurate information about the exact dates, nature, course, and outcome of a set of psychological services. These record retention procedures also provide valuable baseline data for the original psychologist–provider when a previous user returns for additional services.

2.3.5 *Providers of clinical psychological services maintain a system to protect confidentiality of their records.*[15]

INTERPRETATION: Clinical psychologists are responsible for maintaining the confidentiality of information about users of services, from whatever source derived. All persons supervised by clinical psychologists, including nonprofessional personnel and students, who have access to records of psychological services are required to maintain this confidentiality as a condition of employment.

The clinical psychologist does not release confidential information, except with the written consent of the user directly involved or his or her legal representative. Even after consent for release has been obtained, the clinical psychologist clearly identifies such information as confidential to the recipient of the information.[16] If directed otherwise by statute or regulations with the force of law or by court order, the psychologist may seek a resolution to the conflict that is both ethically and legally feasible and appropriate.

Users are informed in advance of any limits in the setting for maintenance of confidentiality of psychological information. For instance, clinical psychologists in hospital, clinic, or agency settings inform their patients that psychological information in a patient's clinical record may be available without the patient's written consent to other members of the professional staff associated with the patient's treatment or rehabilitation. Similar limitations on confidentiality of psychological information may be present in certain school, industrial, military, or other institutional settings, or in instances in which the user has waived confidentiality for purposes of third-party payment.

Users have the right to obtain information from their psychological records. However, the records are the property of the psychologist or the facility in which the psychologist works and are, therefore, the responsibility of the psychologist and subject to his or her control.

When the user's intention to waive confidentiality is judged by the professional clinical psychologist to be contrary to the user's best interests or to be in conflict with the user's civil and legal rights, it is the responsibility of the clinical psychologist to discuss the implications of releasing psychological information and to assist the user in limiting disclosure only to information required by the present circumstance.

Raw psychological data (e.g., questionnaire returns or test protocols) in which a user is identified are released only with the written consent of the user or his or her legal representative and released only to a person recognized by the clinical psychologist as qualified and competent to use the data.

Any use made of psychological reports, records, or data for research or training purposes is consistent with this Guideline. Additionally, providers of clinical psychological services comply with statutory confidentiality requirements and those embodied in the American Psychological Association's *Ethical Principles of Psychologists* (APA, 1981b).

Providers of clinical psychological services remain sensitive to both the benefits and the possible misuse of information regarding individuals that is stored in large computerized data banks. Providers use their influence to ensure that such information is used in a socially responsible manner.

Guideline 3
ACCOUNTABILITY

3.1 *The clinical psychologist's professional activity is guided primarily by the principle of promoting human welfare.*

INTERPRETATION: Clinical psychologists provide services to users in a manner that is considerate, effective, economical, and humane. Clinical psychologists make their services readily accessible to users in a manner that facilitates the users' freedom of choice.

Clinical psychologists are mindful of their accountability to the sanctioners of clinical psychological services and to the general public, provided that appropriate steps are taken to protect the confidentiality of the service relationship. In the pursuit of their professional activities, they aid in the conservation of human, material, and financial resources.

The clinical psychological service unit does not withhold services to a potential client on the basis of that user's race, color, religion, gender, sexual orientation, age, or national origin. Recognition is given, however, to the following considerations: the professional right of clinical psychologists to limit their practice to a specific category of users (e.g., children, adolescents, women); the right and responsibility of clinical psychologists to withhold an assessment procedure when not validly applicable; and the right and responsibility of clinical psychologists to withhold evaluative, psychotherapeutic, counseling, or other services in specific instances in which their own limitations or client characteristics might impair the effectiveness of the relationship.[17,18] Clinical psychologists seek to ameliorate through peer review, consultation, or other personal therapeutic procedures those factors that inhibit the provision of services to particular users. When indicated services are not available, clinical psychologists take whatever action is appropriate to inform responsible persons and agencies of the lack of such services.

Clinical psychologists who find that psychological services are being provided in a manner that is discriminatory or exploitative to users and/or contrary to these Guidelines or to state or federal statutes take appropriate corrective action, which may include the refusal to provide services. When conflicts of interest arise, the clinical psychologist is guided in the resolution of differences by the principles set forth in the American Psychological Association's *Ethical Principles of Psychologists* (APA, 1981b) and "Guidelines for Conditions of Employment of Psychologists" (APA, 1972).

3.2 *Clinical psychologists pursue their activities as members of the independent, autonomous profession of psychology.*[19]

INTERPRETATION: Clinical psychologists, as members of an independent profession, are responsible both to the public and to their peers through established review mechanisms. Clinical psychologists are aware of the implications of their activities for the profession as a whole. They seek to eliminate discriminatory practices instituted for self-serving purposes that are not in the interest of the users (e.g., arbitrary requirements for referral and supervision by another profession). They are cognizant of their responsibilities for the development of the profession. They participate where possible in the training and career development of students and other providers, participate as appropriate in the training of paraprofessionals or other professionals, and integrate and supervise the implementation of their contributions within the structure established for delivering psychological services. Clinical psychologists facilitate the development of, and participate in, professional standards review mechanisms.[20]

Clinical psychologists seek to work with other professionals in a cooperative manner for the good of the users and the benefit of the general public. Clinical psychologists associated with multidisciplinary settings support the principle that members of each participating profession have equal rights and opportunities to share all privileges and responsibilities of full membership in hospital facilities or other human service facilities and to administer service programs in their respective areas of competence.

3.3 *There are periodic, systematic, and effective evaluations of clinical psychological services.*[21]

INTERPRETATION: When the clinical psychological service unit is a component of a larger organization, regular evaluation of progress in achieving goals is provided for in the service delivery plan, including consideration of the effectiveness of clinical psychological services relative to costs in terms of use of time and money and the availability of professional and support personnel.

Evaluation of the clinical psychological service delivery system is conducted internally and, when possible, under independent auspices as well. This evaluation includes an assessment of effectiveness (to determine what the service unit accomplished), efficiency (to determine the total costs of providing the services), continuity (to ensure that the services are appropriately linked to other human services), availability (to determine appropriate levels and distribution of services and personnel), accessibility (to ensure that the services are barrier free to users), and adequacy (to determine whether the services meet the identified needs for such services).

There is a periodic reexamination of review mechanisms to ensure that these attempts at public safeguards are effective and cost efficient and do not place unnecessary encumbrances on the providers or impose unnecessary additional expenses on users or sanctioners for services rendered.

3.4 *Clinical psychologists are accountable for all aspects of the services they provide and are responsive to those concerned with these services.*[22]

INTERPRETATION: In recognizing their responsibilities to users, and where appropriate and consistent with the users' legal rights and privileged communications, clinical psychologists make available information about, and provide opportunity to participate in, decisions concerning such issues as initiation, termination, continuation, modification, and evaluation of clinical psychological services.

Depending on the settings, accurate and full information is made available to prospective individual or organizational users regarding the qualifications of providers, the nature and extent of services offered, and where appropriate, financial and social costs.

Where appropriate, clinical psychologists inform users of their payment policies and their willingness to assist in obtaining reimbursement. Those who accept reimbursement from a third party are acquainted with the appropriate statutes and regulations and assist their users in understanding procedures for submitting claims and limits on confidentiality of claims information, in accordance with pertinent statutes.

Guideline 4
ENVIRONMENT

4.1 *Providers of clinical psychological services promote the development in the service setting of a physical, organizational, and social environment that facilitates optimal human functioning.*

INTERPRETATION: Federal, state, and local requirements for safety, health, and sanitation are observed.

As providers of services, clinical psychologists are concerned with the environment of their service unit, especially as it affects the quality of service, but also as it impinges on human functioning when the service unit is included in a larger context. Physical arrangements and organizational policies and procedures are conducive to the human dignity, self-respect, and optimal functioning of users and to the effective delivery of service. Attention is given to the comfort and the privacy of users. The atmosphere in which clinical psychological services are rendered is appropriate to the service and to the users, whether in an office, clinic, school, industrial organization, or other institutional setting.

FOOTNOTES

[1] The footnotes appended to these Specialty Guidelines represent an attempt to provide a coherent context of other policy statements of the Association regarding professional practice. The Guidelines extend these previous policy statements where necessary to reflect current concerns of the public and the profession.

[2] The following two categories of professional psychologists who met the criteria indicated below on or before the adoption of these Specialty Guidelines on January 31, 1980, are also considered clinical psychologists: Category 1—persons who completed (a) a doctoral degree program primarily psychological in content at a regionally accredited university or professional school and (b) 3 postdoctoral years of appropriate education, training, and experience in providing clinical psychological services as defined herein, including a minimum of 1 year in a clinical setting; Category 2—persons who on or before September 4, 1974, (a) completed a master's degree from a program primarily psychological in content at a regionally accredited

university or professional school and (b) held a license or certificate in the state in which they practiced, conferred by a state board of psychological examiners, or the endorsement of the state psychological association through voluntary certification, and who, in addition, prior to January 31, 1980, (c) obtained 5 post-master's years of appropriate education, training, and experience in providing clinical psychological services as defined herein, including a minimum of 2 years in a clinical setting.

After January 31, 1980, professional psychologists who wish to be recognized as professional clinical psychologists are referred to Guideline 1.7.

The definition of the professional clinical psychologist in these Guidelines does not contradict or supersede in any way the broader definition accorded the term *clinical psychologist* in the Federal Employees Health Benefits Program (see *Access to Psychologists and Optometrists Under Federal Health Benefits Program*, U.S. Senate Report No. 93-961, June 25, 1974).

[3] The areas of knowledge and training that are a part of the educational program for all professional psychologists have been presented in two APA documents, *Education and Credentialing in Psychology II* (APA, 1977a) and *Criteria for Accreditation of Doctoral Training Programs and Internships in Professional Psychology* (APA, 1979). There is consistency in the presentation of core areas in the education and training of all professional psychologists. The description of education and training in these Guidelines is based primarily on the document *Education and Credentialing in Psychology II*. It is intended to indicate broad areas of required curriculum, with the expectation that training programs will undoubtedly want to interpret the specific content of these areas in different ways depending on the nature, philosophy, and intent of the programs.

[4] Functions and activities of psychologists relating to the teaching of psychology, the writing or editing of scholarly or scientific manuscripts, and the conduct of scientific research do not fall within the purview of these Guidelines.

[5] The definitions should be compared with the APA (1967) guidelines for state legislation (hereinafter referred to as state guidelines), which define *psychologist* and the *practice of psychology* as follows:

> A person represents himself [or herself] to be a psychologist when he [or she] holds himself [or herself] out to the public by any title or description of services incorporating the words "psychology," "psychological," "psychologist," and/or offers to render or renders services as defined below to individuals, groups, organizations, or the public for a fee, monetary or otherwise.
>
> The practice of psychology within the meaning of this act is defined as rendering to individuals, groups, organizations, or the public any psychological service involving the application of principles, methods, and procedures of understanding, predicting, and influencing behavior, such as the principles pertaining to learning, perception, motivation, thinking, emotions and interpersonal relationships; the methods and procedures of interviewing, counseling, and psychotherapy; of constructing, administering, and interpreting tests of mental abilities, aptitudes, interests, attitudes, personality characteristics, emotion, and motivation; and of assessing public opinion.
>
> The application of said principles and methods includes, but is not restricted to: diagnosis, prevention, and amelioration of adjustment problems and emotional and mental disorders of individuals and groups; hypnosis; educational and vocational counseling; personnel selection and management; the evaluation and planning for effective work and learning situations; advertising and market research; and the resolution of interpersonal and social conflicts.
>
> Psychotherapy within the meaning of this act means the use of learning, conditioning methods, and emotional reactions, in a professional relationship, to assist a person or persons to modify feelings, attitudes, and behavior which are intellectually, socially, or emotionally maladjustive or ineffectual.
>
> The practice of psychology shall be as defined above, any existing statute in the state of ____ to the contrary notwithstanding. (APA, 1967, pp. 1098–1099)

[6] The relation of a psychological service unit to a larger facility or institution is also addressed indirectly in the APA (1972) "Guidelines for Conditions of Employment of Psychologists" (hereinafter referred to as CEP Guidelines), which emphasizes the roles, responsibilities, and prerogatives of the psychologist when he or she is employed by or provides services for another agency, institution, or business.

[7] This Guideline replaces earlier recommendations in the 1967 state guidelines concerning exemption of psychologists from licensure. Recommendations 8 and 9 of those guidelines read as follows:

> Persons employed as psychologists by accredited academic institutions, governmental agencies, research laboratories, and business corporations should be exempted, provided such employees are performing those duties for which they are employed by such organizations, and within the confines of such organizations.
>
> Persons employed as psychologists by accredited academic institutions, governmental agencies, research laboratories, and business corporations consulting or offering their research findings or providing scientific information to like organizations for a fee should be exempted. (APA, 1967, p. 1100)

On the other hand, the 1967 state guidelines specifically denied exemptions under certain conditions, as noted in Recommendations 10 and 11:

> Persons employed as psychologists who offer or provide psychological services to the public for a fee, over and above the salary that they receive for the performance of their regular duties, should not be exempted.
>
> Persons employed as psychologists by organizations that sell psychological services to the public should not be exempted. (APA, 1967, pp. 1100–1101)

The present APA policy, as reflected in this Guideline, establishes a single code of practice for psychologists providing covered services to users in any setting. The present position is that a psychologist providing any covered service meets local statutory requirements for licensure or certification. See the section entitled Principles and Implications of the Specialty Guidelines for an elaboration of this position.

[8] A closely related principle is found in the APA (1972) CEP Guidelines:

> It is the policy of APA that psychology as an independent profession is entitled to parity with other health and human service professions in institutional practices and before the law. Psychologists in interdisciplinary settings such as colleges and universities, medical schools, clinics, private practice groups, and other agencies expect parity with other professions in such matters as academic rank, board status, salaries, fringe benefits, fees, participation in administrative decisions, and all other conditions of employment, private contractual arrangements, and status before the law and legal institutions. (APA, 1972, p. 333)

[9] See CEP Guidelines (section entitled Career Development) for a closely related statement:

> Psychologists are expected to encourage institutions and agencies which employ them to sponsor or conduct career development programs. The purpose to these programs would

be to enable psychologists to engage in study for professional advancement and to keep abreast of developments in their field. (APA, 1972, p. 332)

[10] This Guideline follows closely the statement regarding "Policy on Training for Psychologists Wishing to Change Their Specialty" adopted by the APA Council of Representatives in January 1976. Included therein was the implementing provision that "this policy statement shall be incorporated in the guidelines of the Committee on Accreditation so that appropriate sanctions can be brought to bear on university and internship training programs that violate [it]" (Conger, 1976, p. 424).

[11] See also APA's (1981b) *Ethical Principles of Psychologists*, especially Principles 5 (Confidentiality), 6 (Welfare of the Consumer), and 9 (Research with Human Participants); and see *Ethical Principles in the Conduct of Research With Human Participants* (APA, 1973a). Also, in 1978 Division 17 approved in principle a statement on "Principles for Counseling and Psychotherapy With Women," which was designed to protect the interests of female users of clinical psychological services.

[12] Support for this position is found in *Psychology as a Profession* in the section on relations with other professions:

> Professional persons have an obligation to know and take into account the traditions and practices of other professional groups with whom they work and to cooperate fully with members of such groups with whom research, service, and other functions are shared. (APA, 1968, p. 5)

[13] One example of a specific application of this principle is found in Guideline 2 in APA's (1973b) "Guidelines for Psychologists Conducting Growth Groups":

> The following information should be made available *in writing* [italics added] to all prospective participants:
> (*a*) An explicit statement of the purpose of the group;
> (*b*) Types of techniques that may be employed;
> (*c*) The education, training, and experience of the leader or leaders;
> (*d*) The fee and any additional expense that may be incurred;
> (*e*) A statement as to whether or not a follow-up service is included in the fee;
> (*f*) Goals of the group experience and techniques to be used;
> (*g*) Amounts and kinds of responsibility to be assumed by the leader and by the participants. For example, (*i*) the degree to which a participant is free not to follow suggestions and prescriptions of the group leader and other group members; (*ii*) any restrictions on a participant's freedom to leave the group at any time; and
> (*h*) Issues of confidentiality. (p. 933)

[14] See APA's (1981a) *APA/CHAMPUS Outpatient Psychological Provider Manual.*

[15] See Principle 5 (Confidentiality) in *Ethical Principles of Psychologists* (APA, 1981b).

[16] Support for the principle of privileged communication is found in at least two policy statements of the Association:

> In the interest of both the public and the client and in accordance with the requirements of good professional practice, the profession of psychology seeks recognition of the privileged nature of confidential communications with clients, preferably through statutory enactment or by administrative policy where more appropriate. (APA, 1968, p. 8)
>
> Wherever possible, a clause protecting the privileged nature of the psychologist–client relationship be included.
> When appropriate, psychologists assist in obtaining general "across the board" legislation for such privileged communications. (APA, 1967, p. 1103)

[17] This paragraph is directly adapted from the CEP Guidelines (APA, 1972, p. 333).

[18] The CEP Guidelines also include the following:

> It is recognized that under certain circumstances, the interests and goals of a particular community or segment of interest in the population may be in conflict with the general welfare. Under such circumstances, the psychologist's professional activity must be primarily guided by the principle of "promoting human welfare." (APA, 1972, p. 334)

[19] Support for the principle of the independence of psychology as a profession is found in the following:

> As a member of an autonomous profession, a psychologist rejects limitations upon his [or her] freedom of thought and action other than those imposed by his [or her] moral, legal, and social responsibilities. The Association is always prepared to provide appropriate assistance to any responsible member who becomes subjected to unreasonable limitations upon his [or her] opportunity to function as a practitioner, teacher, researcher, administrator, or consultant. The Association is always prepared to cooperate with any responsible professional organization in opposing any unreasonable limitations on the professional functions of the members of that organization.
> This insistence upon professional autonomy has been upheld over the years by the affirmative actions of the courts and other public and private bodies in support of the right of the psychologist—and other professionals—to pursue those functions for which he [or she] is trained and qualified to perform. (APA, 1968, p. 9)
>
> Organized psychology has the responsibility to define and develop its own profession, consistent with the general canons of science and with the public welfare.
> Psychologists recognize that other professions and other groups will, from time to time, seek to define the roles and responsibilities of psychologists. The APA opposes such developments on the same principle that it is opposed to the psychological profession taking positions which would define the work and scope of responsibility of other duly recognized professions. (APA, 1972, p. 333)

[20] APA support for peer review is detailed in the following excerpt from the APA (1971) statement entitled "Psychology and National Health Care":

> All professions participating in a national health plan should be directed to establish review mechanisms (or performance evaluations) that include not only peer review but active participation by persons representing the consumer. In situations where there are fiscal agents, they should also have representation when appropriate. (p. 1026)

[21] This Guideline on program evaluation is based directly on the following excerpts from two APA position papers:

> The quality and availability of health services should be evaluated continuously by both consumers and health professionals. Research into the efficiency and effectiveness of the system should be conducted both internally and under independent auspices. (APA, 1971, p. 1025)
>
> The comprehensive community mental health center should devote an explicit portion of its budget to program evaluation. All centers should inculcate in their staff attention to and respect for research findings; the larger centers have an obligation to set a high priority on basic research and to

give formal recognition to research as a legitimate part of the duties of staff members.

. . . Only through explicit appraisal of program effects can worthy approaches be retained and refined, ineffective ones dropped. Evaluative monitoring of program achievements may vary, of course, from the relatively informal to the systematic and quantitative, depending on the importance of the issue, the availablity of resources, and the willingness of those responsible to take risks of substituting informed judgment for evidence. (Smith & Hobbs, 1966, pp. 21–22)

[22] See also the CEP Guidelines for the following statement: "A psychologist recognizes that . . . he [or she] alone is accountable for the consequences and effects of his [or her] services, whether as teacher, researcher, or practitioner. This responsibility cannot be shared, delegated, or reduced" (APA, 1972, p. 334).

REFERENCES

American Psychological Association, Committee on Legislation. A model for state legislation affecting the practice of psychology. *American Psychologist*, 1967, *22*, 1095–1103.

American Psychological Association. *Psychology as a profession*. Washington, D.C.: Author, 1968.

American Psychological Association. Psychology and national health care. *American Psychologist*, 1971, *26*, 1025–1026.

American Psychological Association. Guidelines for conditions of employment of psychologists. *American Psychologist*, 1972, *27*, 331–334.

American Psychological Association. *Ethical principles in the conduct of research with human participants*. Washington, D.C.: Author, 1973. (a)

American Psychological Association. Guidelines for psychologists conducting growth groups. *American Psychologist*, 1973, *28*, 933. (b)

American Psychological Association. *Standards for educational and psychological tests*. Washington, D.C.: Author, 1974. (a)

American Psychological Association. *Standards for providers of psychological services*. Washington, D.C.: Author, 1974. (b)

American Psychological Association. *Education and credentialing in psychology II*. Report of a meeting, June 4–5, 1977. Washington, D.C.: Author, 1977. (a)

American Psychological Association. *Standards for providers of psychological services* (Rev. ed.). Washington, D.C.: Author, 1977. (b)

American Psychological Association. *Criteria for accreditation of doctoral training programs and internships in professional psychology*. Washington, D.C.: Author, 1979 (amended 1980).

American Psychological Association. *APA/CHAMPUS outpatient psychological provider manual* (Rev. ed.). Washington, D.C.: Author, 1981. (a)

American Psychological Association. *Ethical principles of psychologists* (Rev. ed.). Washington, D.C.: Author, 1981. (b)

Conger, J. J. Proceedings of the American Psychological Association, Incorporated, for the year 1975: Minutes of the annual meeting of the Council of Representatives. *American Psychologist*, 1976, *31*, 406–434.

Smith, M. B., & Hobbs, N. *The community and the community mental health center*. Washington, D.C.: American Psychological Association, 1966.

Appendix C

Blue Cross of Oregon

READ INSTRUCTIONS BEFORE COMPLETING OR SIGNING THIS FORM

TYPE OR PRINT ☐ MEDICARE ☐ MEDICAID ☐ CHAMPUS ☐ OTHER

PATIENT & INSURED (SUBSCRIBER) INFORMATION

1. PATIENT'S NAME (First name, middle initial, last name)
2. PATIENT'S DATE OF BIRTH
3. INSURED'S NAME (First name, middle initial, last name)
4. PATIENT'S ADDRESS (Street, city, state, ZIP code)
5. PATIENT'S SEX — MALE ☐ FEMALE ☐
6. INSURED'S I.D. No. or **MEDICARE No.** (include any letters)
7. PATIENT'S RELATIONSHIP TO INSURED — SELF ☐ SPOUSE ☐ CHILD ☐ OTHER ☐
8. INSURED'S GROUP NO. (Or Group Name)
9. OTHER HEALTH INSURANCE COVERAGE - Enter Name of Policyholder and Plan Name and Address and Policy or Medical Assistance Number
10. WAS CONDITION RELATED TO:
    A. PATIENT'S EMPLOYMENT — YES ☐ NO ☐
    B. AN AUTO ACCIDENT — YES ☐ NO ☐
11. INSURED'S ADDRESS (Street, city, state, ZIP code)
12. PATIENT'S OR AUTHORIZED PERSON'S SIGNATURE
    I Authorize the Release of any Medical Information Necessary to Process this Claim and Request Payment of MEDICARE/CHAMPUS Benefits Either to Myself or to the Party Who Accepts Assignment Below
    SIGNED DATE
13. I AUTHORIZE PAYMENT OF MEDICAL BENEFITS TO UNDERSIGNED PHYSICIAN OR SUPPLIER FOR SERVICE DESCRIBED BELOW
    SIGNED (Insured or Authorized Person)

PHYSICIAN OR SUPPLIER INFORMATION

14. DATE OF: ◄ ILLNESS (FIRST SYMPTOM) OR INJURY (ACCIDENT) OR PREGNANCY (LMP)
15. DATE FIRST CONSULTED YOU FOR THIS CONDITION
16. HAS PATIENT EVER HAD SAME OR SIMILAR SYMPTOMS? YES ☐ NO ☐
17. DATE PATIENT ABLE TO RETURN TO WORK
18. DATES OF TOTAL DISABILITY — FROM THROUGH
    DATES OF PARTIAL DISABILITY — FROM THROUGH
19. NAME OF REFERRING PHYSICIAN
20. FOR SERVICES RELATED TO HOSPITALIZATION GIVE HOSPITALIZATION DATES — ADMITTED DISCHARGED
21. NAME & ADDRESS OF FACILITY WHERE SERVICES RENDERED (If other than home or office)
22. WAS LABORATORY WORK PERFORMED OUTSIDE YOUR OFFICE? YES ☐ NO ☐ CHARGES:
23. DIAGNOSIS OR NATURE OF ILLNESS OR INJURY. RELATE DIAGNOSIS TO PROCEDURE IN COLUMN D BY REFERENCE TO NUMBERS 1, 2, 3, ETC. OR DX CODE
    1.
    2.
    3.
    4.

24.

A DATE OF SERVICE	B* PLACE OF SERV-ICE	C FULLY DESCRIBE PROCEDURES, MEDICAL SERVICES OR SUPPLIES FURNISHED FOR EACH DATE GIVEN — PROCEDURE CODE (IDENTIFY:)	(EXPLAIN UNUSUAL SERVICES OR CIRCUMSTANCES)	D DIAGNOSIS CODE	E CHARGES	F

25. SIGNATURE OF PHYSICIAN OR SUPPLIER
    SIGNED DATE
26. ACCEPT ASSIGNMENT (GOVERNMENT CLAIMS ONLY) YES ☐ NO ☐
27. TOTAL CHARGE
28. AMOUNT PAID
29. BALANCE DUE
30. YOUR SOCIAL SECURITY NO.
31.
32. YOUR PATIENT'S ACCOUNT NO.
33. YOUR EMPLOYER I.D. NO.

* PLACE OF SERVICE CODES

1 —(IH) — INPATIENT HOSPITAL	4 —(H) — PATIENT'S HOME	7 —(NH) — NURSING HOME	O —(OL) — OTHER LOCATIONS
2 —(OH) — OUTPATIENT HOSPITAL	5 — DAY CARE FACILITY (PSY)	8 —(SNF) — SKILLED NURSING FACILITY	A —(IL) — INDEPENDENT LABORATORY
3 —(O) — DOCTOR'S OFFICE	6 — NIGHT CARE FACILITY (PSY)	9 — AMBULANCE	B — OTHER MEDICAL/SURGICAL FACILITY

FORM 1105 REV 1/77

APPROVED BY AMA COUNCIL ON MEDICAL SERVICE 6-74

Appendix D

OUTPATIENT PSYCHOLOGICAL TREATMENT REPORT   PEER REVIEW CASE #

I. TREATMENT STATUS

Patient'a DOB: __/__/__   Sex: __M __F

Date of this report: __/__/__

Date treatment began: __/__/__

Continuing: ___

Terminated: ___ Date: __/__/__

# of sessions to date: _____

# of hours testing: _____

# of hours additional assessment: _____

Expected total # of additional sessions: _____

List relationship of other family members currently in treatment with you:

conjointly ____________________

separately ____________________

with other providers ____________________

Ratings: *Complete ratings for progress toward reaching goals previously established for this review point, and for the current severity of dysfunction, for the 6 areas listed below.*

Severity scale: 0=none 1=mild 2=moderate 3=severe 4=extreme

Progress scale: 0=none 1=some 2=moderate 3=substantial 4=complete 5=N/A

1. Home/Family	2. Job/School	3. Interpersonal Relations
S __ P __	S __ P __	S __ P __
4. Bodily Function	5. Protection of Self & Others	6. Personal Comfort
S __ __	S __ P __	S __ P __

IS PATIENT'S SIGNATURE PRESENT? ☐ YES ☐ NO

Specific Components of treatment

	Therapy to date	Planned for future
A. Primary therapy		
1. type	______	______
2. frequency	___ per wk mo *(circle one)*	___ per wk mo *(circle one)*
3. session length	___ minutes	___ minutes
B. Additional therapy		
1. type	______	______
2. frequency	___ per wk mo *(circle one)*	___ per wk mo *(circle one)*
3. session length	___ minutes	___ minutes
C. Collateral contacts		
1. type	______	______
2. frequency	___ per wk mo *(circle one)*	___ per wk mo *(circle one)*
D. Consultations		
1. type	______	______
2. frequency	___ per wk mo *(circle one)*	___ per wk mo *(circle one)*

E. Medication and physical examination: *When applicable, give the date and describe the significant results of physical examination. Name each drug, dosage, and dates began and ended.*

Patient's Concurrence: *(see instructions)*

I have reviewed the Service Plan and agree with it

(check one) ___ fully ___ partially

My estimate of progress toward goals previously established for this review point is:

___ none ___ some ___ moderate ___ substantial

___ complete ___ N/A *(this is first review point)*

LEVEL II REVIEWER: *Confirm the presence of the Patient's signature by checking the appropriate box above. Then detach the portion of the Treatment Report below the dotted line before sending the remainder to Peer Review.*

____

Patient's Signature   Date

II. IDENTIFYING INFORMATION

Patient's Name: ____________________

Sponsor's Name: ____________________

Sponsor's SS or CHAMPVA No.: ____________________

Date Submitted: __/__/__

Relationship of Patient to Sponsor:

___ Self ___ Spouse ___ Other: ____________________

Provider Name and NO.: ____________________

Provider's Phone No.: (   ) ____________________

Patient's Diagnosis: 1. __ __ __ . __ __

__ ICDA __ DSM *(check one)*   2. __ __ __ . __ __

I certify that to the best of my knowledge and belief the information provided on this Treatment Report is complete and correct.

____

Provider's Signature

III. PROGRESS TO THIS REVIEW POINT: __ 8 __24 __40 __60 __Other: _______ *(specify)*

Evaluate the extent to which previously established goals for this review point have been achieved. Describe specific interpersonal, behavioral, emotional, or cognitive changes.

IV. CURRENT FUNCTIONAL IMPAIRMENT(S):

Desribe specific behaviors, emotions, thought processes. Include SEVERITY, FREQUENCY, and SITUATIONAL FACTORS (Where and when is the dysfunction apparent?). Be specific: Do not use terms like "very" or "often."

V. GOALS FOR NEXT REVIEW POINT:

__24 __40 __60 __Other: _________*(Specify)*

Goals must be related to dysfunction and must include estimate (# of sessions) for achieving each goal.

1.

VI. SERVICES PLANNED:

State procedures, techniques, strategies, for obtaining goals outlined in Part E.

1.

INDEX

[redacted]